Abortion and Divorce Law in Ireland

Abortion and Divorce Law in Ireland

JENNIFER E. SPRENG

McFarland & Company, Inc., Publishers
Jefferson, North Carolina, and London

Library of Congress Cataloguing-in-Publication Data

Spreng, Jennifer E., 1968–
Abortion and divorce law in Ireland / Jennifer E. Spreng.
p. cm.
Includes bibliographical references and index.

ISBN 0-7864-1675-0 (softcover : 50# alkaline paper) ∞

1. Abortion — Law and legislation — Ireland. 2. Divorce — Law and legislation — Ireland. I. Title.
KDK1771.A25S695 2004
342.41508'4 — dc22 2004012137

British Library cataloguing data are available

Cover image: Statue of Justice at Dublin Castle (*Clipart.com*)

Manufactured in the United States of America

McFarland & Company, Inc., Publishers
Box 611, Jefferson, North Carolina 28640
www.mcfarlandpub.com

For Emily

Acknowledgments

I have never been involved with the writing of anything worthwhile that was not, at its heart, a group project, and this book is no exception.

In academic research, we all stand on the shoulders of giants. I would like to thank William Binchy, Ronan Fanning, Dennis Murphy, Kevin Myers, and Gerry Whyte for meeting with me and helping me shape my thoughts on Irish history and legal issues during the fall of 1997. Each was immensely generous in giving his time and insight to one previously unknown to him. I also appreciate the painstaking work over the years by every author listed in the bibliography. My thoughts have not always echoed theirs, but I would never deny the importance of their work in forming my own.

Research cannot proceed without access to information, and so often those who seek knowledge are reliant upon the generosity and public spiritedness of others. I have the deepest appreciation for the librarians and donors at the Smurfit Irish Law Center at Saint Louis University School of Law, Saint Louis University. Without this archive of Irish legal materials of such high quality in the U.S. Midwest, I am confident I could not have written this book. Sincere thanks also go to the librarians and administrators of the Trinity College (Dublin) libraries, who granted me privileges as a reader in September and October 1997, thereby providing me access to materials virtually unavailable in the United States and an authentic Irish perspective on these subjects. Of course, that experience would also not have been possible without the hospitality of Richard and Vickie Nash, who cheerfully provided me a place to "hang my hat" while in Dublin. I further appreciate both the collections and assistance I received at the University of Louisville Brandeis School of Law Library; the Louisiana State University Law Library; the Garret W. McEnerney Law Library at Boalt Hall; the University of Alaska, Fairbanks, Elmer E. Rasmusen Library; the Fairbanks North Star Borough Public Library; and the

Daviess County Public Library. The supreme court of Ireland, the Law Library of Ireland, the Irish government's publications sales office, and the Irish Revenue Commission also responded quickly and helpfully with answers to questions and requests for documents.

My own intellectual and professional background has shaped my presentation of the arguments in this book, and the great teachers with whom I have been blessed deserve recognition. Professor R. Randall Rainey first introduced and honed a Catholic perspective on constitutionality in his Constitutional Law I and II and Law and Religion classes at Saint Louis University School of Law. Professor Barry Cushman taught me to recognize the rhythms of legal history. Any thoughts I have about political theory and philosophy originate with William F. Connelly, Jr., Edward Kutler and John McClaughry. My first exposure to public choice theory and the common good was from James Gwartney and Michael Novak, with the generous support of the Liberty Fund, which was reinforced soon afterward in courses sponsored by the Heritage Foundation. I also appreciate the insights and support of John Whitehead during my early studies of the law of religious freedom.

Many friends, family and colleagues have listened for what probably seemed like interminable hours to my "ideas about Ireland" and provided in turn numerous key insights and critical support along the way. In particular, I would like to thank Daniel Caslin, Rich Ewald, Chad Gesser, Ron Haskins, Susie Headlee, Andy Leman, Emily Lowery, Michael Raibman, Joshua Settles, Frank Spreng, Jane Spreng, Evan Taylor, Justin Thorp, Jacquelyn Tretter, Brad Wendel and Kim Wood. They would know more than most that "everything always comes down to Ireland." I also appreciate the opportunity Dan Heckel and Matt Francis, editorial page editors of the *Owensboro Messenger-Inquirer*, gave me to hone some of the themes in this book in my monthly newspaper column during 2001 and 2002.

Few could have helped more on the nitty-gritty of getting this work to press with their careful substantive and technical editing than Eric Keltz, Emily Lowery, Frank Sreng, Jane Spreng and my able assistant, Rebecca Howard, who cheerfully endured countless revisions and gives new meaning to the term "team player."

Any errors are my own.

Contents

Preface

> 'Twas down the glen one Easter morn to a city fair rode I, When Ireland's lines of marching men in squadrons passed me by, No pipe did hum and no battle drum did sound its dread tattoo, *But the Angelus bell o'er the Liffey's swell* rang out in the foggy dew.
>
> –"The Foggy Dew," traditional

I discovered my Irish roots in 1995. That year I stumbled onto the Chieftains' "An Irish Evening, Live at the Grand Opera House, Belfast" and bought it on a whim. I was hooked.

One thing led to another. Irish culture being the political creature it is, that accidental exposure to Irish music led inexorably to volumes of Irish history read and reams of Irish newspapers perused. At a superficial level, I paid my cultural dues: I drank my Guinness, dabbled with Joyce's *Ulysses*, sang along with Tommy Makem in concert, and read Gerry Adams's *Free Ireland*. But it was never enough. I knew what I was missing—I wanted to *feel* what it meant to be Irish—and that just was not happening.

I was looking for Ireland in what turned out to be all the wrong places: at Kilmainham Gaol, the museum of the Irish Republican movement; in the *Irish Times* and the *Irish Independent*, savored at that Dublin institution known as Bewley's Oriental Café; during an evening of *craic* at O'Donoghue's pub with a group of young Dubliners; in the ancient round towers and stone huts of the Glendalough monastery and on the mesmerizing Aran Islands; on the battle-scarred streets of Belfast and Derry; in a Limerick church for the feast of St. Martin de Porrés; among the Sligo's inspirations for some of W. B. Yeats's best poetry. Memorable as those moments were, something was always just eluding the grasp of my understanding.

When Ireland did open its heart to me, I almost missed it. I was distracted—shopping for Aran sweaters along the banks of the Liffey River between the Ha'penny and the O'Connell Street bridges—when I heard church bells. They were the Angelus bells that ring out twice daily above the traffic and bustle of the inner-city streets, calling good Catholics to a prayer even the most devout of their coreligionists in the United States have long ago forgotten. I had heard them many times in Ireland, but in that moment, I stopped and listened.

It was a revelation.

Until that moment on the Liffey River, my heart had swelled with a strong sense of Irish nationalism, but my head had to admit that it was difficult to tell the difference between Ireland and its longtime historical antagonist, Great Britain. Even the mailboxes and double-decker buses looked like someone hijacked a load headed for London, diverted them to Dublin, and then spray-painted them green. Yet while I noticed few people stopping to pray when the Angelus bells peeled, I sensed something deep in the core of what it was to be Irish that was different from my previous understanding of nationality: a shared cultural experience of religious influence and material privation, concerns about national identity, and interdependence. Being a nation could be about more than a social contract that free individuals chose to enter; instead, peoples could be crocheted together over and over again by a shared, collective experience forming their means to communal and individual fulfillment—and perhaps be the better for it.

Later when I read American critiques of the galloping change in Irish abortion and divorce law of the 1980s and 1990s, I often remembered that awakening by the Ha'penny Bridge. Both established American academics and students scratch bald spots into their heads wondering about a nation that considers it unconstitutional for a private women's health clinic to refer a pregnant woman to an abortion clinic in Great Britain. Otherwise moderate Americans chatting over dinner blithely condemn Irish constitutional thought based on the substance of abortion law that probably provides equivalent access to the procedure as is available to many American women. A frequent trend in both scholarly work and popular media is to brand heavy-handed Irish Catholicism as the scapegoat for the apparent Irish rebellion from enlightened liberal individualism, in spite of the comparatively thoughtful Irish public discussion of foundational constitutional philosophy, which only infrequently garners a mention. Surprisingly, given the number of Irish Americans and their constructive contributions to Americana, we tend to miss the point about Ireland: that based on events not wholly of their own making, the Irish have developed a constitutional philosophy informed and perfected by the creative tension between liberalism and communitarianism and have perhaps been the better for it.

As a practicing Catholic trying, but not always succeeding, to be a good one, I initially came to the subject intending to challenge the all-too-frequent assumption that Catholicism had perniciously imposed any sort of unholy legal regime on the Irish. My experience as an American Catholic did not involve the church "imposing" anything on me, at least. The church was and still is an institution to which I feel privileged to belong. Religion, doctrine, belief—these were things people *chose*, often at some personal cost and against the grain of the popular culture. Writers who saw it otherwise did not understand, and I would explain. Or so I thought.

As usual, the truth lies somewhere in between and matters in important but different ways from what I had realized. As I explored what attracted the Irish to Catholicism and what that religion says about who the Irish are as a people, I realized that the true impact of Catholicism on Irish constitutional law is that it opened the nation to an intellectually sophisticated, communitarian political philosophy which complemented their practical national experience and which they then translated into their own political voice by setting it in the liberal democratic tradition they inherited from the British. The influence of the church on Irish politics declined precipitously in the second half of the twentieth century, but the communitarianism that was so well suited to the Irish character has remained. Catholic church teaching did have a direct causal effect on the public philosophy the Irish adopted, but that teaching was not exclusively "religious" or doctrinal, and the resulting institutions, law and politics have produced demonstrable secular good.

The history is quite clear: The Irish have freely chosen, over and over, to find wisdom, solace and inspiration in Catholic teaching and to admit the consequences of Catholic teaching to both their public and private lives. Moreover, these choices have been advantageous; because of their openness to religion in public life, Irish politics and culture have been enriched to their benefit with communitarian ideals. As Trinity College (Dublin) Professor Gerry Whyte has recognized at this time when the Irish are reexamining so many first principles, understanding and respect for the positive role the church's social and political teaching has played in forming the foundations of its society may be necessary to avoid sacrificing what is best about being Irish. More importantly for Americans, such an understanding may show us how we may shape our foundational principles to better facilitate the fulfillment and flourishing of all our citizens.

This book is an attempt to explain the Irish constitutional story as it relates to abortion and divorce law in a way that enables Americans to understand and benefit from it and the Irish to take deserved pride in it, for they have done something uniquely their own. Each of the three sections of the book uses different analytical approaches. Part I is primarily historical with an eye to relevant portions of the legal landscape. Chapter One discusses current issues and law. Chapter Two provides a brief background of Irish history with a primary focus on the Irish famine of the 1840s, the formative event of modern Irish history, and the resulting ascendance of Irish "group voices"—of nation, church, family, and community—through the early period of Irish independence. Chapter Three focuses on the vision, drafting and philosophy of the Irish constitution of 1937, which balanced Catholic communitarianism with principles of liberal democracy, particularly in provisions related to the family and personal rights. Chapter Four describes the increasing tension between the Catholic church and the Irish state during the mid–1900s, in which the church's influence on public opinion steadily diminished and that of secular influences took center stage.

Part II focuses on a legal analysis of modern Irish abortion and divorce law. Chapter Five describes the constitutional amendment struggles over the issues of right to life and divorce of the 1980s and 1990s. Chapter Six focuses on *Attorney General* v. *X*, in which a thirteen-year-old rape victim challenged an injunction that stopped her from traveling to London for an abortion, and the Irish Supreme Court ruled that when carrying a pregnancy to term creates a substantial risk to right to life of the mother, including a threat of self-destruction, the mother may have a legal abortion on Irish soil. Chapter Seven explores two high-profile abortion and euthanasia cases and another divorce referendum from the 1990s. The balance between liberalism and communitarianism in Irish law is shifting, and its ultimate settling point is by no means clear.

Part III takes a comparative approach to the philosophies undergirding Irish and American law. Chapter Eight explores women's aspirations from a communitarian perspective and argues that Irish law may actually contribute more to the fulfillment and flourishing of Irish women than American law does for American women. Chapter Nine compares more concrete Irish and American legal supports for women's aspirations and concludes that decentralized lawmaking—preferring state to nation, and nation to international law—is more likely to enhance liberty and minimize tyranny.

These theoretical matters would themselves captivate, but the history of Irish abortion and divorce law is more than the story of how two dry political philosophies—liberalism and communitarianism—converged and informed the spectrum of Irish law. Instead, it is a great drama of world history, first a drama of marquee players whose stories deserve to be told and told again: of the larger-than-life Taoiseach, Eamon de Valera, whose talents both for standing on and then compromising principle produced a constitution of genius, and of Trinity College (Dublin) law professor Dr. William Binchy, the intellectual leader of the modern Irish prolife and antidivorce movements, who has almost singlehandedly stemmed the tide of liberalism in Irish family law that has washed over the rest of Western Europe. It is a drama of awesome historical forces and their cruel effects: of the great Irish famine which robbed the nation of a quarter of its population and transformed its culture; of a nation born in deprived circumstances that experienced the full range of political growing pains within a few generations and right under the noses of developed, "Old World" nations; and finally of an economic dynamo, the Celtic Tiger, the most profound modern source of renewal and challenge to Irish culture, which has reversed two centuries of emigration and economic deprivation, the historical scourges of the Irish. It is also a drama of great legal and philosophical concepts, such as "human dignity," "freedom," "human flourishing," and "community," made concrete and tangible in the lives of ordinary citizens practicing a very human-scale politics. Finally, it is a drama of a nation, of a people, of a group of individuals, each with value by virtue of their humanity, thrown together not by choice but by birth, crocheted together through shared cultural experience and aspirations, and the kind of country they chose, and will in the future choose, to be.

Few dramas could be grander than that.

Owensboro, Kentucky
August 2004

Part I

One

After the "Coffee and Condoms Revolution"[1]: Communitarianism in 21st Century Irish Law

> I repeat, the ultimate protection of human rights in a democracy lies with the people themselves.
>
> —J.M. Kelly, *Fundamental Rights in the Irish Law and Constitution*[2]

In 1991, the Irish people chose as their president a female, women's rights crusader, Mary Robinson, bypassing in the process an established and respected legislator from Ireland's long-time party of government. The choice was especially noteworthy because while Robinson was well known as a champion of legalized birth control and divorce and for having scorned antiabortion efforts in Ireland, in the ten years before her election, the Irish had supported overwhelmingly a referendum to constitutionalize the unborn's right to life and had resoundingly rejected efforts to legalize divorce even in narrow circumstances. Commentators were quick to jump on the bandwagon to anoint Robinson's election as a harbinger of the end of "reactionary Ireland," and statistical analysis did reveal a growing, fundamental liberal-conservative cleavage in Irish society.[3] Given the election results, Ireland seemed poised for massive social and legal change in the 1990s, and Robinson was not shy about using her mostly ceremonial office to nudge the country along. *Irish Times* columnist Fintan O'Toole argued later that the Irish people "didn't know they wanted a president like her until they got one,"[4] but what became apparent as the 1990s proceeded was that even though the Ireland at the dawn of the third millennium would be very different from that of the date of Robinson's inauguration, many fundamentals would remain the same.

As late as the early 1980s, Ireland had seemed almost untouched by the movement to liberalize abortion laws which had gripped the United States, Great Britain and much of Western Europe for the prior fifteen years. Abortion had been a misdemeanor at common law and a much more serious statutory crime for almost two centuries in Ireland. While the British parliament was passing what turned out to be the very permissive Abortion Act of 1967 and the 1973 U.S. Supreme Court was handing down *Roe* v. *Wade*, no more than a handful of souls were champing at the bit to do anything of the sort in Ireland.

In fact, many Irish people wanted to make sure no one ever did. In the late 1970s, the Oireachtas, the Irish parliament, passed legislation in response to a court decision describing limited circumstances under which contraceptive devices would be available to the general public, albeit only to married persons and by prescription. The statute had been a long, arduous time in the making, mostly because the wide availability of contraceptives was unpopular,[5] and despite the fact that, for years, many Irish women had discretely used oral contraceptives apparently prescribed for medical purposes other than birth control. Both the erudite and the Irish "person in the street" recognized the uncomfortable parallel between how contraception had been legalized in Ireland and how abortion had come in one fell swoop to the United States. By a two-to-one margin in 1983, the Irish ratified a constitutional amendment popularly understood to outlaw abortion in all circumstances and to eliminate the possibility of a future Irish *Roe* v. *Wade*. Yet the amendment went further than outlawing abortion; it also made a positive statement about the relative values of different humans' lives and the state's role in vindicating the right to life:

> The State acknowledges the right to life of the unborn and, with due regard for the equal right to life of the mother, guarantees in its laws to respect, and, as far as practicable, by its laws to defend and vindicate that right.[6]

This was merely the calm before the storm. A decade later, the Irish Supreme Court held that the constitution permitted abortion where there was a "real and substantial risk" to the mother's life, including perhaps not completely convincing suicide threats.[7] Not only was this a popular decision — the Irish had taken to the streets demanding it so that a fourteen-year-old rape victim would be permitted to abort her child in either England or Ireland — the Irish did not repent it at leisure. Instead, they upheld the decision by rejecting a constitutional amendment that would have effectively overruled it and by ratifying another pair of amendments that facilitated Irish women's access to abortion in foreign countries. Despite this firm electoral statement, the Irish went as far as they went, and no farther. No movement to liberalize Irish abortion law developed any further momentum.

What it all meant seemed clear. During 1992, the Irish as a nation traveled the road from having the most restrictive abortion law in western Europe to a state of flux. In the late 1990s, Irish constitutional law experts were uncertain as to precisely what abortions would ultimately be labeled "legal" or "illegal"; the Irish government was paying for teenaged girls to obtain abortions in England, and a report from a high-profile government committee was leading the way toward yet another referendum. Added to that maelstrom, a national referendum legalized divorce in 1995, and an Irish Supreme Court decision ruled that the state could end the life of a ward who was in a permanent vegetative state on the basis that the action was in the ward's best interest.

Moreover, this apparently dramatic legal change occurred in tandem with other fundamental economic, social and cultural changes in Irish society. In the early 1960s, British television, along with other new communications technologies, became widely available to the Irish, and they challenged longstanding Irish institutions in ways with which those institutions were ill prepared to cope. This was particularly true of the Irish Catholic church, about which *Irish Times* columnist Nuala O'Faolain argued as late as 1995 that:

> Most Irish Catholics I know are happy to be Catholics, and privately it is a serious matter with them to try to be good Catholics.... The country is full of decent, reasonable people who are committed Catholics. But the hardest thing to find in the country is a decent, reasonable Catholic who can argue and debate the big questions facing Irish Catholicism. I blame the institutional church which kept its people dumb. It never taught them language for fear that their profit from it would be that people would know how to curse, that the faithful would want seminars as well as processions.[8]

Moreover, though the Irish experienced extreme economic difficulty during the 1970s and 1980s, during the 1990s and beyond, for the first time since independence, the Irish economy has enjoyed a sustained period of enviable growth, which has offset 150-year old economic and social scourges, such as widespread emigration and unusually anemic, long-term economic growth. During the 1980s and 1990s, the Irish also finally wearied of the political and philosophical conundrum of laying territorial claim to the portion of their homeland, the six counties of Northern Ireland, clearly under the political thumb of a much stronger nation, Great Britain, and gave shrill voice to a deep-rooted skepticism about the Catholic church and its hierarchy.

Yet, more subtle developments may be just as critical to understanding what gives every appearance of being profound changes in Ireland. For example, the modern Irish intellectual and political set has championed an infusion of public life with increased respect for greater religious and philosophical pluralism — which in the Irish context is similar to what Americans call "diversity"— and it has increasingly informed public discussion. Jurists and other Irish have also become fluent in the language of individual rights and individualism, while concerns of community and family seem to have lost some of their comparative cachet. Though many Irish view the church and its leaders with greater skepticism than in the past, Catholic social teaching, as stated in the documents of Vatican II, has reinforced these more subtle changes in Irish culture and outlook.

"It has been a coffee and condoms revolution in Ireland," *Irish Times* columnist Kevin Myers marveled in 1997.[9] Myers argued that while legislators and judges (and perhaps by extension, the intelligentsia, generally) had facilitated aspects of this revolution, the true engine had been the minds and actions of individuals sitting in homes, pubs and shops drinking coffee, and especially the increased confidence of Irish persons in their individualism, their sexuality, and in the individualism and sexuality of others. The Irish had left behind a "fierce, illiberal, intolerant" society "which invariably served instant coffee wherever you went" and "discovered that coffee came from beans."[10]

Myers' most profound observation, however, may be the one he made only in spite of himself: that whatever changes had occurred in the way Irish people thought of themselves, their family law, and their country, they were still drinking coffee! The external fabric that clothed Irish society might have changed, but the soul of Ireland had survived. Challenged? Certainly. Refined and reshaped? Yes, that too. But as this book will show, the soul of Ireland retains the essential character that it always had in ancient Celtic times, in the clans, during the devastation and aftermath of the famine, and through the formation of the Irish state. True, that soul has not always revealed itself as "good," for the same families and villages that cleaved together to weather the memory of the famine also flung their seemingly dispensable children and neighbors to the far corners of the earth, but it has survived even the upheaval of modernity essentially intact. The soul of Ireland, yet alive in the law as well as so many other unseen and, all too often in modern society, unappreciated places, is the concept of "community." "Community" still shapes the people's fundamental values as recognized and vindicated not only by legislators and courts in law but also in the simplest ways individual Irish persons relate to each other and flourish together.

Therefore, it is not surprising that since the legal battles of the early and mid–1990s as to abortion, divorce, and death-and-dying law, an uneasy stalemate has emerged. Fianna Fáil, the ruling party in the late 1990s and the early years of the twenty-first century, known for its conservatism on social issues, consistently promised a constitutional referendum on abortion, ostensibly to add limitations to the locus of legal abortions, and it commissioned a comprehensive "green paper" on which to base the drafting. Nevertheless, until 2002 it was never politically expedient *actually to hold* the referendum, and when the Irish eventually voted, the process generated more heat than light, with an ambiguous constitutional and legislative package going down to a razor-thin defeat. Though some pundits proclaimed—and mourned—the death of the prolife movement as a bankable political force after the election, prolife leaders found themselves on both sides of the referendum debate, as a strategic rift developed within the movement between practicality and purity: those who saw the referendum as a practical solution to the potential liberalities in Irish law and those who were unwilling to support any measure that failed to provide absolute protection to human life from the moment of conception. On the one hand, the complicated referendum package eliminated threats of suicide as a justification for a legal abortion in Ireland and protected conscientiously objecting health-care providers from requirements that they perform abortions, but on the other, the package also would have secured the legality of abortifacients such as the intrauterine device and the morning-after pill, which terminate a pregnancy after conception but prior to fertilization and are therefore anathema to ardent prolifers. Only careful statistical research will say one way or another, but it is possible that the purists voting against the referendum made the difference, testifying yet again to the Irish people's strong prolife commitment. The Irish give lip service to their dissatisfaction with the uncertain state of their law, but as a practical matter, there is no strong consensus for any particular change.

Moreover, the Irish government recently committed itself to providing a perhaps more meaningful cornucopia of programs and services to decrease the number of crisis pregnancies that result in abortions, from sex education to improved social services for single mothers and health services for women who have had abortions abroad. As a government publication promoting the new legislation explains, an important part of the strategy to decrease the rate of Irish women having abortions abroad is "working with society as a whole in promoting a more supportive attitude" in the face of crisis pregnancies.[11] Such measures might have more effect on mothers who are considering abortions and the fact of abortion in Ireland than any tinkering with the range of legal abortions.

It is very Irish to lack discomfort with the sorts of moral and legal ambiguities exemplified by their current abortion law; the Irish themselves refer to such ambiguities self-deprecatingly as "an Irish solution to an Irish problem." Nor are those ambiguities unique in Irish constitutional law and policy; after all, for years the Irish constitution insisted that the government's jurisdiction reached over the entire island, including the six counties accepted internationally as part of the United Kingdom of Great Britain and Northern Ireland. Nevertheless, some of the country's political inertia may arise more from uncertainty about what to do than from any real satisfaction with the current state of the law. If so, the Irish inertia would hardly be surprising. The breadth and depth of social change in Ireland during the past decade and a half must raise for the discerning Irish citizen the questions, "Who are we?" and "What kind of country do we want to be?" These are not questions with easy answers.

They are questions with high stakes, however. As Rory O'Connell points out, Irish law leads to the conclusion that "[i]f you believe in the right to life of the foetus, you are committed to restricting the rights of women."[12] Abortion law forces such hard choices over and over again, in all its manifestations.

A state's law related to abortion, the circumstances of its making, and the actual conduct of the people governed by it, speaks intimately about the core beliefs of that society and the fundamental choices that society has made. The law of abortion and its relation to the daily life of the people is a rare legislative and jurisprudential package containing a society's foundational principles about life and the rights and duties of one living person to another that are the bases of a good constitution, what one Irish scholar calls "the fundamental jural presuppositions of the lived accommodation."[13] In this view of constitutionalism, similar to the "invisible hand" of Adam Smith as well as the thinking of Edmund Burke and Fredrich von Hayek, the written document may be only one part of the true constitution, or "the daily accommodation that arises between those who live together, the lived agreement to live here and with these people."[14] This true constitution is the set of terms under which people hazard their fortunes together and suggests, if not unanimity of support for those terms, at least broad-based acceptance of the political order. After all, in the modern, mobile society — especially the modern, mobile Europe — those who do not like the social order in which they live have more of a tangible option to leave than ever before.

A debate over an issue such as abortion rights has relevance far beyond judicial chambers because it is really a public debate "to which the judiciary contribute."[15] Abortion regulation implies answers to some of the most fundamental questions individuals and society may face: "What is alive?" "What is human?" "Does one's humanity matter?" "Under what circumstances and in what way must we choose between one human life and another?" "What does it mean for women to be equal to men before the law in the face of inherent differences?" "What does it mean for women to engage in a meaningful pursuit of happiness?" "Even if we know what it means for women to pursue happiness and we want them to do so, what deleterious effect can that be permitted to have on others?" And, circling back to the start: "Who are those 'others?'" These questions go to the core ordering of society, which makes a society's response to the moral, social and legal questions abortion raises foundational issues of any day. The fact of abortion requires all persons to face the foundational questions with which the Irish are struggling in the twenty-first century: "Who are we?" and "What kind of people do we want to be?"

As this book argues, the Irish have done better in grappling with these questions during recent history than Americans have. Americans and Irish started from different social and political philosophies in their constitutional development generally and their abortion debates particularly, and both nations have conducted them very differently. Both processes have seemed complex to participants and observers; the Irish process with its continual referenda may seem the messiest. Nevertheless, it is the Irish who have much to teach both Americans and the world about how to address these types of foundational problems in the future. The Irish success is not complete and not necessarily evinced by the ultimate substantive outcome but instead is rooted both in the starting point and in the process—the process of a community of citizens coming together and making fundamental decisions about how they will hazard their fortunes together.

The Irish view of the fundamentals of societal order formed during the colonial experience (particularly the famine of the 1840s) with its resulting dehumanization of large groups in Irish society and the difficult founding period of the Irish state in the first half of the twentieth century. What arose from that history was not a rage for individualism as a means to freedom and fulfillment, but the fluency of the "group voices" of family, community, church and nation. Individual voices were, and still are, weak in Ireland, but group voices were and remain strong. The state's law and dominant cultural institutions articulated a strong sense of duty to and relationship between the individual and the relevant group, be it the nation (and later the state), community, family or church. This sense of social interconnection and overlapping circles of community were consistent with Irish history and religious tradition. Through the colonial and famine experiences, the Irish cleaved together and to their institutions with unusual loyalty. In contrast to dominant American and British Protestantism, Catholic philosophy emphasizes the pursuit of the common good as the fundamental purpose of political and social institutions—as is specifically stated in preamble of the Irish Constitution—and was therefore well suited to provide philosophical and political order to a necessarily community-oriented culture. That same focus on the common good pervades the personal rights articles of the Irish Constitution, written in 1938 at the high point of modern Irish national and politico-religious identity.

In fact, until recently, modern Irish society was unmistakably communitarian, or as one Irish academic calls it, a "Christian democracy,"[16] constantly sparring with the remains of a liberal democratic ethos left behind by evacuating foreigners. "Communitarianism" has enjoyed recent notoriety and has many prophets and precepts. Brian Stiltner identifies three strains of the basic philosophy: narrative communitarianism, which "highlights the pervasive role a community and its stories play in the formation of its members characters, values and beliefs ... [t]herefore, the common good in its fullness is found only within a fairly homogeneous community"; discourse communitarian, which "locates the common good in a form of society that allows all members to discuss and articulate their conceptions of the good"; and egalitarian communitarianism, which "highlights how people are fulfilled as individuals only by being connected to one another in community."[17] Communitarianism in the Irish sense "encompasses a broad range of political views which essentially advocate increased involvement in public life and endorse the public pursuit of those shared ends which define the community's way of life"[18] and in practice resembles an amalgamation of Stiltner's narrative and egalitarian models. Irish public philosophy accepts that the lives of individuals are integrated with communities and that human flourishing is dependent on the goodness of the community as a whole,[19] which arose from, was nurtured by, and was made fluent over time in the Irish group voices of family, village, nationalism and church.

The resulting "black letter" rule of Irish abortion law—that only where there is a real and substantial risk to the mother's *life* may an abortion be performed on Irish soil, though Irish women will not be stopped from leaving the country to seek an abortion elsewhere that would be otherwise illegal in Ireland—is ideologically inconsistent and is open to the criticism that it is somewhat irresponsible, in that it "resolves" the underlying philosophical problem by exporting its consequences to other European countries where abortion is legal as evidenced by the thousands of Irish women who seek abortions in Britain and elsewhere every year. Nevertheless, even though the rule is a victory of sorts for individualism, and especially individualism's emphasis on the vindication of individual "rights," the rule still retains a significant remnant of the communitarian concerns and Catholic social teaching from which the Irish Constitution and surviving Irish political philosophy arose. Yet a fork in the road is rapidly approaching. Whether the Irish will follow the American example of pure individualism and abandon communitarianism and Christian democracy is the great constitutional and foundational decision the Irish must make.

While American authors criticize and American activists lobby on both sides to change Irish law, American citizens could learn much from the Irish about how to manage the philosophical and political challenges abortion creates. As in Ireland, the common law criminalized most abortions in the United States, and the reach of the criminal ban on abortion extended to every state through the mid-1900s. Though some state legislatures liberalized their abortion laws during the 1960s, the modern national debate about the legality of abortion had scarcely begun before the U.S. Supreme Court anointed the "right to an abortion" with constitutional magnitude in *Roe* v. *Wade*, thereby removing the debate over these foundational issues from the democratic process. By avoiding the issue of whether the unborn were human beings with constitutional standing, the Court recognized a constitutional right to terminate the life of a fetus without meaningfully engaging the possibility that the unborn fetus might have a right or liberty interest in life that the born were bound to respect. This reflected — and to some extent caused — the emerging, radically individualistic, jurisprudential basis of American constitutional law. It focused solely on the rights of individuals without, by comparison to many European regimes, consideration of correlative duties and interests of those individuals within a wider society or the possible rights and needs of the unborn.[20] American abortion law has instead focused on reconciling the limited interests of *the state* in "the life of the fetus that may become a child"[21] with the fundamental rights of adult women to privacy and bodily integrity.[22] Of course, this forensic tactic effectively ends the discussion before it begins— after all, how can a state's interest in protecting something that may not be human trump a fully human being's fundamental rights on more than the rarest occasions? It also means that the American discussion's pedantic framing of the issues pales in comparison to the stakes in the Irish debate: the right to life of the fully human unborn child versus the equal right to life of the equally fully human mother. Now that's a real moral conundrum.

Yet even the terms of the Irish debate create consequences for the development of law and public policy. In Ireland, prolife supporters took control of the early debate on the legality of abortion, and they chose to frame the constitutional debate in terms of competing rights of individuals—the right to life of the unborn child versus various other personal rights, particularly the mother's right to life. While this had the effect of memorializing a strong, simple principle with the potential to provide firm guidance for future decision making, it did not apparently take into account Ireland's rich heritage of societal interconnectedness and interlocking communities—the "group voices" of family, church and village—in this foundational conflict. Though Irish judges have not ignored this vibrant constitutional heritage, it is no more than a glimmer in the most recent Irish jurisprudence on life issues. Therefore, even though in Ireland, abortion seems illegal and in the United States we think of it as essentially legal, the underpinnings of both countries' laws are becoming increasingly similar. Regardless of the outcome, both countries now judge the legality of an abortion based on the relative individual rights of the unborn child and the mother and their relationship with the state, as opposed, for example, to their mutual roles, duties and obligations, as well as their roles, duties and obligations to and within the communities around them and those communities' roles, duties and obligations in response. Failure to take serious account of this broader set of roles, duties and obligations will color future developments in Irish abortion law and may have a profound impact on that most foundational of questions, "What kind of country do we want to be?"

Obviously for the unborn, these philosophical debates are not idle, but neither are they for women. The Irish experience shows that the abortion right's status as the crown jewel in the series of legal shifts designed to liberate women and help them to flourish by providing them greater power in their relationships with men and more choices in their public lives[23] does not stand up to scrutiny. Methods of both artificial and natural birth control are now so reliable and available that few American women truly need the availability of abortion to protect their sexual and personal freedom. Admittedly, studies show that the use of birth control devices and techniques raises potent relationship fault lines which often discourage women from using birth control,[24] but an all-encompassing "right to abortion" is plainly not the only or even necessarily the best way of addressing those hard problems of sexual politics. In fact, it may be counterproductive. Catherine MacKinnon argues that the right to privacy on which American abortion rights are based tends "to cut women off from collective verification and state support in the same act" and "isolate[] us at once from each other and from public recourse." Therefore "[t]his right to privacy is a right of men 'to be let alone' to oppress women one at a time."[25] As a matter of the civil and criminal law that may influence these matters, the U.S. Supreme Court jurisprudence has always made assumptions about what liberates women —from early-twentieth-century rhetoric about protecting women from their physical frailties[26] to the more modern view that legislative decisions should not be driven by "archaic and stereotypic notions"[27] about women's abilities and interests— without reference to much hard evidence on the subject on any of these occasions. Providing women with more "rights" is no great challenge, but what good does that do? Do those rights meaningfully help women flourish and pursue happiness? The question "what do women want?" or perhaps more aptly stated, "what should women want?" is fraught with difficulty. What if what many want is the opportunity to live and flourish in the interlocking communities that excessive attention to individual rights undermines? Can their interests be protected, or must they be abandoned along the wayside in the rush to liberalism? It is precisely those questions that the Irish are better equipped to address than Americans.

Differing values in Irish society and American society and the more penetrating public debate in Ireland reveal that abortion rights and easy divorce, while arguably attractive legal developments, do not necessarily empower women or put them on the road to greater personal growth. Instead, they simply pick a different set of "winners and losers" among women. Because the Irish are more skeptical about the relative merits of the empowerment thesis, they are correspondingly better placed philosophically to recognize the importance of something far more practically useful than rhetorical "rights": greater opportunities for women to experience valuable and fulfilling lives and the type of society that will nurture them. Therefore, it is hardly surprising that, in an otherwise sophisticated country such as Ireland that has not already created an expectation that abortion should be widely available as a woman's right, there is considerable public reluctance to make it so.

In fact, in Western European and North American polities there is considerable skepticism that a woman's "right to an abortion" either exists or should be protected, despite efforts of feminist groups to promote both in individual countries and within human rights organizations. Whether a right exists, is a philosophical determination, but whether it should be protected, to what extent, and what the political determinations are speak much of how the members of the polity perceive their individual and communal interests, including the necessities for flourishing. There can be "a significant discrepancy between a country's legal norms regarding abortion and the practice of abortion it tolerates," but even merely labeling something as a "right" communicates important messages to society and can remove individual members of the polity from the educative and creative process of "imagin[ing] reality."[28]

In several of the largest western jurisdictions, such as the United States, France, and Great Britain, people are sharply divided both as to whether abortion is a legitimate right and, if so, whether and how it should be protected as such. The United States, for example, has recognized a constitutional right to an abortion, and Great Britain permits virtual abortion on demand, but as a consequence, very large minorities in both countries are dissatisfied or, worse, feel themselves imposed upon in this sensitive, defining area of law. In polities where this individual right is protected either explicitly or implicitly, there may be more discontent than in Ireland, where it is not, including more discontent among women. Because Ireland has compromised its way to a policy most can live with, even if they do not consider it ideal, fewer Irish citizens experience the tyranny of a government and society that vindicates values antithetical to those that they find fulfilling, both as multidimensional individuals in their autonomy and members of communities. "Nobody" likes the Irish law, but through trade-offs and compromise it has become over time a consensus position. The same cannot be said of American abortion law. More rights do not necessarily mean more freedom and happiness, particularly where small groups of like-minded citizens are willing to give up certain freedoms and rights in order to vindicate other values.[29]

This book addresses the fundamental questions the Irish now face by taking a step back to explore abortion in Ireland within the context of slightly less searing ones, such as "Who were the Irish?" "What kind of country was Ireland?" and "What kind of country were the Irish trying to be?" From an overarching Irish context — historical, cultural, political, economic, and philosophical — there have been three driving influences on the Irish law and mores generally, including those related to abortion and divorce. First is almost two centuries of economic insecurity, most notably manifested in the 1845–49 famine and its horrific aftermath, which led to a culture of emigration, late and rare marriage among other forms of sexual conservatism, and devotion to the church as a stabilizing influence and attractive career path. This influence was not, until the 1990s, significantly eliminated. Second is a sense of group loyalty and identification at a variety of levels, particularly within families and churches, which has some of its roots in Ireland's geographic location on the periphery of Europe, famine experience, and colonial history when Irish institutions, particularly the church, were repressed. This group identity and loyalty in turn gave rise to a strong sense of shared history and culture, consensus public philosophy, the ethic of nationalism, intense devotion to parish and church, familial loyalty, both cultural preservation and defensiveness, and a comparative lack of modern interest in individualism and pluralistic government. The final, driving influence is Catholic social and political teaching about the common good — not merely abortion or family law — which is consistent with and has reinforced the group loyalties that arose from the secular experience and ultimately served as one of the philosophical bases for the Irish Constitution.

What these driving influences did, in both their positive and negative manifestations, was to create a society in which group voices have been strong and individual voices have been comparatively weak; where individuals define themselves, cleave together, and develop within and in the context of their group membership and identification; and where community consensus and interpersonal relationships hold comparatively more cachet than individual rights or expression. Not surprisingly, these are values and characteristics praised in Catholic social teaching, which informs much of the written Irish Constitution. Given these sources, it is also no surprise that Irish constitutional development in general, and abortion law in particular, is quite distinctive compared to the American. The infusion of communitarian Catholic social and political philosophy within the liberal framework that was the British political legacy in Ireland preserved a communal context for the flourishing of free individuals as envisioned in Catholic social thought, balanced by liberal principles. That communal context in turn fertilized widely held, substantive notions of the common good that could be conducive to many Irish citizens' flourishing.

Regardless of where its abortion law ultimately settles, Ireland, that least individualistic of countries, has much to teach about how to recognize and protect the most important opportunities for individual human flourishing because instinctive within Irish public philosophy is the notion that individuals flourish in some part through their membership and interaction in one or more communities. The Irish know that the rights discussion is not merely "a confrontation between the individual and the State" and that they must consider "the vital social dimension to human conduct" within their constitutional scheme.[30] The Irish have gleaned much from liberalism and the American experience specifically, particularly American case law on abortion and contraception, but the Irish have a substantive and rhetorical fluency in discussing these issues that Americans would be well served to notice, appreciate and emulate. For Americans, this may be a challenge, but perhaps one worth accepting:

> So deeply embedded in [the American] intellectual climate are the assumptions of liberalism that our intelligentsia is unfamiliar with any

> living intellectual tradition that simultaneously differs fundamentally from liberalism, is at least its equal in depth and intellectual power, and is fully compatible with a principled commitment to the free society.[31]

One can learn about such an intellectual tradition by studying Ireland.

The Catholic Church and Catholic social teaching have left their imprint on Irish abortion and divorce law, but the reader will not be confused at the end of this book: There is more to know about the genesis of family law in Ireland than the state's Mass attendance rate. More important than the fact that so many Irish over the centuries have been and are now Catholic is the question of *why* the Irish were and are Catholic. That question of "why" then becomes "how": *how* those underlying rhythms influenced relevant issues in Irish society, particularly the Irish Constitution and abortion law. What will become apparent is that the Irish are Catholic both because they are believers and because cultural Catholicism has met profound social needs related to the colonial and famine experiences. The whole ethos of what it means to be Catholic in a universal and nonparochial sense is consistent with and supportive of what it has meant for hundreds of years to be Irish. What it means to be Irish, however, has perhaps never been in such doubt. The ambiguity of modern Irish abortion law mirrors shifts in those underlying cultural rhythms.

The irony of an Irish history that sometimes seems defensive and fearful is that the Irish put into practice productive ways of thinking and talking about fundamental public policy issues such as abortion and divorce that have served them quite well. Even as notions of individual rights have gripped Irish thought, the Irish have retained a sharply tuned sense of interpersonal responsibility and a communitarian culture. The Irish are open to a balanced solution to the abortion problem perhaps because of their implicit recognition of the responsibilities that society and other groups may have for individual women as well as the social realities and relationships created by a woman's fundamentally social and creative capacity for motherhood. Not only may a study of Irish abortion law within its historical and cultural context provide a blueprint for the next step in Irish thinking about the abortion challenge, but perhaps it may also help identify the appropriate breadth of a woman's right to an abortion, while protecting and valuing women and their many roles in modern society. Ireland has within its culture and tradition powerful tools to balance appropriately the competing concerns that inform the debate on abortion in its Catholic communitarian tradition, and thereby limit the number of abortions performed on Irish women. The United States has much to learn from tiny Ireland in this area.

Two

"The Land of Happy Wars and Sad Love Songs"

> But there is one memory of that Lughnasa time that visits me most often; and what fascinates me about that memory is that it owes nothing to fact. In that memory, atmosphere is more real than incident and everything is simultaneously actual and illusory.
>
> — Brian Friel, *Dancing at Lughnasa*[1]

The original Irish intermarried with Celtic invaders and amalgamated. Neither Roman nor barbarian invaders graced Irish shores, and therefore a uniquely Irish civilization flourished before Christ and through the first few hundred years after his birth. The Irish had their own, nonclassical system of law, the Brehon laws, a complex system of compensation for all sorts of crime and disapproved behaviors, carefully preserved by the Brehons, a group of legal scholars separate from political and religious authority. This system remained at least in partial effect until the early 1600s, when James I's packed Dublin Parliament abolished it.

The Gaelic system of marriage and family was looser than that which we tend to associate with the modern Irish. The family was the central unit of society, and nine different types of marriage were available, as well as formalized concubinage, perhaps not unlike the extralegal modern reality. Divorce was theoretically permitted for numerous just causes, abortion and infanticide being among them, with marital property divided based on fault, the amount of separate property brought to the marriage, the status of the marriage, and the proportion of household work borne by each partner, a system remarkably like our own. Despite the availability of these procedures, they were probably rarely used except by the wealthy.

When St. Patrick converted the Irish to Christianity in the fifth century A.D., the new religion fit neatly into the Brehon social framework, partly because Patrick and his successors did not require conformity to a Roman sort of Christianity and partly because the Irish genuinely wanted both the old customs and the new religion. Women, though not completely legally incompetent under Brehon law, improved their legal standing through Patrick's religion, because Christians set great store by converting women; women established monasteries of equal status as those founded by men; nuns obtained legal rights not granted to laywomen; and the church lobbied to make crimes against women more serious offenses, sometimes more serious than crimes against men.

As far as "Roman" Christianity was concerned, there was not much of Rome left, barbarians having sacked it in A.D. 410 when its civilizing influence was already on the wane. Many of its intellectual treasures had already been lost or destroyed. The melding of pagan Celtic culture with Christianity and the new converts' enthusiasm for the intellectual treasure trove otherwise lost to the world inspired joyful worship and a thirst for knowledge. Through the energy of scholarly Irish clergy from A.D. 600 to 800, most of the world's classical intellectual treasures were saved by Irish monks, who copied and then decorated them with artwork of fantastic beauty,[2] and the Irish further regenerated their new religion by setting up contemplative monasteries and abbeys, a number with female leadership, both in obscure spots as well as at the crossroads of Europe. Ireland became a land of saints and scholars, with a religion that was uncentralized, "pure, spiritual, intensely personal, dedicated only to the absolute word of God."[3]

The English first landed in Ireland in the 1100s, not with thoughts of conquest, but because they were invited to assist in the defense of the island against Viking raiders. The pope had "given" Ireland to Henry II for the purpose of instituting religious reforms that the Irish were doing a good job of instituting without his help. Henry, uninterested in Ireland and far more interested in his French domains than his island kingdoms, allowed a lieutenant to sort things out in Ireland and to take advantage of opportunities that might present themselves. Several did, including the opportunity to marry the Earl of Leinster's daughter and succeed to the kingship of the province of Leinster. This made Henry sit up, take notice, and secure his position by taking control of the politically important "Pale," a small area surrounding Dublin. The English have controlled Ireland in some direct capacity ever since.

The English presence was tiresome, but it was a sideshow to Irish clan warriors, whose political loyalties were never more than temporary. Until Henry VII established Tudor authority in England in the late 1400s, English rulers were, like Henry II, more concerned either with retaining and enlarging possessions in France or in maintaining their thrones against the other strong English houses, who were forever attempting to usurp, often with success. Only in the Pale did the King's writ run. Catholic Ireland eventually became a victim of Henry VIII's acquisition of religious power in England—Ireland's religious treasures such as St. Patrick's Cathedral and Christchurch Cathedral fell into the Anglican Church of Ireland's hands—but Ireland was too independent and too remote to be significantly touched by the substance of the Reformation, the Counterreformation, or the Enlightenment periods that followed.

Ireland remained politically sensitive during the Tudor and Stuart period as a soft underbelly through which England might be militarily and religiously undermined, and Irish Catholics suffered for it. Elizabeth I instituted a settlement program which supplied loyal Protestant settlers and nobles with land taken from local Catholics. One of the ubiquitous Irish revolts—this one over Stuart insistence on the plantation policy and other meddling with land titles, always a sore point with the Irish—arguably helped precipitate the English civil war. Parliamentary forces sacked Ireland, with Puritan commander Oliver Cromwell himself declaring that Irish Catholics could go to "Hell or Connaught," the island's most underdeveloped province.

To replace Oliver Cromwell, the English invited the easy-going and politically pragmatic Stuart, Charles II, back to the throne. His Catholic brother, James II, succeeded him and set about with all the zeal of the convert he was to return the now solidly Protestant England to the Roman fold. James was deposed, but over the next century, he and his progeny, such as Bonnie Prince Charlie, gamely tried to regain the throne, James himself taking the traditional route through Ireland and giving Irish Protestants the military victories over his Catholic forces that they still celebrate today, the Battle of the Boyne and the Apprentice Boys' brave defense during the siege of Derry.

Ireland remained a thorn in the side of the British. It is debatable whether British management of the island was as bad as nationalist and folk historians have described it, but it could not have been good. The activities of the Catholic church, the church of a huge majority of the population, were repressively circumscribed after James's forces were defeated. The terms and enforcement of the Banishment Act of 1697 and other such legislation were so severe on the Catholic clergy that the emperor of Austria accused the English of attempting "the entire extirpation of the Catholic religion."[4] Due to the plantation policy and confiscation of Catholic lands, the portion of Irish land owned by Catholics fell from 60 percent in the mid–1600s to 14 percent of the total by the early 1700s.[5] Catholics who did own land were required to bequeath it to all their male heirs instead of keeping holdings together for future generations, which not only impeded the concentration of Catholic economic power but also meant that only a few Catholics could meet the property qualifications for voting when the franchise was extended in 1793. Catholics could not hold public office because they could not take the required oath rejecting transsubstantiation. Irish Catholics were also forbidden to carry swords, sit on juries, join the legal profession, obtain numerous forms of education, and own guns or horses worth more than five pounds. While the industrial revolution was making tentative inroads in Britain, the Catholic Irish remained firmly rural, with most people living in little better than dirt huts and farming land owned by others for a barely subsistence diet of potatoes. On the eve of the Irish famine of the mid–1800s, the British prime minister grimly described his government's "Irish question" as "a starving population, an absentee aristocracy, and an alien church, and in addition, the weakest executive in the world."[6]

A group of intellectuals, mostly Protestant, watched the exciting revolutions in both the United States and France and hoped Republican values might take root in Ireland. Led by Theobald Wolfe Tone, a young Protestant from Ulster, its adherents rose in Ireland in 1798. Like most such risings in Ireland, it failed, but Tone's political philosophy and ambitions ignited imaginations. Even today, modern players such as the two largest political parties in the republic, the Provisional Irish Republican Army and the Sinn Féin party led by Gerry Adams, trace their roots to Tone. Tone's revolt provoked the Act of Union in 1800, which eliminated the Irish Parliament in return for nonproportional representation in the British House of Commons and rule from London, where Irish representatives would always be outvoted. The Irish Parliament had voted itself out of business as a result of the persuasive power of British bribery, but in return the British had also dangled the possibility of Catholic emancipation. On that promise, the British predictably did not deliver.

Lethargy, degradation, and humiliation became the national mood, while the British busied themselves with military and coercive means of ensuring that the Irish would not again rise.

> A century of misery, want, and persecution preceded [the Act of Union]. A century of famine, emigration, and hopelessness followed. However much the Union might have benefitted Britain, to Ireland it seemed like the prelude to the slow bleeding to death of a nation.[7]

Into this hopeless situation arrived Catholic leader Daniel O'Connell, who successfully organized Catholics into a political force outside the mainstream institutions, won election to parliament, despite the law that did not allow him to serve, and eventually won Catholic emancipation in 1829. Tragically, the glory of this victory was depressingly short lived.

Any understanding of modern Irish history must start with the famine of the 1840s.[8] It killed at least one million of the island's prefamine eight million citizens, and at least another million left the country during the famine and its immediate aftermath — the direct loss of a quarter of the island's population. But the indirect loss was even more staggering. Between the famine and 1911, emigration, much of which may have been famine related, and famine-related deaths reduced the country's population by half. Most amazing about the Irish famine is that the nation survived it at all to claim its independence little more than seventy-five years later.

Outside the northern industrial counties of Ulster, six of which are now known as "Northern Ireland," much of the island contained essentially a rural, subsistence culture, leaving the Irish particularly badly positioned to survive such a disaster. The immediate cause of the famine was *phytopthora infestans*, known as "blight," which infected Irish potatoes. The potato was not merely Ireland's staple food, particularly for laborers and small farmers of the west; for much of the working poor, the potato, along with milk, was the *only* food.[9] Potatoes had numerous dietary merits, and Irishmen were larger and stronger on average than Englishmen of the time. Enough to feed a family for nine months could be produced on the tiny plots of land many young husbands received when their fathers subdivided their property, and one Irish historian has argued that landowners may have encouraged reliance on the potato because the small amount of land needed to raise them would leave land available for more lucrative crops.[10] In any event, even the poorest young Irish could marry early in the "haphazard, happy-go-lucky" affairs that such marriages were and produce large families.[11] Even before the famine, such unions struck outsiders as imprudent, but when asked why the poorest Irish married so young, one Catholic bishop tellingly pointed out that nothing could be gained by waiting. "They cannot be worse off than they are and ... they may help each other."[12] The situation stretched to the breaking point in the 1800s, with up to ten families sometimes occupying land intended for just one. Their children were the first to die when the potato crops rotted in the ground.

Over the prior fifty years, the Irish had faced many comparatively minor famines, and had the infection obliterated only the 1845 potato crop, the event would have been a minor footnote in Irish history. But the infection struck again in 1846. The next year, 1847, seemed hopeful, but the crop rotted again in 1848. The following year, 1849, was no better. People who did not starve to death caught "famine fever" (a colloquial term for typhus), relapsing fever or some other equally horrible disease.

Why, in a colony of and nearest neighbor to the richest country in the world, a famine occurred and was not alleviated has been a subject for endless debate. The British government did not provide what many Irish considered meaningful famine relief, even while Irish-produced food was flowing from Belfast to Liverpool, after having been collected under armed guard from towns where starvation was worst. One problem was that neither the government nor the landowners had suspended the rent system, whereby the Irish raised wheat, oats, and barley to make the rent payment for land on which they grew potatoes for themselves. Without a rent payment, a farmer would be evicted; without rented land, no farmer could grow potatoes; and without potatoes, he and his family would starve. It was that simple, especially since many Irish did not understand that wheat, oats and barley could be used as food and would not have known how to prepare them if they had. In any event, as Cecil Woodham-Smith explains in what remains the definitive account of the famine, "it was a desperate man who ate up his rent, with the certainty before him of eviction and 'death by slow torture.'"[13]

Further, it is fair to remember that the attitudes of British politicians in charge of famine relief and other opinion makers were strongly influenced by a belief in the recuperative forces of market capitalism, even though the long-term in which the invisible hand might be expected to work was not a time frame available to the Irish once the famine hit full force. The British failed to recognize that the famine broke all the normal rules and therefore other rules might have to be broken in response to avoid results that few other than Malthusians would countenance. The British were by no means opposed to providing relief, but over and over again, the philosophies and available resources governing the scope of famine relief were grossly disproportionate to the need. Nothing they tried worked. The British started by limiting famine relief to only those in distress due to potato blight, but failure of the potato crop had set into motion such economic destitution that the restriction was impossible to enforce. The British relief team tried to rely on local landowners to provide first-order relief in the form of direct aid or higher rates, but landowners were insolvent and unable to provide for their tenants. The government limited relief in some areas to those who would participate in public works, only to be overrun with applicants for unneeded projects. The government organized the public importation of only the most minimal amount of food for fear of pushing private importers, who they believed were most capable of obtaining the needed food, out of the market, but the "market" the government had hoped to protect through its inaction did not even exist, because there were no importers in Ireland of sufficient magnitude to address a food shortage of such scale; even if private importers could have gotten enough food to Ireland in time, rural areas lacked a retail economy to distribute it; people had no money with which to buy food anyway.

Pain would have to be felt in England and perhaps across the world economy to help the Irish meaningfully, and many British leaders simply lacked enough respect for the Irish people to take any risks or accept any pain on their behalf. Among the unhelpful comments from opinion formulators and policymakers included the following:

- Paying more than a person's "labour is worth ... would stimulate every man to marry and populate as fast as he could, like a rabbit in a warren," and "it is no man's business to provide for another," said the *Economist.*[14]
- Britain's chancellor of the exchequer told the prime minister that he was "perfectly ready to give [the Irish] as near nothing as may be."[15]
- The *Times* of London, noting that many British subjects were struggling in the mid–1840s, wrote that "[i]t appears to us to be of the very first importance to all classes of Irish society to impress on them that there is nothing so peculiar, so exceptional, in the condition which they look on as the pit of utter despair."[16]
- "The only way to prevent the people becoming habitually dependent on the Government, is to bring the [relief] operations to a close. The uncertainty about the new crop only makes it more necessary," wrote the British relief coordinator, Charles Trevelyan, in 1845, when the famine had more than three years to continue.[17] On another occasion, Trevelyan noted again that relief would lead only to "general reliance on our depot, a general relaxation of private effort ... and general failure and disappointment in the end."[18]
- The English economist Nassau Senior expected that the Irish famine would kill "not more than a million people, [but] that would scarcely be enough to do much good."[19]

The famine demonstrated to many the Irish nationalist's claim that as long as the union and British control of Irish affairs continued, the destiny of the Irish was in the hands of an alien society with antithetical interests.

Few individuals or societies would fail to do what it took to protect themselves against another calamity such as a famine, and changes in Irish citizens' economic, social and religious conduct had transformative, aggregate effects which produced a more conservative and group-oriented society. For example, the number of instances of personal religious devotional activity — saying the rosary, praying novenas, observing forty hours, dedication to the Sacred Heart of Jesus, and devotions to the Child of Prague — soared in the aftermath of the famine. More generally, institutional Catholicism played a key role in helping "Irish society cope with the psychological impact of disruption,"[20] and for the first time in Irish history, the Roman church and hierarchical Catholicism earned the genuine loyalty of the Irish people.[21]

Among the most profound and far-reaching secular changes were those in marriage, land tenure practices and estate planning. The practice of subdividing land prior to the famine had allowed young men to obtain what they needed to support the families they produced from early marriages, and that relative sexual freedom, though it may have already been declining, ended abruptly after the famine. That the more land a family owned or controlled, the more likely it was to have survived the famine may well not have gone unnoticed, and it is well established that many Irish families deliberately sought higher standards of living after the famine. Postfamine families systematically increased their land holdings and financial position by refusing to subdivide and making advantageous marriages, but the flip side of this new regime was that many men were never able to afford to marry.[22] Marriage merged with inheritance issues to become a complex legal and financial transaction. Brides were expected to bring hefty dowries to the altar, and it became de rigueur for the groom to have land or a place in business. Because an heir might wait years to inherit, average marriage ages — particularly those of men — rose, and the practice of late marriage, if at all, continued into the 1950s.

Liam Kennedy has pieced together one such estate-planning arrangement among the members of the Looby family of Limerick.[23] In 1927, Edmond Looby transferred his farm to his son at the younger man's marriage. In return, Looby Senior received an annuity, the right to live on the farm, and his daughter-in-law's dowry. He also required the son to pay an annuity to the son's otherwise disinherited sister, Ellen. As a result, Ellen probably eventually received a dowry in an amount approximately equal to that of her new sister-in-law, Mary.

The Looby example demonstrates the merits of circumspection in postfamine Irish marriages. Careful planning allowed the Loobys to provide financial security for father, son and daughter. Had the Looby son chosen, or been forced by premarital pregnancy to choose, a poor girl for his wife, he would have condemned either himself or his father to poverty and his sister to not only poverty but also celibacy and possible emigration because she would not have succeeded to Mary's dowry, and therefore could not have afforded to marry. In a world where many women hoped to marry but marriageable men were scarce, even with a small independent income, a pregnancy outside of marriage or an irregular sexual union, for either of the sisters-in-law, could have spelled disaster for Ellen.

For many, these were idle concerns. Many men lived their whole lives with neither land nor sufficiently lucrative employment, and so they neither wed nor procreated. Many of their sisters and potential mates lacked dowries. The lucky ones had a choice between emigration or a religious vocation, and the incidence of both increased dramatically after the famine, also saying much about Irish culture of the time. While many Irish emigrants to England as well as far-flung places such as the United States and Australia experienced economic and social opportunity beyond anything that could be hoped for in Ireland and at the same time vitalized the cultures of their geographic destinations, Irish historian Joseph Lee argues that the mass emigration experience proves the fundamentally materialist national character of those who remained, because "[f]ew peoples anywhere have been so prepared to scatter their children around the world in order to preserve their own living standards."[24]

On the other hand, if emigration as a form of upward mobility highlighted the grimmer aspects of the Irish survival instinct, perhaps the rise in religious vocations is more meritorious. A career in the service of the Almighty was an attractive option for a bright young person unlikely to inherit land in Ireland between 1850 and 1950. It provided an opportunity for one otherwise facing emigration or extremely reduced circumstances effectively to become a gentleman or a lady doing meaningful and sometimes intellectually challenging work in interesting and perhaps even comfortable surroundings. Such young people constituted a large proportion of the teachers, health-care professionals and administrators, and local intellectual and spiritual leaders, providing their neighbors with valuable service. Others traveled the world to do missionary work and to care for the less fortunate. Celibacy was no disadvantage to the religious life because most would have remained celibate anyway. Irish historian Ronan Fanning argues that even if the aggregate and personal ardor of religious devotion is held constant, the number of new entrants to the clergy or religious life under the Irish will tend to decline precipitously as economic conditions improve, which explains what has actually occurred since 1960 despite the fact that through much of that period, Irish religious devotion has remained comparatively strong.[25]

Revisionist Irish historians and economists question the extent to which this transformation in Irish culture would have occurred regardless of the famine, whether it occurred due to the aggregate effect of individual behavior changes, and whether the transformation is nothing more than a result of the fact that the more conservative and personally devout larger farmers and shopkeepers from the towns were more likely to have survived the famine than subsistence farmers. Nevertheless, recent research indicates that the revisionists have failed to dispel the longstanding theory of both academic and lay Irish that the famine did change individual behavior, which when aggregated, changed a society.[26] Granted, early marriage ages had tended to characterize the poorest Irish in the west, who suffered the most in the famine, while wealthy eastern counties had the latest average ages for marrying in the latter part of the nineteenth century.[27] The same appears to be true for the increasing number who avoided marriage after the famine.[28] Nevertheless, the traditional theory, supported by strong circumstantial evidence, is standing the test of time, despite considerable efforts to undermine it.

The fact remains that seventy years after the famine, Irish rural life had undergone a transformation and become deeply religious, materialist, conservative and marked by extreme sexual restraint. Noninheriting children who tried their luck in nearby towns as shopkeeping assistants (and eventually shopkeepers themselves) spread these rural attitudes to more urban areas. The swollen ranks of the clergy and religious, including the hierarchy, came from the farming and shopkeeping classes, a career in the church being a source of almost immediate upward mobility,[29] and they brought their conservative social attitudes with them to the seminaries, where the culture of those institutions did not challenge them. The clergy formed a significant portion of local and national leadership, and they policed their jurisdictions to minimize transgressions of the new social order. These conservative marriage practices continued into the 1950s and characterized the conduct of both Catholics and Protestants. As Terence Brown has written of the period:

> Irish rural life was like a raft afloat in the calm after a great storm. The Famine had betrayed so many that the survivor, conscious of the frailty of his craft and of the likelihood of future buffetings, calculated its precise seaworthiness and supported a social order that allowed no significant role in the countryside for those sons and daughters who could neither inherit the land nor make an appropriate marriage. For them emigration was the only possible route to a life without the frustrations and indignities of their position as helpers about the farm they neither owned, nor, accidents apart, would ever own.[] So in the first two decades of independence emigration was much less a reflection of demoralization in the countryside than a measure of continuity in Irish life and an indication of how powerfully the values that had taken hold in the second half of the nineteenth century still held sway.[30]

The intensity of the movement for land reform and home rule increased during the last half of the nineteenth century. During the decades surrounding the turn of the century, an Irish intellectual class, including such luminaries as the poet W. B. Yeats, led a renaissance of interest in Gaelic language, sport, and arts. A parallel group, including many of the same characters, began to organize into semimilitary units of volunteers and the more secret Irish Revolutionary Brotherhood, while Protestants in the north formed similar groups in anticipation of the passage of an Irish home rule bill in Parliament. Notions of an "Irish Ireland" were in the ascendance, and in 1914 parliamentary nationalists achieved victory: a home rule bill did pass the Parliament. Events quickly rendered the bill obsolete, however. The First World War intervened, and it was never expedient for the British to implement the bill.

Impatient radicals descended intellectually from Wolfe Tone, espousing an ideology known as "republicanism" and drawn from the core of the Irish culture and militia movements, took matters into their own hands. Republicanism in Ireland was "a shorthand term for insurrectionist anti–British nationalism, usually, but not invariably, combined with a rather vaguely expressed preference for political democracy, representative institutions, and human rights."[31] Where it differed from nationalism, which had been promoting the right to vote, land reform and home rule was that republicanism "proclaims the abstract rights of the nation and the inalienable and non-debatable right of 'the Irish people' to separation and complete independence, irrespective of the ballot box, counting of heads and majorities or minorities."[32] By contrast, the nationalism of Daniel O'Connell and the standard-bearer who followed him, Charles Stuart Parnell, kept its faith in the traditional mobilization of voters, party politics and the parliamentarian process. By the early 1920s, the old-fashioned nationalist movement would essentially cease to exist, though its commitment to traditional politics would survive in varying degrees.

Republicans rose in Dublin on Easter, 1916, hoping to dispense with the intermediate step of home rule, overthrow the British, and establish a republic in their place. Dubliners did not welcome the rising, but many were more disgusted by the ruthless execution of the principals. Public outcry forced the British to halt the executions when they reached a secondary leader, Eamon de Valera, who was, inconveniently, an American citizen, because he had been born in the United States before returning to Ireland as a boy. De Valera, the seniormost figure in the rising who lived to tell his tale, took the mantle of leadership, and public opinion quickly coalesced around him and his colleagues. They formed a republican party, Sinn Féin, or "Ourselves Alone," and its stunning electoral success demolished the other political parties in Ireland.

After the First World War, the British sent not an army to put down the Irish rebellion, but a souped-up, vicious, police force known as the Black and Tans, who were riddled by the guerilla tactics of the Irish Republican Army (IRA). By 1921, the British had wearied of bloodshed in Ireland and negotiated a controversial treaty to create the "Irish Free State," or Saorstát na hÉireann in Irish. This was not the republic for which the martyrs of the Easter rising had died — the treaty required an oath of allegiance, a governor general, British military bases on Irish soil, and the loss of the northern counties. Perhaps unwisely, De Valera, then the president of Dáil Éireann, the one-house Irish Parliament, decided not to back the treaty, and the country split down the middle. The two groups fought a bloody civil war, but eventually a competent, if not inspiring, protreaty, free state government established itself, and the civil war petered out.

Much of the political history of Ireland since the Easter rising and into the 1950s can be characterized as a struggle between the core constituencies of republicanism and nationalism: those who wanted the people to do "right" and those who thought the people had the "right to do wrong."[33] The treaty debate revealed a fault line in Sinn Féin between the adherents of "majority right and divine right."[34] Antitreatyites, republicans who thought success of the treaty polls revealed "that the will of the people was tainted, because the Irish had a collective slave mind and would have to be taught how to be spiritually free by the minority of true republicans," fell into the first category. Treaty supporters, on the other hand, who thought the people's will was sovereign "even if that involved voting for William Cosgrave [the treatyites' leader] rather than for Eamon de Valera," were the second.[35] The Irish fought their civil war over whether it was more important that their nation be virtuous, defined as a republic, than it was that all the people participate in the process of making the country what it would be, virtuous or not.

Many hoped that the political revolution would be an opportunity for a broad-scale economic, social and cultural revolution as well. It did not happen. Dire economic conditions and the lack of a "self-confident national bourgeoisie" provided the nation with little margin for experimental error.[36] Physical and political casualties in the Irish civil war had robbed the new country of the political talent that had been interested in radical change. Influential minority groups that might have contributed a broader range of ideas were lost to the mainstream political process, including antitreaty Sinn Féin members who refused to take the oath of allegiance to the king, and the overwhelming majority of Irish Protestants. This left the legislative process to the "gloomy, negative, and deeply conservative"[37] new protreaty party, Cumann na Gaedhael. The opportunity for a profound break with the past was lost.

The constitution of the Irish Free State was an odd document, completely satisfactory to few, openly detested by many, and describing a regime that bore limited resemblance to the one that actually came to power following the civil war. It was very much a British document when being British wasn't cool. As agreed in the treaty, the new constitution saddled the Irish with a British governor-general, Commonwealth status, and an oath to King George V for members of the Irish Parliament. The un–British provisions, such as those providing for referenda, initiatives, and extern ministers, never made it to the final document.

The Free State Constitution also included liberal democratic provisions such as protections for due process; the privacy of the home; freedom of conscience, religion and speech; free elementary education; and equal rights for women, though the document did not mention a "right to life." These provisions were nice, but they were not at the top of the Irish national agenda; establishing an independent Irish state was the prime concern, and during the 1920s, that translated into the less lofty ambitions of maintaining public order and convincing numerous malcontents to respect the legitimacy of the state. As a result, the Irish Free State became a somewhat authoritarian entity, despite its constitution's liberal rhetoric.

One of the ways the free state government tried to cajole the public acceptance that would translate into legitimacy and authority was by promoting an anti–British national definition. Many idealized the Irish nation as "pure and unpolluted from outside trashy influences."[38] Heavy-handed government programs nurtured Gaelic culture, particularly the language, but the policy failed dismally, despite the enthusiastic language and Gaelicization movement prior to independence. The Irish people did not want to be "West Britons," but the Gaelic culture movement was not the method toward which they ultimately gravitated.

What did become a badge of national identity was the church. Being Catholic was a way to be "not British," and many Irish expressed their nationalism through devoted religious participation. Outside the northern counties, Ireland was almost completely Catholic. Prior to the Easter Rising, when Protestants dominated most secular institutions, the parish priest was frequently the most important, and perhaps the only institutional, local Catholic leader. Though the hierarchy had not supported the independence movement, many parish priests coordinated nationalist activities on the local level.

The church, therefore, wielded considerable social power. In search of both popularity and legitimacy, as well as because they thought them the proper things to do, the free state lawmakers enacted a host of measures on the church's wish list: a ban on divorce, limits on religiously mixed marriages, censorship laws that forbade dissemination of information about contraception and other taboo subjects, curtailed drinking hours, regulation of dance halls, and clerical control of education. The incidence of government favoritism to Catholics and the institutional church, as well as discrimination against Protestants, were legion, though they were far less severe than the disadvantages Catholics had experienced under British rule. In return for its recognition that "there were truths that the majority had no right to flout,"[39] the government received the support it needed from the church.

It is common and by no means wholly inaccurate to criticize the free state government for "enshrining" Catholic teaching in the law and the church for being overbearing, but this is a one-dimensional characterization of a three-dimensional social phenomenon. Disappointment at the partition of the country, IRA and antitreaty malcontents roaming the countryside, and a teetering financial situation made anarchy a constant threat. Legitimacy for the new government was crucial, and laws congruent with Catholic moral teaching were consensus policies among both Catholic and Protestant Irish for a mixture of religious reasons, economic and moral defensiveness and the fledgling nation's rage for a national identity. As Terence Brown characterizes the thinking of the time, "[i]f Britain had its material empire the Irish could assert their dignity in terms of a patriotism and a Catholic spirituality which both transcended the island itself."[40] The rural Irish were particularly shocked by the contraception movement of the 1920s, for example, even before the Church made strong condemnatory statements. In any event, the so-called Catholic legislation actually changed little in people's daily lives. Many of these policies might have been effective in fact if not in form had legislation never been passed.

The free state government did not outlaw abortion because it did not need to. That abortion was and should be illegal was a settled issue, just as it had been settled in the other Western nations since the time of Christ.[41] This is not to say that abortion and infanticide were unknown to Irish culture, of course; occasional appearances in Irish folklore as well as disproportionately high infant mortality rates among the illegitimate suggest that infanticide was an occasional response to an unwanted pregnancy. After the Act of Union in 1800, British common law criminalizing abortion controlled such incidents in Ireland. Aborting a pregnancy after the unborn child had quickened in the womb was a misdemeanor at common law, but in 1803, the British Parliament made abortion subsequent to quickening a capital offense; prior to quickening it was also a felony but subject to a lesser punishment. The distinction between quick and nonquick women was difficult even for doctors to make, however, and in 1839, the statute first took the form it still has in Ireland today.

As reenacted in the Offenses Against the Person Act of 1861, any woman or third party who *unlawfully* attempts to procure her miscarriage commits a felony with the possibility of a life sentence. Anyone supplying an instrument or drug with intent to procure a miscarriage is guilty of a misdemeanor. The act also makes it a misdemeanor to conceal the birth of a child born dead or dying after birth. Under the terms of the Irish separation from Britain, the Offenses Against the Person Act retained its force on the island, and Irish authorities investigated and prosecuted a number of backstreet abortion cases early in the history of the Irish Free State.[42] Ironically, the Irish have a strict criminal prohibition on abortion and related activity not because they are Catholic, but because they inherited it from the Protestant British.

In a situation that would later create uncomfortable déjà vu for the Irish, the British courts faced the question of what constituted a "lawful" abortion under the statute in 1939. In *Rex* v. *Bourne*,[43] the evidence showed that a fourteen-year-old girl had been brutally raped, had conceived a child in the process and would suffer considerable emotional damage if she brought the child to term. The defendant doctor performed an abortion on the girl and was charged with a felony under the Offenses Against the Person Act. Just a decade earlier Parliament had made the intentional killing of a child "capable of being born alive" a felony punishable by life imprisonment, unless the act causing the death of the child was done in good faith "for the purpose only of preserving the life of the mother."[44] The court looked to, though it did not rely on, this statute in formulating its instructions to the jury concerning the law it was to apply to determine the doctor's guilt or innocence. The judge urged the jury to find the defendant doctor "not guilty" if it believed that the abortion had been performed in good faith for the sole purpose of saving the life of the girl, thereby concluding that an action lawful under the new act concerning the preservation of infant life must also be a lawful abortion under the Offenses Against the Person Act. If the doctor was of the reasonable opinion that continuing the pregnancy would make the woman a physical or mental wreck, the jury should construe the abortion as an effort to preserve the life of the mother.

The judge's justification for this test — that threats to life, as a function of health, could not be easily distinguished from health — was prescient for the coming abortion debate in Ireland:

> What then is the meaning to be given to the words "for the purpose of preserving the life of the mother." There has been much discussion in

> this case as to the difference between danger to life and danger to health. It may be that you are more fortunate than I am, but I confess that I have found it difficult to understand what the discussion really meant, *since life depends upon health, and it may be that health is so gravely impaired that death results.* A question was asked by the learned Attorney-General in the course of his cross-examination of Mr. Bourne. "I suggest to you, Mr. Bourne," said the Attorney-General, "that there is a perfectly clear line — there may be border-line cases — there is a perfectly clear line of distinction between danger to health and danger to life." The answer of Mr. Bourne was: "I cannot agree without qualifying it; I cannot say just yes or no. I can say there is a large group whose health may be damaged, but whose life almost certainly will not be sacrificed. There is another group at the other end whose life will be definitely in very great danger." And then he adds: "There is a large body of material between those two extremes in which it is not really possible to say how far life will be in danger, but we find, of course, that the health is depressed to such an extent that life is shortened, such as in cardiac cases, so that you may say that their life is in danger, because death might occur within measurable distance of the time of their labour." If that view commends itself to you, you will not accept the suggestion that there is a clear line of distinction between danger to health and danger to life.[45]

The jury returned with an acquittal, and *Bourne* became the law in Britain, though not in Ireland. Nevertheless, the problem of the legal distinction between abortions to save the life versus the health of the mother would eventually haunt the Irish courts as well, and prosecutions related to illegal abortions apparently dropped dramatically in Ireland after the *Bourne* decision.

Back in Ireland, by the early 1930s, Irish society was marked by people's awareness of their mutual interdependence and sense of self as defined by participation in groups and institutions, particularly their families, church, and nation. Group voices were strong in Ireland, and compared to Great Britain and the United States, they drowned out those of individuals. The ascendency of group voices in Ireland can trace its lineage to three enduring, historical experiences. First is the island's relative geographic isolation, which insulated the Irish from many of the formative experiences of other Europeans, such as the Roman Empire, the dominance of the Roman church, the Reformation and Counterreformation, and the Enlightenment. Second, the colonial experience enhanced the position of the Catholic Church as a receptacle for local loyalty and power and produced a reaction in the form of a national ideology and identification. Finally, the famine encouraged substantive respect for citizens' interdependence, efforts at mutual reliance, and loyalty to the institutional church.

By the early 1930s, however, colonialism had ended, the Irish having shown for ten years that they could keep their newly independent state afloat and fertilize a non–Anglo culture. Technology was making the island ever less isolated. Only the famine — now in the form of continued economic stagnation — was not receding from memory. Ireland was about to bring back a leader with strong views on all those subjects.

Three

The de Valera Vision: The Irish Constitution

> I have not lived solely amongst the intellectuals. The first fifteen years of my life that formed my character were lived among the Irish people down in Limerick; therefore, I know what I am talking about; and *whenever I wanted to know what the Irish people wanted I had only to examine my own heart and it told me straight off.*
>
> —Eamon de Valera[1]

In 1932, the Irish installed the party of the antitreatyites, Eamon de Valera's Fianna Fáil (Warriors of Destiny), behind the levers of power. De Valera himself is one of the most fascinating, hated, loved and infuriatingly elusive characters in modern Irish history:

> Eamon de Valera was highly intelligent, charming, compassionate, vindictive, volcanic and cold, vicious, and generous. He played every part; he left out no emotion. The pulsings within him, his will, daring, guile, and lust for power were phenomenal, a continuous astonishment. De Valera was not an idealist, but he served ideals when it suited and pleased him. He was not a reactionary, but he fanned reaction when it helped him advance himself. De Valera's career was one person's experience of nearly everything important in Irish public life since 1916, and he was as personally responsible for Irish history between 1917 and 1959 as any other man of his time.[2]

The "Man Who Was Ireland"[3] or the "cute hoor," as his detractors called him, had his full share of ideological and political slipperiness, but he made up for it in his well-defined, oft-discussed vision for the Irish nation, and two generations rewarded him with Dail majorities for it. The years between 1927, when de Valera's Fianna Fáil decided to take the oath of allegiance to the king and enter the Dail, and 1932, when it formed its first government, were a contest "between rival legitimacies: between the

Irish Free State and de Valera's Ireland."[4] In 1932, de Valera's Ireland won. For a time.

De Valera envisioned a nation of "small agricultural units, each self-sufficiently supporting a frugal family; industrious, Gaelicist and anti-materialist. His ideal ... was built on the basis of a fundamentally dignified and ancient peasant way of life,"[5] drawing on a long tradition of Irish nationalist and Republican romanticization of the island's rural culture, particularly in the west and on the islands where the Irish language survived. In de Valera's melodious words delivered on St. Patrick's Day, 1943:

> That Ireland which we dreamed of would be the home of a people who valued material wealth only as a basis of right living, of a people who were satisfied with frugal comfort and devoted their leisure to the things of the spirit — a land whose countryside would be bright with cosy homesteads, whose fields and villages would be joyous with the sounds of industry, with the romping of sturdy children, the contests of athletic youths and the laughter of [happy] maidens, whose firesides would be forums for the wisdom of serene old age. It would, in a word, be the home of a people living the life that God desires that man should live.[6]

De Valera's thinking was not unique. In a slightly less rarified form, his treaty rival Michael Collins had been developing similar themes himself prior to his untimely death, and the Catholic church of the 1930s was independently promoting an ideal of an Ireland founded on "the chivalrous honour of Irish boys and the Christian reserve of Irish maidens."[7] These ideas had legs because the Irish people believed in them. As *Irish Times* columnist John Waters explains it:

> In the Ireland of the 1950s, there existed a set of beliefs which, though difficult to classify neatly, were nonetheless recognisably of a monolithic nature. People believed in God, in land, in community, in locality, in the past, in nationhood and in particular notions of tribe and family. These beliefs are nowadays presented as being of a piece, as an integrated ideology which was used to dominate Irish society. But nothing could be more ludicrous. People did not believe in the values of the land, of the past or of a deity as distinct ideologies— in fact, they did not believe in them as ideologies at all. They represented simply a set of beliefs which made sense. Most Irish people lived on the land and derived their living from it. They lived within families, communities, and ultimately, within a nation, and these loyalties gave them an added sense of belonging and self-knowledge. But they were not going around the place thinking of themselves as adhering to a preordained set of beliefs, in the manner of a Maoist or a Thatcherite.

> Their view of the world was complex, contradictory, ironic and muddled, and they changed their minds in an incremental manner in response to the experience and assimilation of changing circumstances. In short, they did not live in an ideological construct.[8]

Instead, Irish thinking in the 1930s and 1940s had coalesced around a clear, substantive notion of a common good, and the Irish were giving their politicians a mandate to promote it.

It is easy to see how many Irish in the 1930s and 1940s might have found de Valera's an attractive vision, making a virtue of their reduced circumstances and providing hope of dignity for the future as it did, though the romantic rhetoric of the St. Patrick's Day speech was perhaps better packaging for nostalgic emigrants than financially pinched natives. In a famous story, a Fine Gael shopkeeper pointed out to an elderly customer that de Valera's policies had caused the prices of food to be higher than they would otherwise be. The customer retorted, "I would vote for him if it meant having to starve." Of course, many of the poor "also believed that de Valera would take good care to ensure that they would not starve."[9] Such was their belief in Eamon de Valera.

De Valera's vision was also a description of an ideal based on interrelationships among people and the communities they create, which also made that vision a useful organizing principle for Irish political thought. As Gearóid Ó'Crualaoich argues, in a very difficult time for the new state, de Valera's vision gave the Irish people "a mentality deriving not from the consciousness of 'class', in any modern sense, but rather from the consciousness of collectivities whose focus is primarily neither political nor economic."[10] Therefore, it gave form, substance and purpose to the strong notions of overlapping communities and group identification within Ireland.

In the long run, de Valera's vision turned out to be a mirage. It was the description of a dream, not a reality—the title of the speech is, after all, "The Ireland which we *dreamed* of"—and if the cultural inspiration for this vision had ever really existed, it was dying by the 1930s and 1940s. The masterpiece of Irish poet Patrick Kavanagh, *The Great Hunger*, preceded the de Valera speech by merely a year, and its description of the desperate existence of Patrick Maguire, an unmarried, middle-aged, peasant landowner who takes care of his mother and sister, is afraid to speak to available young women, grapples with the contrast between the ideological glorification of his way of life and the reality of its joylessness, and "will hardly remember that life happened to him,"[11] stands in stark contrast to the de Valera vision. Nevertheless, de Valera and many others believed in the merits of this vision, which he translated in practice to policies of cultural and economic protectionism through tariffs, language revival efforts and censorship, and at least in his enigmatic and rhetorical sort of way, he pursued it vigorously.

Eamon de Valera left the stamp of his personality and visionary aspirations all over what became *Bunreacht na hÉireann*, the Irish Constitution of 1937, which he drafted to replace the free state document. De Valera believed that to understand the aspirations of the Irish people, he needed only to look into his own heart, and what was in his heart was a nationalist ideology that grew out of the unique Irish experience but was set in the context of the more generous and responsible Christian democratic thinking in vogue at the time. He concluded, probably correctly, that the aspirations and values bound up with his rural, Catholic and almost utopian vision for the state — a communitarian vision — constituted the aspirations and values of the Irish people. This vision became the root of his Irish Constitution.

De Valera conceived a constitution that would serve not as a beginning, but as an end — an end to the British-imposed Irish Free State and the constitution of 1922 so that the Irish state might achieve true independence. The Free State Constitution was a seriously flawed document. To the extent that a constitution should reflect the core principles of the people, the Irish Free State Constitution had failed; it was mostly ignored, except on the twenty-seven occasions when it was amended in the fifteen years after its ratification. In de Valera's eyes, the British had imposed the Free State Constitution on the Irish through an infamous treaty process, and this constitution's primary achievement had been to preserve by force what was British in Irish society. As a result, the Free State Constitution lacked the loyalty of the people, and therefore the government on which it was based was not wholly legitimate. As an antitreatyite, de Valera himself had come to power disputing whether the institutions of the state were legitimate and deserved his allegiance. Restless, well-armed Republicans in rural areas continued to threaten. De Valera's "aim was to enact a constitution that would satisfy what he regarded as justifiable republican aspirations and thereby secure the legitimacy of the state."[12] In the process he "largely succeeded in squaring the circle between the parliamentary 'will of all' and the republican 'general will.'"[13]

He did it the Irish way, and the Irish way was Catholic. Few were better qualified than de Valera, a devout Catholic and Carmelite Third Order, called the "lay cardinal" by one of his biographers,[14] to draft a Catholic constitution for a Catholic country. According to John Murphy:

> [T]here was ... something ecclesiastical and priestly about his persona, and an element of the preacher in his bearing, his attire and his

> rhetoric. His speeches to the people of Ireland tended to be secular sermons ... De Valera was very much at home with the clergy, mixed with them on terms of equality and enjoyed a day out at an episcopal consecration just as much as one of his political successors would do at a Munster hurling final.[15]

On the other hand, de Valera was also "unquestionably both courteous and not only just but generous in his approach to minority traditions,"[16] and Fianna Fáil itself was considered the anti–Catholic party of its day. Moreover, a Catholic constitution was not de Valera's first-order goal: his primary objective was to create a state legitimately founded on the core beliefs of the Irish people. It just so happened that the core beliefs were very Catholic, and therefore, so was the Irish Constitution.

Despite the fact that de Valera accepted remarkably little assistance from anyone other than a few relatively obscure clerics, a close-knit band of civil servants, and, on a few key points, the archbishop of Dublin — and most of the assistance he did receive, he ignored — he produced a constitution of genius.[17] Despite occasional lapses, most notably the Irish Civil War, and especially in comparison to other Catholic European leaders of his day, de Valera was at heart a liberal democrat, and his constitution retained virtually all of the liberal democratic government forms and individual rights that the Irish had inherited from the British, in some cases lifting the structures and even the vocabulary straight from the free state document. On the other hand, while Ireland remained a liberal democracy procedurally, the underlying substantive social and political philosophy in de Valera's Irish Constitution is fairly unadulterated Catholic social teaching. The constitution's great achievement is the way these two philosophies check and balance each other.

In the years just before World War II, Catholic social teaching was in the process of modernization from a medieval philosophy advocating the unity of church and state, and de Valera's work anticipated Vatican II, when that council put its imprimatur on the structures and freedoms of liberal democracy as necessary to promote the common good, both the goal of Catholic political philosophy and the explicitly stated purpose of the Irish Constitution. But the Irish Constitution is not merely an amalgam of pure Catholic social thought with a liberal democratic setting. Only partly by virtue of its Catholicity does the Irish Constitution emphasize and reinforce the significance of groups and collectives in Irish society. Group voices and identities in Irish society were already strong as a result of the colonial and famine experiences. The Irish Constitution may have been cut from the cloth of Catholicism, but it was also a communitarian coat that fitted its wearer well.[18]

Ironically, the provisions of the Irish Constitution most often criticized as inappropriately Catholic have been almost wholly inconsequential to the development of Irish constitutional law and were not, in fact, viewed as sectarian in 1937. The preamble provides several examples:

> In the Name of the Most Holy Trinity, from Whom is all authority and to Whom, as our final end, all actions both of men and States must be referred,
> We, the people of Eire,
> Humbly acknowledging all our obligations to our Divine Lord, Jesus Christ, Who sustained our fathers through centuries of trial,
> Gratefully remembering their heroic and unremitting struggle to regain the rightful independence of our Nation,
> And seeking to promote the common good, with due observance of Prudence, Justice and Charity, so that the dignity and freedom of the individual may be assured, true social order attained, the unity of our country restored, and concord established with other nations,
> Do hereby adopt, enact, and give to ourselves this Constitution.[19]

To modern ears, this preamble sounds overtly Catholic—certainly religious—and it is. Nevertheless, the offending part is most often identified as the reference to the Holy Trinity, even though the reference to the Trinity was intended to be religiously inclusive, given that the reformed Church of Ireland was devoted to the Trinity and the Trinity was viewed in the 1930s as an ecumenical Christian symbol.[20] It is more correct to characterize the preamble of Bunreacht na Eireann as a proclamation of "the acceptance of *Christianity* and of the *Christian ethic* as the basis of government of the state."[21]

The 1937 constitution also recognized the "special position" of the Roman Catholic faith as that professed by the overwhelming majority of the nation's citizens, which suggests, at first glance, a potentially unhealthy favoritism. Sometimes forgotten, however, is the provision's second paragraph:

> The State recognises the special position of the Holy Catholic Apostolic and Roman Church as the guardian of the Faith professed by the great majority of the citizens.
> The State also recognises the Church of Ireland, the Presbyterian Church in Ireland, the Methodist Church in Ireland, the Religious Society of Friends in Ireland, as well as the Jewish Congregations and the other religious denominations existing in Ireland.[22]

The irony of this second paragraph, placed as it is in a provision that now rings as sectarian in modern ears, is that it attracted criticism from the

Catholic hierarchy and key members of the laity for not recognizing the Catholic church *more*. By contrast, support from non–Catholic clerics for this provision was quite enthusiastic, and de Valera actively courted them for their support of the entire document. In light of the antipathy in Ireland for Anglicism and of the growing antipathy across Europe for Jews, the second paragraph was a magnanimous gesture.[23] By the standards of the eve of the Second World War, de Valera had gone to great lengths to be inclusive; in fact, his choice not to identify the Catholic church as the "one true faith" almost derailed his constitution and his government, and he had to appeal all the way to Rome to save them. When the time came to remove the "special position" provision in 1972, Irish Catholic leaders supported the effort, while Jewish leaders actively opposed any such change. These sorts of provisions— the preamble and the religion clause — and the corresponding balancing of interests they represented, marked de Valera and Fianna Fáil as liberals, not conservatives.

The true Catholic influence on the Irish Constitution may be obscured from the view of those uninitiated into Catholic teaching, and it reflects a broader and more coherent philosophy than the mere engrafting of a particular religious dogma into the civil law of a society. As Irish historian F. S. L. Lyons describes it, "[w]hat gave Mr. de Valera's provisions their particular interest was the way they attempted to combine the liberal, democratic mode in which such declarations were commonly expressed with a very specific Catholic content,"[24] creating a "communitarian" constitution.[25] The key giveaway that the Irish Constitution was influenced by Catholic teaching is in the preamble, but it is not the reference to the Trinity; instead, it is the phrase "common good."

The modern Catholic concepts of personhood and the roles of persons within society describe a fundamentally communitarian vocation for humankind. According to Catholic teaching, a person is "an autonomous subject of moral decision"[26] with a divinely created human nature which bestows dignity and worth on one's individuality and both through and for whom society exists and is built.[27] Human beings are also naturally social and become more fully themselves in and through relationships with other human beings[28]; they are called to "confront and actualize" themselves in terms of other persons.[29]

> The social nature of man shows that there is an interdependence between personal betterment and the improvement of society. Insofar as man by his very nature stands completely in need of life in society, he is and he ought to be the beginning, the subject and the object of every social organization. Life in society is not something accessory to man himself: through his dealings with others, through mutual service

> and through fraternal dialogue, man develops all his talents and becomes able to rise to his destiny.[30]

The church further teaches that human beings are naturally inclined as well as divinely willed to form families, the basic institution of society.[31] Through the family, individuals realize and develop themselves in communion with other members of the group[32]; as the Second Vatican Council put it, "[t]he family is, in a sense, a school for human enrichment."[33] Nevertheless, families are not the only communities through which people may flourish and fulfill their social nature; society is made up of numerous intermediary groups—economic, cultural, social and political[34]—as well as the state itself.

According to the church, the goal of civil society—of all the groups and communities of individuals freely striving for perfection—is the common good.[35] The common good, in Catholic social teaching, is "the sum total of social conditions which allow people, either as groups or as individuals, to reach their fulfillment more fully and more easily,"[36] a definition shared by non–Catholic legal theorists also.[37] Pursuit of the common good has three elements: respect for the person, the social well-being and development of the group itself, and peace.[38] Moreover, respect for the common good is essential; the fast and far-reaching pace of change in modern society is such that people cannot afford the "luxury of a merely individualistic morality."[39] Instead, individuals must affirmatively contribute to the common good to the greatest extent possible, through either public or private institutions if necessary.

The state's role is to defend the common good, the citizens and their mediating institutions,[40] which means that politics itself "becomes a moral enterprise with a moral objective,"[41] preferring freedom, constitutional democracy and limited government. Yet the church rejects the Enlightenment view of negative government. Church teaching insists that the role of the state is positive, though limited; it has the "modest task of creating conditions within which men can 'with relative ease' achieve their own destiny."[42] Political authority "must be exercised within the limits of the moral order and directed toward the common good," and citizens may defend themselves and their rights when public authority oversteps its competence.[43]

The Irish Constitution adopts this Catholic communitarian philosophy almost exactly. According to the preamble, the constitution's primary goal is "to promote the common good, with due observance of Prudence, Justice and Charity, so that the dignity and freedom of the individual may be assured, true social order attained, the unity of our country restored, and concord established with other nations." Further, the constitution emphasizes and protects the social institutions—family, schools, churches, and the national identity—through which individuals are most likely to flourish and achieve their destinies, balancing that emphasis and protection against the imperatives of individual rights.

Both the Irish and the American constitutions emphasize protections for individual freedom, but what "freedom" means to both has diverged over the years. The man who once claimed that the Irish people "have no right to do wrong" envisioned freedom as Lord Acton described it, "the right of being able to do what we ought,"[44] or as the recent *Catechism of the Catholic Church* puts it, "[f]reedom is the power, rooted in reason and will, to act or not to act, to do this or that, and so to perform deliberate actions on one's own responsibility,"[45] but "[t]here is no true freedom except in the service of what is good and just."[46] The Catholic commentator John Courtney Murray argued in the 1950s that while "America has passionately pursued the ideal of freedom" of the "ordered" variety to new lengths, "it has not pursued this ideal so madly as to rush over the edge of the abyss into sheer libertarianism, into the chaos created by ... the conscience that knows no law higher than its own subjective imperatives."[47] On the other hand, modern Americans' use of "rights language" at every turn suggests that now Americans associate freedom and rights with the ability to do what one pleases, when one pleases.[48]

Structurally, the first three-quarters of the Irish Constitution as written by de Valera is a more verbose version of the American. The first major section starts with an emphasis on group identity, including three short articles about "the Nation," which declare its sovereignty and right to self-determination, define the national territory as the entire island of Ireland, and announce the jurisdiction of the constitutional government pending reunification of the nation. The second major section deals with "the State," indicating structurally the dichotomy between the Irish state and the nation; while the Irish state is the entity known as the Republic of Ireland, the Irish "nation" is currently divided between two jurisdictions—the Republic and the United Kingdom—and would take in peoples and institutions spread all over the world from forced and voluntary emigration. In the next set of sections, the constitution describes the structures of its parliamentary government and their interrelationships.

The constitution then includes an extensive and detailed package of fundamental, individual rights similar in subject matter to those that have arisen under the U.S. Bill of Rights and Fourteenth Amendment, but with important substantive and rhetorical differences. For example, the wording of the American provisions has an absolutist quality, while the Irish statements of rights are explicitly limited, and though the United States Supreme Court has limited the reach of many of the American rights provisions in practice, their wording still gives them "a psychological, symbolic force ... which just does not exist in Ireland."[49] Also, instead of the U.S. Constitution's expression of negative rights, the Irish Constitution's individual rights provisions describe relationships between citizens and between citizens and the state necessary to the maintenance of a good society, the sorts of "positive empowerments" that are central to Catholic teaching.[50] The Irish Constitution further places an affirmative responsibility for guaranteeing the protection of rights on the state, while American rights tend to be couched solely in terms of what Congress, and now the states, may not do. Consider, for example, the First Amendment to the United States Constitution:

> Congress shall make no law respecting an establishment, or prohibiting the free exercise thereof; or abridging the freedom of speech, or of the press; or the right of the people peaceably to assemble, and to petition the Government for a redress of grievances.

By its terms, the First Amendment makes no guarantees of these associational liberties; it merely guarantees that the government will not infringe on them. Compared to the U.S. Constitution's emphasis on absolutist protections for individual autonomy, the corresponding Irish provisions also reflect a communitarian philosophy[51] by defining positive duties for the state to protect and promote those rights[52] and balancing those rights against the needs of others, mediating institutions and society at large.

Social equality is central to Catholic principles of social organization. As Alexis de Toqueville observed of Irish American Catholics during the 1800s, "among the various sects of Christians, Catholicism seems to me ... one of the most favorable to equality of condition among men."[53] Though governance of the Catholic faith is hierarchical, most Catholics interact almost exclusively with their priest and fellow members of their congregation, and within that congregation, members are all equal before both God and the priest, as well as subject to the same rules and doctrine regardless of ability or wealth.[54]

Therefore, given both the Irish religious culture and the Catholic experience in both the United States and Ireland, where Catholics were not treated equally by civil authorities, it will come as no surprise that the Irish Constitution's personal rights provisions start with an assertion of the equality of citizens before the law instead of absolutist statements of individual freedoms: "All citizens shall, as human persons, be held equal before the law."[55] True to its Catholic roots, the syntax of the provision confirms the source of that equality as the humanity of each citizen. The provision then goes on to recognize that even equality is not an absolute concept by identifying legitimate classifications into which citizens may sometimes be appropriately divided for differential treatment, such as "differences of capacity" and "differences ... of social function," openings for legal distinctions based on sex.[56]

The Irish Constitution's "rights provisions," which come next, state true rights compared to their American counterparts. The Irish Constitution explicitly "guarantees in its laws to respect, and, as far as practicable, by its laws to defend and vindicate the personal rights of the citizen"[57] and therefore makes the affirmative commitment on behalf of the state to vindicate numerous personal *rights* as opposed to requiring that the state stand aside so that individuals may exercise a variety of *freedoms*. In fact, even merely referring to "rights" as opposed to "freedoms" bolsters the Irish state's correlative duty to vindicate personal rights, compared to the U.S. Congress's more minimal duty to avoid restraining an individual.[58] Therefore, while the U.S. Constitution makes broad, absolutist, rhetorical statements about protected individual activity, the Irish Constitution describes carefully crafted contours of relationships and concomitant duties.

Even before the Irish inserted the right-to-life amendment into this section on rights in 1983, with its specific admonishment that the state should vindicate the unborn's right to life to the extent practicable,[59] the Irish state's constitutional responsibilities toward human life were far more significant than those of the United States government. The organic Irish constitution states that "[t]he State shall, in particular, by its laws protect as best it may from unjust attack and, in the case of injustice done, vindicate the life, person, good name, and property rights of every citizen."[60] By contrast, the Fifth (and Fourteenth) Amendment of the U.S. constitution is more restrained: "No person shall ... be deprived of life ... without due process of law." Like the other amendments in the Bill of Rights, it limits government action, not private action, and requires no affirmative governmental protection for life.

A series of individual rights provisions that corresponds to those in the U.S. constitution follows. First is a rhetorically narrower but practically equivalent procedural "due process clause": "No citizen shall be deprived of his personal liberty save in accordance with law."[61] "Criminal procedure" rights follow; then an assurance of the inviolability of dwellings, a sore spot from the British response to the Irish rebellion of the early 1900s. The Irish constitution then "guarantees liberty for the exercise of" a number of rights related to the exercise of free speech and associations, but balances them against the needs of other citizens, collectives, and the state, making their exercise explicitly "subject to public order and morality."[62] Courts have also recognized additional, unenumerated personal rights, in some cases, arising from the humanity of the rights bearers themselves,[63] including the right to strike, the right of dissociation, the right to privacy, the right to earn a living, the right to communicate, the right of access to courts, the right to legal representation on criminal charges, the right to protect one's health, the right to travel, the right to marry and found a family, the right to know the identity of one's natural mother, and the right to fair procedures (due process) in decision making among others.[64]

At this point, the Irish Constitution contains a series of provisions that has virtually no counterpart in the U.S. Constitution, related to the family, education, private property, and religion. The provisions related to the family in particular do not fail to raise eyebrows when described to the average American or Britisher of today, for whom eliminating legal differences in the treatment of men and women is the order of the day, though oft forgotten is that the Irish provisions were considered somewhat liberal within the context of the day in which they were written. Gone from de Valera's constitution is the Free State Constitution's guarantee that all could enjoy the privileges of citizenship "without distinction of sex"[65] or the 1916 proclamation's statement that "[t]he Republic guarantees religious and civil liberty, equal rights and equal opportunities to all its citizens."[66] On the other hand, the provisions on the family reflect that institution's vital role as "the first school of the social virtues that are the animating principle of the existence and development of society itself"[67] and contain some of the most apparent influences of Catholic communitarian social teaching in the Irish Constitution.[68]

Article 41, titled "The Family," begins with a statement of principle:

> The State recognises the Family as the natural primary and fundamental unit group of Society, and as a moral institution possessing inalienable and imprescriptible rights, antecedent and superior to all positive law.[69]

The article therefore guarantees to protect the family "in its constitution and authority, as the necessary basis of social order and as indispensable to the welfare of the Nation and the State,"[70] consistent with Catholic social teaching that the family is "a school for human enrichment" and "constitutes the basis of society."[71] Use of the language "inalienable and imprescriptible" and "antecedent and superior to all positive law," however, suggests not only the textual superiority of family rights to the Article 40 personal rights, which are balanced against public order and collective needs, but also their fundamental vitality to the common good. [72]

The article goes on to "recognise[] that by her life within the home, woman gives to the State a support without which the common good cannot be achieved,"[73] and "The State shall, therefore, endeavour to ensure that mothers shall not be obliged by economic necessity to engage in labour to the neglect of their duties in the home."[74] This is virtually a restatement of the Catholic social teaching that women should not be compelled to work outside the home in light of the "irreplaceable value" of the maternal role in the special communal unit of the family, through which human beings first and foremost may flourish in all their humanity.[75] The reasoning in these provisions leads to two constitutional conclusions: "[t]he State pledges itself to guard with special care the institution of Marriage, on which the Family is founded, and to protect it against attack,"[76] and "[n]o law shall be enacted providing for the grant of a dissolution of marriage."[77] The constitution permits the government to discriminate in favor of the traditional married state in pursuit of the common good.

The tiny Irish feminist community protested at these provisions in 1937, as its much larger counterpart does today, but their objection had no impact on the final document. The family rights' provisions of the Irish Constitution were popular enough to constitute the collective will of the people.[78] Further, if de Valera's vision of "rural utopianism" was to be achieved, many feminist ideals, such as widespread female employment outside the home, were out of the question.

The next article, concerning education, further confirms the Irish state's role in pursuing the common good as envisioned in Catholic social teaching. The article again "acknowledges" the family's role as the "primary and natural educator" of Irish children, "guarantees to respect the inalienable right and duty of parents to provide" for the education of their children,[79] and permits parents to fulfill this duty in a variety of settings, with free primary education available for the public good. Though parents have freedom in fulfilling their duty of educating their children, that freedom is limited in the interest of the broader society: "The State shall, however, *as guardian of the common good*, require in view of actual conditions that the children receive a certain minimum education, moral, intellectual and social." And the order of those minimal priorities would certainly have mirrored the priorities of the Irish Catholic Church of the 1930s.

Last in the fundamental rights section of the Irish Constitution is the article on religious rights. As other provisions also indicate, the Irish Constitution is not neutral on the question of the existence of a Supreme

Being—"[t]he State acknowledges that the homage of public worship is due to Almighty God. It shall hold His Name in reverence, and shall respect and honour religion"[80]—but "[f]reedom of conscience and the free profession and practice of religion are, subject to public order and morality, guaranteed to every citizen,"[81] "[t]he State guarantees not to endow any religion,"[82] and "[t]he State shall not impose any disabilities or make any discrimination on the ground of religious profession, belief or status."[83] The state is further enjoined from various forms of religious discrimination, and the constitution guarantees integrity to the self-management of religious denominations and protects some of their activities. These provisions are not facially offensive to reasonable notions of religious liberty, sectarian, or overly burdensome to either believers or nonbelievers. They have provoked virtually no constitutional litigation.

Unlike the United States Constitution,[84] there is an economic theory imbedded in the Irish document. Article 43 starts with another statement of externally derived public philosophy: "The State acknowledges that man, in virtue of his rational being, has the natural right, antecedent to positive law, to the private ownership of external goods."[85] Based on that principle, the state's power to regulate is necessarily limited—"[t]he State accordingly guarantees to pass no law attempting to abolish the right of private ownership or the general right to transfer, bequeath, and inherit property"[86]—but the limited power to regulate is not a nonexistent power. The constitution goes on to reflect mild redistributionist principles in muted and pragmatic tones. Further, "[t]he State, accordingly, may as occasion requires, delimit by law the exercise of the said rights with a view to reconciling their exercise with the exigencies of the common good."[87] In other words, the rights of the individual are necessarily tempered by the needs of the larger society and even the needs of other individuals.

The Irish Constitution next includes an Article 45 with absolutely no counterpart in the United States Constitution: "Directive Principles of Social Policy" to guide legislative decision making. These principles essentially assumed the Oireachtas would be guided by basic capitalist, free market principles but urged limits such as recognition of the common good and general welfare of the people as a whole in distributing material resources and credit, so essential commodities would not be held by only a few individuals; protection against unjust exploitation of workers and the economic necessity of working in inappropriate labor; and economic care of the elderly, the infirm and children. In particular, the provisions urge that the legislature work to "establish[] on the land in economic security as many families as in the circumstances shall be practicable,"[88] a plain reference to de Valera's vision. Translated to the Irish situation, this article was very much the Christian Democrat program then coming to the fore in Europe, and de Valera's government bolstered the written constitution's economic and morality provisions with a constitutional scheme in legislation, providing more generous, social welfare benefits, capping the proportion of women in industry, and banning the sale, importation and advertisement of contraceptives. Article 45 itself, coupled with the preamble's statement that the purpose of the constitution is the Irish people's effort to promote the common good, again reflects a Catholic communitarian vision of public policy dedicated to collective, rather than individual, values, but they constitute a set of collective values intended to maximize individual flourishing.

One pivotal word in particular appears at least twice in the Irish Constitution, but never in the United States Constitution: "charity." Article 45 of the Irish Constitution directs that "[t]he State shall strive to promote the welfare of the whole people by securing and protecting as effectively as it may a social order in which justice and charity shall inform all the institutions of the national life."[89] The preamble states that the purpose of the constitution is to assist the people in promoting "the common good, with due observance of Prudence, Justice and Charity, so that the dignity and freedom of the individual may be assured, true social order attained, the unity of our country restored, and concord established with other nations." In recognizing and determining the contours of fundamental rights, judges are exhorted to look to notions of prudence, justice and charity in their decision making:

> Both Aristotle and the Christian philosophers have regarded justice as the highest human virtue. The virtue of prudence was also esteemed by Aristotle as by the philosophers of the Christian world. But the great additional virtue introduced by Christianity was that of charity — not the charity which consists of giving to the deserving, for that is justice, but the charity which is also called mercy. According to the preamble, the people gave themselves the Constitution to promote the common good with due observance of prudence, justice and charity so that the dignity and freedom of the individual might be assured. The judges must, therefore, as best they can from their training and experience interpret these rights in accordance with their ideas of prudence, justice and charity.[90]

This emphasis on charity is perhaps the most important distinguishing feature between the Irish Constitution and the foundational values of Anglo societies and is one of the most Catholic aspects of the document. Prudence, justice and charity are three of the seven human virtues according to Catholic doctrine, but charity is the greatest.[91] Charity is love, "the theological virtue by which we love God above all things for his own sake, and our neighbor as ourselves for the love of God,"[92] and necessarily implies relationship with others and respect for their humanity. A person of charity will naturally keep God's commands and thereby live a life consistent with divine law.

Though aspects of the Irish constitutional scheme ring shrilly in the ears of modern readers, to dismiss them as a thin-lipped, authoritarian etching of Catholic doctrine into a somewhat boorish nation's fundamental law obscures the best aspects of Irish constitutional law and history. The Irish Constitution balances individual rights and other priorities of liberal thought against the common good and needs of the groups and collectives in order that citizens' most precious human selves may flourish and cultivate fulfillment. In this sense, it is a communitarian blueprint, similar to a description of a Christian democracy,[93] and it elevates to an explicit catalog much of what thinkers such as de Toquevillle once respected so much in the United States.[94] It is consistent with the historical and philosophical roots of Irish political thought and the flora into which that thought had grown, and it did "discover and express the fundamental jural presuppositions of the lived accommodation" of the Irish people.[95]

Most criticisms of the Irish Constitution attack either or both sides of the compromises needed to achieve a balance between liberal and communitarian. First, the constitution was much less Catholic than it could have been, and as many at the top of the Catholic hierarchy would have liked it to be. Though a number of provisions reflect strong Catholic influences, the constitution as a whole was an impure jumble of religious natural law and secular rationalist philosophies. Some of the morality provisions, such as the divorce ban, were not congruent with Catholic teaching, and the ideal that the state would assist mothers so that they would "not be obligated by economic necessity to engage in labour to the neglect of their duties in the home" was not only consistent with Catholic social teaching *but also* very popular because a married woman who worked carried with her the stigma of poverty. De Valera needed all his fancy political footwork to sidestep criticisms from both the hierarchy and some in the laity that he had failed to name the Catholic church the "one true church," and the constitution rings with a statist aspect that the hierarchy increasingly resisted; after all, so many of the rights it announces are clearly endowed and primarily protected by the state. Nevertheless, de Valera intended and did well to steer Ireland away from the "confessional, right-wing authoritarianism" that gripped so many majority Catholic European nations in the 1930s; he might have taken on authoritarian or even totalitarian powers, yet he deliberately remained a liberal democrat to the end, repelled by much of the dictatorial politics of

Central Europe at this time.[96] Perhaps as Basil Chubb argues, judicial interpretation and not de Valera's text created the "Catholic Constitution."[97]

Second, unlike the Free State Constitution, which was really a blueprint for a cookie-cutter secular, liberal democracy, de Valera's constitution was specifically designed for the unique experience of the Irish nation. It was a statement of the core beliefs of the free state citizenry at that time. Ireland's history of colonization, religious persecution, and nationhood enduring against the odds was very different from that of Britain, the United States, Canada and other such Anglo nations, and therefore the Irish required a different constitutional order. The picture the constitution painted of Irish citizens' aspirations was accurate and uniquely Irish. Along with de Valera's protectionist international trade regime and neutral foreign policy, they confirmed that Ireland had chosen its own moral and philosophical path, which contrasted profoundly with that of other western nations, particularly Britain.[98]

Finally, the constitution's provisions related to church and state and social issues were consensus matters, at least to the ninety-three percent majority who were Catholic,[99] and not purely for sectarian reasons. Certain aspects of the "religious content" of the constitution were also consistent with a culturally formative strand of political thinking dating back to the origins of the republican movement and the Protestant Wolfe Tone in the eighteenth century, the nationalist Daniel O'Connell in the nineteenth century, and later what became the human rights movement of the late-twentieth century.[100] They had been integral Irish aspirations longer than the Catholic church in Ireland had been legal. Many of the principles criticized for their strong sectarian content are also central to the Catholic form of liberal democracy and have since become central planks in many international human rights charters.[101] Enda McDonald calls the fundamental rights articles "the successful coalition of republicanism and liberal democracy in a Catholic context."[102]

For one man to do all this was genius, made even more impressive by the fact that he had set out to do almost none of it. As Irish historian Ronan Fanning notes in an essay prepared for the 50th anniversary of the Constitution, "[t]o de Valera, the recent constitutional referenda on divorce and abortion would have seemed profoundly distasteful and, probably, irrelevant."[103] He had written a Constitution to create a state that would be respected for its legitimacy and genuineness at a time when the Irish Free State was not.

> To point out our current obsession with such issues as the constitutional regulation of sexual morality, with the role of women, with property, rights, with judicial review—even, perhaps, with the role of

> the North — is not to suggest that these are not appropriate concerns in the present. It is rather to remind ourselves, if I might end as I began, that de Valera's perspective must be distinguished from our own.[104]

Not much changed in Ireland as a result of the new constitution because the new document merely constitutionalized shared values already ordering society through legislation, custom or religious practice. To the extent that restrictions on liberty may be criticized by how much they unnecessarily constrain the minority, de Valera's constitution and the Catholic regime over which he presided may not deserve much. Censored books and contraceptives were often available through the mail from Britain, and after a short domicile in Britain, Irish citizens could even obtain divorces; given that many traveled to Britain regularly for work, the divorce ban, as opposed to religious and societal structures against divorce, may not have induced much hardship. The Irish Constitution also provides protections for minority rights through judicial review, and those protections have tended to be forthcoming. Perhaps within that context, it was appropriate for the overwhelming majority in the Irish Free State to have its way.

Four

What Kind of Country? Social Change from 1950 to 1980

> Ireland was a very inhibiting place at the time and could be still. There were a whole lot of repressions. So much would have been repressed.
>
> — Liam Clancy[1]

> The greatest enemy of the modernization process was the continuing existence of belief.
>
> — John Waters[2]

"Ireland was a very inhibiting place at that time and could be still. There were a whole lot of repressions. So much would have been repressed," remembered folk singer Liam Clancy thirty years later when describing why so many Irish teenagers and twenty-somethings like himself found the United States attractive in the 1950s. "There's freedom," he said, looking about a street in New York. "There's no social mores to which you have to conform: cultural, sexual, sartorial."[3]

There was also money, something in short supply in Ireland in the 1940s and 1950s. Workers poured out of Ireland, most of them searching for thicker pay envelopes. During World War II, two hundred thousand people left Ireland, and in the 1950s, emigration exploded to rates three times as high as those before World War II. The numbers of Irish working in Ireland actually dropped, and the country was no longer replacing its population. De Valera's cabinet was embarrassed when a social worker exposed the almost inhumane living conditions his desperate countrymen found in Britain. Irish workers in Britain were subsisting on tea and buns; men on day work shifts shared beds in boarding houses with women working on night shifts; the incidence of alcoholism, tuberculosis and gastroenteritis was as appalling as the sanitation. An anonymous letter from an Irishman living in England to then–Taoiseach John Costello in 1949 warned:

> Don't think that we are sending out angels & saints in our Irish boy and girl emigrants, most of them are backward and unable to fit into the more civilised mode of living here after the more cramped and less free standards prevailing in Ireland.

"'More cramped and less free'?" wonders Ronan Fanning:

> This lonely and haltingly eloquent indictment of how little independent Ireland had to offer so many of her children echoed throughout the fifties and compelled various élites—whether bishops, bureaucrats or politicians—to bend their energies to stanching the haemorrhage of emigration.[4]

But the Irish had no money to relieve the suffering and no way to stanch the bleeding at its source. Economic stagnation, made even more acute by agricultural disasters, had created severe conditions, requiring, for example, bread rationing, even though the nation had never been at war. The size of the hoards flowing out of the country did not mean that those who remained were benefiting from de Valera's vision. "By the late 1950s Ireland's ability to continue as a viable economic and social entity was in question."[5]

Other social "repressions" were interfering with de Valera's goals as much as they may have been intended to assist, such as the official, religious and private veil of silence where sexual matters were concerned. To be unwed and pregnant in Ireland was only barely easier in the 1940s and 1950s than it had been in earlier decades. An illegal British abortion or the opportunity for an unobtrusive confinement there were the preferred escape routes, while other such women flocked to group homes run by the Catholic Church. Though a refuge for some, allegations of near-slavery conditions have been made of others. Many single mothers raised their children for a time but were then forced to give them up for adoption.

Social control reached its peak during World War II, "the Emergency," as it was known in neutral Ireland. The Emergency Powers Act and Censorship Act permitted the government to preserve its image of neutrality and to take a strong hand with the IRA, but they also dammed up the escape route from so many Irish social ills: traveling to Britain. Under these conditions, prosecutions for infanticides and backstreet abortions exploded, particularly among the poor and unmarried. Forty-six women were tried for infanticide, and many of those found guilty were sentenced to hang.

> So many of the infants' deaths of that era were invested with a tragic symbolism: time after time, they died of asphyxiation as a result of the birth mother's attempts to silence her baby's cries by filling its mouth

> with rags, or clay, or grass, or whatever came to hand, as she pushed her baby out into a world that would punish her for the infant's existence.[6]

Another judge lamented in 1944 that "[i]t is a melancholy reflection that for the past few weeks I have been trying these [backstreet abortion] cases and nothing else."[7] When the full horrors of these circumstances were revealed in the mid–1990s, people were shocked to discover that such things had gone on in de Valera's Ireland.

In less controversial situations from the 1940s and 1950s, Irish criminal courts applied the Offenses against the Person Act indirectly to punish those performing abortions when those operations went wrong. In a 1940 case, an abortionist who caused the death of a woman on whom he was performing an abortion was found guilty of manslaughter.[8] One woman of the period was sentenced to fifty-eight years in prison for performing eight abortions.[9] A 1957 jury found a nurse who killed a woman in the process of performing an abortion on her guilty of felony murder, where the abortion in contravention of the Offenses Against the Person Act was the underlying felony.[10]

In 1949, the Oireachtas enacted the Infanticide Act, which permitted a woman who killed her child under the age of twelve months to be tried for felony manslaughter as opposed to murder if the woman caused her child's death by a "wilful act or omission"; in circumstances that would, but for the Infanticide Act, constitute murder; and "at the time of the act or omission the balance of her mind was disturbed by reason of her not having fully recovered from the effect of giving birth to the child or by reason of the effect of lactation consequent upon the birth of the child."[11] Unfortunately, the act, which was almost a duplicate of the British Infanticide Act of 1938, made little practical or philosophical sense. One Irish journalist who has studied the infanticide problem in the 1940s and 1950s believes the act would have applied to none of the cases she can identify, because "puerperal psychosis"—to which "lactation" refers in the act—is rare, and there is little evidence of a medical connection between actual lactation and mental disorder.[12] In fact, it was on this basis that the Criminal Law Revision Committee of Great Britain seriously considered recommending that Britain substantially reform or repeal its Infanticide Act in 1980.[13] The Act may have done little more than cover up broader social problems by classifying their immediate manifestation—mothers killing their children—as acts of mental illness and even encouraging victims' mothers to take legal responsibility for crimes they did not commit, because all too often, the perpetrator of infanticides was the mother *of the mother* of the victim.[14] To the extent that the act was intended to extend generosity to those in difficult situations who might otherwise have faced murder convictions, at best it created legal fictions and encouraged deception. Great Britain's Butler Committee report on mentally abnormal offenders from 1975 argued that Britain's infanticide laws put pressure on generous psychiatrists "'to conform their medical opinion to the felt need for mercy.'"[15] Such acts are not well-directed solutions for the scourge of infanticide and underscore the disadvantages of medicalization of family law.

The economic and social repressions of the war years, as well as Ireland's neutrality policy itself, have given rise to the characterization of the Emergency years as a period in which Ireland became a historical dropout,[16] but war years had a more complicated effect on Irish culture. "The emotional experience of neutrality" had made the inchoate state the constitution had just defined seem real, because "[m]en had been prepared to bear arms on its behalf" and Ireland had not again slipped under the political thumb of one of the larger combatants.[17] While citizens of other developed nations were off shooting at each other, the immature political entity of the twenty-six counties became a self-aware nation and sowed seeds that would blossom into a full-fledged exploration of the question "who are we?" in the coming generation. In fact, just after the war, Ireland stumbled into two intertwined, foundational debates: over the relationship between the state and the people and the relationship between the state and the church. Both of these fundamentally constitutional debates were played out in great detail in the public arena.

The church and government had enjoyed "mutually reinforcing political and episcopal visions" during the first twenty-five years in the history of the free state, but they parted company when the people's material deprivation became inexcusable.[18] There are simply no good statistics from the period to report. From 1949 to 56, when the average increase in the gross national product (GNP) of Organization of European Economic Cooperation nations was 42 percent, and even the British GNP increased by 21 percent, the Irish GNP increased only 8 percent.[19] National income increased by only 1 percent from 1949 to 53.[20] An optimistic *Irish Banking Review* article of the period rejoiced that Irish standards of living had significantly improved—"compared with the Great Famine of 1845–50!"[21] The notion of economic issues driving politics was a relatively new concept for the Irish. Economics had played a role in the land wars during the last half of the 1800s, but the civil war and treaty debates had been quarrels over independence, sovereignty, and cultural aspirations. The early governments of the 1920s had never promised economic development, and though de Valera experimented with New Deal-type policies and efforts toward industrialization, he publicly discouraged expectations of economic improvement; his vision was of a "frugal" lifestyle, after all, and even as late as 1951 he was commending "the choice of the humble cottage" to emigrating Irish.[22] Yet, behind all these lofty ideals, there had been hope that political, and through it economic, control over Irish resources would provide economic security that would at least stem the tide of emigration. It did not happen. The situation had become unconscionable at the same time members of the Irish hierarchy were becoming interested in a more materialist social teaching. Those two dominant group voices—church and state—were on a collision course.

The church and the state ultimately clashed over two related issues, adoption and health care, and these served as a vehicle for a debate that ended in a draw over the role of the state in individuals' lives and in respect for human dignity. The polite tug-of-war began during the framing of the constitution and continued into the mid–1940s over a matter of Catholic social teaching known as "vocationalism," a vision of social organization that would cut across class lines so that workers and employers in various professional and vocational groups could join forces to promote their mutual interests, a vision which never caught on in Ireland. After the war, the continually less polite quarrel turned to public health issues when a well-respected bishop excoriated the government over the state's health "dispensary" system, which he claimed "is the core, the hub and the heart of the degrading Poor Law system," and demanded the government do better.[23] Though this particular position was a minority view among the bishops, church leaders of a number of philosophical stripes were for the first time openly ignoring their previously symbiotic relationship with state institutions.

Despite considerable public support for legislation legalizing adoption as early as 1948, the two governments of the period shied away from the issue on constitutional and religious grounds. The Catholic hierarchy's opposition to legalized adoption stemmed from the proposed measures' failure to protect the natural family and the rights of natural parents and adoptees. The hierarchy announced in 1952 that it supported legalization as long as those interests were protected; it participated in drafting legislation; and the Adoption Act passed that year.

The hierarchy reacted differently to the health-care issue. Rising infant mortality statistics and new British national health service nurtured public interest in state health schemes for Ireland in the late 1940s. Fianna Fáil had passed a health-care program for mothers and children in 1947 before private channels communicated the news that the church opposed it on doctrinal grounds, including compulsory participation requirements, excessive centralization, and other provisions which were outside the mainstream of western health programs of the time. It was probably the first time the hierarchy had made a formal protest to a particular item of legislation, but Fianna Fáil lost at the polls soon afterward and could not address the hierarchy's concerns themselves. The interparty government that followed was made up of virtually the entire rainbow of political ideologies in Ireland, and it proposed amendments to some of the offensive provisions, but their health minister, Dr. Noel Browne, held firm on other aspects of the revamped mother-and-child plan. Members of the hierarchy corresponded privately with the cabinet to express their concerns that the scheme would interfere with parents' rights and involve the state in sensitive aspects of gynecological care, and over Browne's objections, the government decided to accommodate the hierarchy's wishes. Browne resigned and published the correspondence, and the government fell.

Back in power, Fianna Fáil passed virtually the same mother-and-child program with mostly cosmetic changes, which satisfied the hierarchy. The only significant change the hierarchy (and their allies in medical organizations) exacted from Fianna Fáil was that services would be provided for free only to those who qualified under a means test. Ironically, after all that effort and cost to church and state relations, only fifteen percent of the population was barred from free mother-and-child services, and in the years that followed the passage of the act, government officials agreed that a means-test program was better for Ireland than a British-style national health service would have been.

These two experiences, particularly the mother-and-child controversy, help clarify three aspects of the church's role in policy making by the mid–1950s. First, though the church had genuine disagreements with the government over issues closely related to faith and morals, the hierarchy was most concerned about the increasing size of the public sector, the squeeze on mediating institutions such as the church, and the state's conmitant control over individual behavior. After all, "instruction in regard to sex relations, chastity and marriage" was only one aspect of an extensive mother-and-child health plan, and the possibility that the government would introduce "birth limitation and abortion" was probably small.[24] On the other hand, the mother-and-child plan could also be viewed as a huge power grab by the state, wiping away the system of shifting communities from this broad and sensitive area of public policy and private decision making.

Further, a widespread and all-encompassing program such as the mother-and-child plan would do considerable damage to the principle of subsidiarity, the organizing principle for political institutions that "reflect[s] the primacy of the person over things in the Church's social teaching."[25] As Pope Pius XI explained in the 1931 encyclical, *Quadragesimo Anno*:

> When We speak of the reform of the social order it is principally the State We have in mind. Not indeed that all salvation is to be hoped for from its intervention, but because on account of the evil of Individualism, as We called it, things have come to such a pass that the highly developed social life which once flourished in a variety of prosperous institutions organically linked with each other, has been damaged and all but ruined, leaving thus virtually only individuals and the State. Social life lost entirely its organic form. The State, which now was encumbered with all the burdens once borne by associations rendered extinct by it, was in consequence submerged and overwhelmed by an infinity of affairs and duties.
>
> It is indeed true, as history clearly proves, that owing to the change in social conditions, much that was formerly done by small bodies can nowadays be accomplished only by large corporations. Nonetheless, just as it is wrong to withdraw from the individual and commit to the community at large what private enterprise and industry can accomplish, so, too, it is an injustice, a grave evil and a disturbance of right order for a larger and higher organization to arrogate to itself functions which can be performed efficiently by smaller and lower bodies. This is a fundamental principle of social philosophy, unshaken and unchangeable, and it retains its full truth today. Of its very nature the true aim of all social activity should be to help individual members of the social body, but never to destroy or absorb them.[26]

The principle of subsidiarity maximizes freedom by allowing decisions to be made by the smallest and most local groups possible, thereby minimizing the number and significance of the occasions when citizens must live according to rules with which they disagree.[27] In the case of a health-care scheme, the principle of subsidiarity might have benefited both Catholics and non–Catholics in 1950s' Ireland.

Therefore, both the political and moral issues the mother-and-child plan raised were extremely important both to the church and many practicing members. The church gave voice to widespread concerns about the increasing size of the state in light of communist and other socialist victories on the continent; even as late as the early 1950s the government "still had not grasped that, to many Irishmen, the greatest menace was ... the power of a centralising government department."[28] It certainly was to the church.[29] Small victories, such as limited means testing, providing choice of a doctor and preserving the church's role as a widespread health-care provider, are much more significant in light of those political goals. In both cases, the church was backing "human dignity" and individualism, at least to the extent that the latter was a check against centralized power, while the state's primary concerns were homogeneity and bureaucracy in a quest for efficiency. In the adoption situation, the church wanted to protect "freedom of religion" or at least "freedom to ensure your child would grow up Catholic" for natural parents; in the mother-and-child case, the church's concern was freedom of choice and freedom to opt out of state-supported health care or to tailor one's state health benefits to one's individual (read: religious) needs.

The two episodes also highlight the church's ambiguous political role in Irish society. In some respects, the church behaved as interest groups with considerable support will do; it tried to make sure its concerns were represented in the ultimate legislation, though perhaps with some of the arrogance of one who is not used to hearing "no." If the church was a supplicant, however, it was a very compelling one given its large membership and the fact that its hierarchy speaks with what its members, including government ministers, viewed as a higher authority properly demanding their obedience. Even during the mother-and-child crisis, the Taoiseach John Costello stated that "I am an Irishman second; I am a Catholic first."[30] Further, the church's influence may have been more pronounced when making requests based on faith and morals, such as the nature of gynecological care and the rights of natural parents and children to their religious views, because these issues are more widely accepted as within the hierarchy's competence.[31]

The watershed nationwide debate that followed Browne's resignation and publication of the hierarchy's correspondence was perhaps the first time a high-profile group publicly criticized the hierarchy's political activities, and the criticism may have gotten the better of the electoral argument. The interparty government that capitulated in response to church pressure on the popular mother-and-child measure was swept from power soon afterward. The electoral beneficiaries, de Valera's Fianna Fáil, may have been inclined to be moderately deferential to church doctrine in fashioning policy during the 1950s, but their leaders were not always of the same mind as the hierarchy. The mother-and-child controversy had flared up at just the moment that the hierarchy had begun to take a more intrusive role in criticizing Irish public policy, and it bungled that role somewhat. A small movement to amend the religion provision in the constitution to recognize the Catholic faith as the "one true faith" failed during the same period.

Moreover, it is not wise to equate the political machinations of one nation's hierarchy with the view from Rome, as de Valera was reminded for the second time when he appealed the Irish hierarchy's verdict on his health policies to the Vatican and received a much more favorable response from Rome. The Irish bishops did force Fianna Fáil to amend the scheme before it was enacted, and de Valera was quick to state that the church had the final say on the morality of any law in Ireland, but the final plan was virtually the same program Browne had proposed two years earlier. Flouting church teaching did not pay electoral dividends in Ireland in the mid-twentieth century, but the mother-and-child debate also showed that simply allowing the church to dictate policy was a strategy of equally limited utility. A role, but not a veto pen, appears to have been the happy medium on which everyone could compromise. As Dermot Keogh concludes, "[l]ittle evidence can be found in this episode to confirm the 'Rome rule' thesis."[32]

The mother-and-child debate may have been the hierarchy's last policy hurrah. No longer would the church be part of the state's institutional support structure, because the state did not need the church anymore. In fact, the state could afford to be a little pushy. As Ireland got to the point where it could afford more social welfare programs, the state encroached directly on matters formerly left to the church, such as health and education, and indirectly through government incentives that had the effect of influencing the voluntary actions of individual church members. This was an obvious threat to the practice of such a communal religion as Roman Catholicism, and not surprisingly, the bishops were worried. To maintain the same balance between the state and religious spheres in society, however, the state would have to be more, rather than less, accommodating to the needs of Catholic practitioners,[33] which was partly what the church was clumsily seeking when it spoke of individual rights. In any event, the days of lobbying the government for dance hall restrictions were over. In the next few decades, the church would have its work cut out for it keeping its own flock in line.

The sum of these events may have made the "repressions" of the 1950s that Liam Clancy remembers seem more real than they were. Emigration, censorship and unwed motherhood stories horrify, but part of the pain many Irish felt in the midcentury stemmed from the fact that their national goals and expectations were changing. The debates over adoption and health showed that there were limits to how rigid a society — dominated by either the hierarchy's agenda or a centralized government's— the people would tolerate. Of course, these changes were still "embryonically in the making,"[34] but Ireland was clearly moving on. The social control of the 1940s and the confusion of the early 1950s may have been the darkest hour before the dawn.

The fate of the censorship policy confirms the applicability of such symbolism. The notion of state censorship of publications is anathema to modern Americans, but it can be justified by an ethic of public policy based on "the rational conviction that there are certain basic moral principles, rooted in the very nature of the human person, which are fixed and unchanging," as opposed to the vision of societal order based on "deals made by individuals and groups" and determined at any time by the "pull and drag between the State and individuals."[35] This is essentially the difference between the vision of social order based on natural law and that based on pluralism or individualism. Certainly, the natural law requires that censorship laws be just laws, but freedom of expression still may be regulated in the common good.

Until 1929, British censorship laws remained in effect in Ireland, but they targeted "home-grown" pornography, and since most published material came from abroad, they were insufficient to maintain even the same power and control that the British had. During the first years of independence, all the usual suspects in the Free State public philosophy exerted themselves, and the Irish decided they wanted more power and control in their censorship laws anyway:

> Once [the] need for change was recognised, the Free State had the opportunity to devise a law to suit itself. Religious fervour, nationalism, a desire to be different, a determination not to be a cultural appendix of Britain: all of these factors led to a movement to reform the law on obscenity—not just to introduce technical changes but to increase its scope: and, in addition, to do something to stem the growing propaganda for birth control which was coming into the country.[36]

The Irish parliament passed a major censorship bill in 1929 in response to these concerns.

The 1929 censorship regime did its job in keeping pornography—even a pretty high standard for pornography—out of sight and, for many people, out of mind, but the policy always produced overly broad results. Especially for the Irish, who pride themselves on their literacy, too much legitimate, serious work showed up on the banned list. It is so well known that it barely requires notice that writers such as William Faulkner, Graham Greene, Ernest Hemingway, Aldous Huxley, Marcel Proust and an embarrassingly thorough list of Irish writers including Samuel Beckett, Austin Clarke, St. John Ervine, James Joyce, Maura Laverty, George Moore, Kate O'Brien, Sean O'Casey, Frank O'Connor, Sean O'Faolain (a leading activist against censorship), and Liam O'Flaherty had works on the censored lists.[37]

Censorship came under increasingly aggressive attack in the 1940s and 1950s. During the Emergency, the Senead engaged in a public debate over the wisdom of censoring books that referred to monitoring the "safe period" as a means of family planning. Post-Emergency reforms, which created an appeals structure, just produced an even longer list of banned works. Writers and intellectuals continued their assault on the censorship laws for the next ten years, and in 1957, Fianna Fáil appointed a more liberal board:

> No longer did the Censorship Board see itself as waging a war against an alien campaign of cultural and moral contamination but operated as a body "making it difficult for the average person to read books which were pornographic and had no literary merit."[38]

In the wake of tightening controls that could not realistically have been sustained over the long run, the censorship regime shifted almost overnight to a sensible system with public support. After an additional reform in 1967, the question for Irish censorship was not whether it was too strict, but whether it was strict enough.[39]

In 1959, Eamon de Valera surprised everyone by turning over the reins of power to his deputy, Sean Lemass, and running for the almost completely ceremonial office of the presidency. All the pressures for modernization and change found their release in Lemass' succession. He initiated a series of multiyear economic strategic plans which abandoned de Valera's economic protectionism for free trade, encouraged infrastructure construction, and provided public incentives for the development of key industries. The Irish economy finally burst ahead.

De Valera had the joy of choosing to end his political career at exactly the time it might well have been ended for him. Ireland would have taken its first tentative steps into modernity in the 1960s regardless of who held the reins of power. Vatican II would change the relationship of lay Catholics and their church and encourage dissension and discussion among both the laity and the clergy. A constitution review committee would propose radical changes such as dropping the territorial claim over Northern Ireland, references to the Catholic Church and the ban on divorce. The economic possibilities of the European Common Market were increasingly attractive, and Ireland finally joined in 1972. De Valera himself is believed to have voted against a constitutional referendum to permit Common Market membership, and "there is pathos in the thought of the elderly President being among the one-sixth of voters who said 'No' to a measure that subverted fundamentally the democratic basis of legislation as he had provided for it in the Constitution he had drafted thirty-five years before."[40]

Perhaps the most important instrument of social change, Radio Telefís Éireann, the Irish television station, began broadcasting on New Year's Eve in 1961. Both de Valera, as president, and Lemass, as Taoiseach, commented on the advent of the new medium; their remarks say as much about the chapters that were opening as about those that were closing in Ireland's history. De Valera welcomed television, but cautiously:

> Never before was there in the hands of man an instrument so powerful to influence the thoughts and actions of the multitude.... A persistent policy pursued over radio and television, in addition to imparting knowledge, can build up the character of a whole people, including sturdiness and vigour and confidence. On the other hand, it can lead, through demoralisation to decadence and dissolution.[41]

Lemass's approach was different. He was wholeheartedly enthusiastic about television as a means for opening Ireland to the world.[42] He could find no fault with the medium.

Depending on one's precise view of "sturdiness," "vigour," "demoralization" and "dissolution," both men were correct. Television changed Ireland as much as any other force acting on the republic; as Fianna Fáil TD[43] Oliver Flanagan lamented, "There was no sex in Ireland until the BBC," a statement that readers may take as they will.[44] Journalist and author Mary Kenny remembers that she was introduced to "the pill" while watching the BBC's *Panorama* program in 1960.[45] The ubiquitous metaphor for this process was Gay Byrne's *Late, Late Show*, a long-running Irish talk show taking on the most controversial issues and said to be the main topic of conversation after Sunday Mass in the 1960s and 1970s. The Irish Women's Liberation Movement used the show (or was it the other way?) to launch a manifesto, *Chains or Change*, in early 1971. *The Late, Late Show* rattled the sensibilities of the viewing public at first and the bishops for long afterward, because they realized that such programming "would challenge and eventually replace the Church as the teaching authority in manners and morals, as indeed it has ... done."[46] In part, the church had itself to blame, because it had failed to provide the Irish with the rich meat of an intellectual faith that could sustain itself in the face of such challenges.[47]

Patrick McCabe's prescient novel, *The Dead School*, dramatizes the fall of de Valera's Ireland with almost sympathetic delicacy when his protagonist, Raphael Bell, who watched his father die in a Black and Tan war ambush years earlier and is now the headmaster at a respected boys' school, watches an interchange on a thinly disguised 1975 *Late, Late Show* broadcast. The panelist happens to be a member of the parents' committee seeking to "reform" Raphael's school by arguing, among other "heresies," that the boys need not carry rosary beads at school or visit sites of the 1916 Rising on school trips:

> "Yes," [the panelist] said, "I had an abortion. I had an abortion when I was seventeen years old and I see no reason why, as a citizen of this country, I should be vilified for that. As far as I am concerned what I do with my own body is my business."
>
> And that wasn't all she had to say. Oh no. Mrs. Evans had a lot more to say than that. She was only getting warmed up. Herself and her cronies had smuggled condoms into the Irish Republic, she said. "The Holy Catholic Irish Republic!" she said, sneering. Then she opened her bag and took out a handful of them and she threw them into the audience. Laughing. Laughing! That was only the start, she said. The next plan was to open a family planning clinic in Dublin. Any woman who wanted to would from now on be able to take control of her own body.
>
> As he listened to her going on and on, Raphael felt sick. He hated the way her lips moved. He hated the way she waved her hands. He hated her eyes. The more he looked at her the more he got a pain in his head, directly over his right eye — throb throb throb, thanks to her. Why did she not bother Nessa [his wife]? he asked himself. Was it just him?
>
> When he asked her, Nessa said the soul of Mrs. Evans, like everyone else's, was her own responsibility. She would, please God, eventually see the error of her ways and repent, she said. The nerve over Raphael's eye started throbbing twice as much. "She won't!" he cried. "You don't know her! She won't stop! Not until she has destroyed everything! Don't you see that, Nessa! Why can't you see it?"
>
> Far away, [the presenter] laughed and clapped along as Evans and her buddies sang a song of solidarity. They invited all women everywhere to join them at the Reclaim The Night march against rape to be held in Dublin. Raphael had to go to the toilet. He thought he was going to vomit. But he didn't. He just stood there over the bowl with his eyes glazed.[48]

Television may have been interrupting the relationship between the church and its members during the 1960s and 1970s, but the Catholic Church was itself redefining that relationship. One of the Second Vatican Council's most critical debates had been over whether the church was a hierarchical institution to which people belong to take advantage of spiritual benefits, or whether the church was the whole People of God, which happens to have a hierarchical structure for its mission's purposes. The former had been the traditional view, but the council adopted the latter, which certainly suggested that the international church would pursue a relationship between the membership and the hierarchy that was very different from the one that had existed between the two in Ireland in recent decades.

Partly because of Vatican II's momentum, and partly coincident with it, relationships between the hierarchy and the church and also between the church and the laity revolutionized in the 1960s and 1970s. First, the men at the top of the hierarchy were replaced with more moderate and flexible clerics who simply managed church-state relations better, and they were certainly assisted by a new generation of government leaders who were glad to help them appear to minimize their influence by minimizing it in fact. Second, Pope John XXIII's encyclical *Mater et Magistra*, the Vatican II document *Gaudium et Spes* and other intellectual developments in Catholic social teaching made church leaders in Ireland and all over the world not only less skeptical of state intervention but also supportive of it as the answer to problems of poverty and what many church leaders viewed as social injustice. Cardinal William Conway went so far as to suggest that the hierarchy got it wrong in the mother-and-child debate by being overly concerned about the size and role of the state. The third critical change was Vatican II's encouragement of open discussion among the laity, which paralleled the advent of television and its challenging program content, loosening of censorship, economic improvement apparently stemming from state involvement, the adoption of a free trade policy, and entry into the European community. Finally, economic improvement in Ireland permitted the government to get its hands dirty providing education and other social services previously left to the church during times when the state was more financially strapped. Contemporary commentators noted a "psychological change" in the Irish people — greater optimism and self-confidence — that made it unlikely they would be easily controlled against their will by anyone.

Whether Cardinal Conway's 1969 television statement that "the notion that Ireland was governed from the Irish seminary at Maynooth was fantastic" had been true in the past, it certainly would be true in the future, as much due to the church's free choice as the government's.[49] In case there was any confusion, Cardinal Conway went farther, announcing just at the time the Northern Ireland civil rights movement turned bloody:

> I personally would not shed a tear if the relevant sub-section of Article 44a [the "special place" provision] were to disappear. It confers no legal privilege whatever on the Catholic Church and, if the way to convince our fellow Christians in the North about this is to remove it, then it might be worth the expense of a referendum.[50]

This was change, a mere thirty-two years after another leader of the Irish hierarchy had excoriated Eamon de Valera for not recognizing the Catholic Church more. Vatican II promoted ecumenism and religious freedom in

Church thinking after years of suspicion of both, and Sean Lemass's Committee on the Constitution of the late 1960s—an interesting spectacle according to Basil Chubb, because it was "an all-party committee deliberately raising an apparently contentious issue and interpreting Vatican documents for themselves"—also concluded from the Vatican II documents that the "special place" provision ought to be removed from the Constitution.[51] Ironically, one of the minority who was disappointed in 1972 when by an all-party agreement and 84 percent of the vote, the "special place" section as well as the portions recognizing other faiths was removed was the then–Chief Rabbi of Ireland, the Irish Constitution having been the only one in Europe giving express recognition to the Jewish congregations.[52]

All this new openness and encouragement did not obscure the difference between the substantive core of doctrine from the way it was presented. In 1968, at the end of the Vatican II meetings, Pope Paul VI issued the encyclical *Humana Vitae* (Of Human Life), which clarified the church's moral teaching on artificial means of birth control, abortion and sterilization: All were described as illicit means of regulating birth. "[E]very marriage act ... must remain open to the transmission of life," Pope Paul wrote.[53] "[W]e must once again declare that the direct interruption of the generative process already begun, and, above all, directly willed and procured abortion, even if for therapeutic reasons, are to be absolutely excluded as licit means of regulating birth."[54] The Irish hierarchy presented a united front: It supported and would implement and promulgate the directives in the encyclical.

Use of artificial birth control had taken tentative root in Ireland prior to *Humana Vitae*, and it is possible to see how Irish Catholics might have become confused on the content of church teaching, resulting in a "moment of silent crisis" when the encyclical appeared.[55] The Catholic Church had permitted use the of the pill to treat various genuine medical complaints, and such use was even approved in *Humana Vitae*.[56] Individual priests spoke out in opposition to the letter, and many Catholics using natural or artificial means of birth control apparently decided not to change their conduct to conform to the letter. As to contraception, *Humana Vitae* was the resolution of a doctrinal uncertainty that might have gone either way, but abortion was a different story. As to abortion, *Humana Vitae* was not a change in direction or even a hardening of doctrine; it was merely a reaffirmation of what had gone before.[57]

Though contraception and abortion both arise from sexual activity and seem to have similar practical effects—the avoidance of a child being born—they raise different moral imperatives. Pope Pius XI's 1930 comprehensive encyclical *On Christian Marriage* presented a compassionate but firm statement against abortion, sterilization and artificial birth control in response to the legalization of abortion in Russia and feminist thinking adopting the cause of abortion as a necessary element of women's liberty. As a general matter, all three types of regulating births were morally repugnant because "the conjugal act is destined primarily by nature for the begetting of children, those who in exercising it deliberately frustrate its natural power and purpose sin against nature and commit a deed which is shameful and intrinsically vicious."[58] Abortion was also condemned for an additional reason, however: It was "direct murder of the innocent."[59] Later, in *Evangelium Vitae* (The Gospel of Life), Pope John Paul II invoked his papal infallibility to declare that "*direct abortion, that is, abortion willed as an end or as a means, always constitutes a grave moral disorder,* since it is the deliberate killing of an innocent human being."[60]

The philosophical distinction between contraception and abortion made it possible for the church to permit what were then crude, natural, family planning techniques in certain circumstances in the 1950s and thereby give hope to some Catholics that forms of artificial birth control might become permissible. According to church teaching, engaging in sexual activity exclusively during the nonfertile parts of a woman's cycle does not necessarily mean a couple is not open to the possibility of procreation, and it still permits a couple to give to each other totally during intercourse; the couple is really only taking advantage of a natural process. On the other hand, *Humana Vitae* confirmed that artificial contraceptive methods are sufficiently manipulative and interfering of the unitive and procreative meanings of human sexuality to be forbidden.

Moreover, many popular forms of artificial contraception, such as birth control pills and the intrauterine device (IUD), frequently act as abortifacients because they prevent not conception, but implantation in the womb. By contrast, the condom, for example, is a prophylactic contraceptive, which stops conception by keeping sperm away from the egg entirely; since the "unborn child" never comes into existence at all, there is nothing to abort. Use of abortifacients is inconsistent with church teaching that an unborn child is a fully human being from the moment of conception because abortifacients simply induce very early abortions, but for other faiths and traditions that focus on implantation as opposed to conception, abortifacients create less significant moral issues. These concerns created moral challenges even for the Irish, where the Irish Family Planning Association estimated in 1969 that twelve thousand women were on the pill — not necessarily for pregnancy avoidance — and even though the pill's character as an abortifacient may not have been understood.

On the legal front of Irish cultural change, nothing had a greater impact than Irish lawyers' "discover[y of] the constitution"[61] during the 1960s and 1970s as a legal stick in the courtroom. That Irish constitutional law even permits judicial review is somewhat surprising; after all, Eamon de Valera was hostile both to Irish courts as British leftovers and judicial review in general. The Irish courts had, of course, dealt with issues of constitutional magnitude before the 1960s, but they had inherited and arguably expanded on the British common law deference to parliamentary action — perhaps justifying de Valera's suspicions— and they did little to develop the fundamental rights provisions of that document. Most in the legal profession were Fine Gael supporters, and William Binchy theorizes that they may have lacked interest in a de Valera-drafted document.[62] In any event, constitutional cases were rare; until 1959, no private citizen had brought an original lawsuit to challenge the constitutionality of a legislative act.[63]

Once they found the constitution, however, the Irish courts busied themselves with establishing rules for its interpretation. The process was not easy. On the one hand, the Irish Constitution would be a living document, with different interpretations appropriate as society changed and developed unconstrained by historical or "original meaning" interpretations of the constitution,[64] a significant concern during the nip-and-tuck debates over abortion rights to come. On the other hand, the justices sometimes found it hard to stick to that rule, resulting in inconsistent analysis.[65] The court eschewed the doctrine of strict construction of the constitutional text where it would "allow the imperfection or inadequacy of the words used to defeat or pervert any of the fundamental purposes of the Constitution," opting instead for a more holistic, purposive interpretive scheme,[66] a realistic response to the fact that de Valera had neither drafted nor intended to draft the personal rights sections of the constitution, for example, carefully enough to withstand strict construction. Particularly in light of the supreme court's choice not to bind its constitutional decision making by stare decisis, the principle that courts should follow their own decisions and those of higher courts, there would be few clear and objective boundaries on the range of constitutional analysis.[67]

Further, the justices developed different approaches to reconciling conflicting provisions, particularly in the personal rights area. According to one approach, where rights conflicted, the justices would have to develop a hierarchy, and the right closest to the top of the list would prevail.[68] Others preferred a balancing approach that would give "due and harmonious effect" to even directly conflicting provisions in order to effect the constitution's underlying purpose,[69] similar to a well-known canon of construction that statutory or contractual provisions should not be read to render one superfluous or meaningless. These approaches tended to bleed into each other, with many justices alternately opting to apply a strict hierarchical approach only where rights could not otherwise be harmonized or developing a hierarchy based on the constitution's underlying purposes.[70] In some cases, as High Court Justice Declan Costello argued, the text itself should drive the analysis because it specifically indicated that some rights preceded the constitution and were "inalienable and superior to other law" while others were merely positive and clearly limited by democratic and majoritarian exigencies.[71] In any event, while these varying approaches might theoretically produce radically different constitutional regimes, no great jurisprudential debate brewed on the supreme court over the reconciliation of conflicting personal rights during the 1960s and 1970s.

In fact, until the 1960s, the long-standing interpretation of the personal rights article, Article 40.3, hampered efforts to protect individual liberty through constitutional adjudication. On the one hand, Article 40.3 guarantees that the state shall defend and vindicate the personal rights of citizens, and according to Article 40.4, citizens shall not be deprived of personal liberty "save in accordance with law." But "save in accordance with law" did not mean "due process of law" as Americans understand it. For many years, "save in accordance with law" was simply interpreted to mean "as the legislature may by law decide," which effectively cut off judicial review of legislation that had the effect of depriving citizens of personal liberty.[72]

Irish judges eventually came to see Article 40.3 as a vehicle for substantive notions of due process of law. In *Ryan* v. *Attorney General*,[73] the supreme court held that the Article 40.3 of the Constitution protected unenumerated natural rights arising from the "Christian and democratic nature of the State," thereby upholding a high court decision relying on an encyclical of Pope John XXIII.[74] During the next decade, the Irish courts identified other constitutional provisions as sources of natural personal rights the state was bound to defend and vindicate, including the "special place" of the Catholic Church, the constitutional acknowledgment that God was the source of all authority, the preamble's instruction that the law of the state was to be grounded in prudence, justice and charity in order to ensure the dignity and freedom of the individual and judicial precedent recognizing that Ireland was a religiously pluralistic country. These provisions and the jurisprudential thinking that sprang from them reflected a Thomistic approach to personal rights mandating that judges derive "political truths from the eternal law of God."[75]

Irish personal rights jurisprudence quickly abandoned what appeared to be a purely Catholic character. Catholic notions of natural justice clearly informed the constitution, but so did an amalgam of rational secular and liberal philosophies, and Irish courts of the 1960s and 1970s were quick to establish that a citizen might have a right that was contrary to Catholic teaching. Moreover, judges applying natural law analysis did not always specify the underlying school of natural law they were following, which produced conclusory and inconsistent decisions.[76] They further left unanswered whether they were relying on natural law as superior to the constitution; whether natural law notions were simply a gap filler where the constitution did not speak explicitly; or whether they believed judges should even rely on natural law at all. The apparent force of natural law in Irish constitutional jurisprudence may stem from the intellectual and political personalities of the judges who espoused it, particularly Supreme Court Justice Brian Walsh,[77] to whom his chief justice delegated the responsibility of writing most of the constitutional law decisions of the period. Justice Walsh's landmark *McGee* opinion of the 1970s reflects a marked decline in specifically "Catholic" as opposed to merely "Christian" or more generic "natural law" reasoning, which continued in the individual rights cases that followed.[78]

Concepts of personhood and human dignity formed the basis for Irish personal rights jurisprudence. Some justices clearly saw human dignity as the fundamental constitutional value, and the others relied on competing concepts of human dignity to flesh out constitutional meaning.[79] To establish that a claimant was protected by an unenumerated right, one generally had to show that the right was a logical extension of another provision of the constitution,[80] that it arose from the Christian and democratic nature of the state[81] or that it arose "by virtue of [the claimant's] human personality."[82] Personal rights would not generally be considered absolute, and alleged violations would have to be justified as proportional to the significance of the state interest involved, though not with the doctrinal rigidity of American constitutional law.

These principles were developing, though not fully formed, when the Irish courts heard the moving case of *McGee* v. *Attorney General*.[83] Mrs. McGee, a fisherman's wife in her late twenties living in a cramped mobile home with four children born only twenty-three months apart, had a variety of medical difficulties that had made her third pregnancy, when she gave birth to twins, life threatening. Though she had survived, the risk of death or deformity if she became pregnant again mounted precipitously. She believed it would be unfair to both herself and her husband to cease sexual intercourse, and so they resorted to birth control. Natural and certain artificial family planning methods had serious drawbacks in the McGees' specific situation, and Mrs. McGee and her doctor concluded that the only satisfactory form of birth control would be a diaphragm with a contraceptive jelly. When Mrs. McGee attempted to import the jelly, customs officials seized it pursuant to statutes that banned both the sale and importation of contraceptives, which therefore had the effect of virtually banning their use as well.[84] Mrs. McGee claimed that the seizure violated her rights under Articles 40 (equal treatment and unenumerated personal rights), 41 (family rights), 42 (parental rights), 44 (freedom of religion) and 45 (declaration of social policy).

McGee became the high-water mark for natural law analysis and the application of the principle of subsidiarity in Irish jurisprudence, though, ironically, the majority held that Article 40.3 protected a right to marital privacy that extended at least far enough to permit the McGees to import the contraceptive jelly. Justice Walsh's important decision arose from three key themes. First, the Irish Constitution recognized that the community of the marital couple and its constituent members each has more privileges than individuals acting outside of marriage[85] and that the marital community mediates between the individual and the state on the sensitive issue of determining family size. Second, the principle of subsidiarity supported leaving decisions about family size to families, the institution closest to the individual with the requisite competence to make that decision.[86] This view is consistent with that of the Irish bishops' statement of the period noting that while contraceptive use was morally wrong, that did not necessarily mean the sale or importation of contraceptives should be prohibited by the state.[87] Identifying a "right to privacy" was another way of making a political decision about the person or institution who should make a particular decision in the common good, though the common good itself might require such a decision to be made by a different person or institution if circumstances changed. The third theme was Justice Walsh's respectful compassion for the McGees. He noted that the Irish people had enacted the constitution to promote the common good, with "due observance of prudence, justice and charity," and that the key component of charity was mercy.[88] He left no doubt about what he believed mercy required in the case.

The *McGee* justices were also very explicit that they were going so far and no farther. Though Justice Walsh observed that state interference in family planning decisions would normally be "an intolerable and unjustifiable intrusion in the privacy of the matrimonial bedroom," he identified a situation where an abortion was under consideration as one in which the state would be justified in intruding.[89] Two justices also emphasized that the right of privacy would not be extended to overturn a legal ban on the sale or use of abortifacients. Despite the apparent similarities between *McGee* and the U.S. Supreme Court's decision in *Griswold* v. *Connecticut*,[90] which recognized a zone of privacy sufficiently broad to invalidate a state law criminalizing the use of contraceptives and is now considered a progenitor of *Roe* v. *Wade*,[91] the Irish Supreme Court was clear: There would be no Irish *Roe* on its watch.

The 1960s had seemed so giddy, almost fun. A curtain between Ireland and the rest of the world had risen. *McGee* is symbolic of the growing realization in the early 1970s that life does not exist in a vacuum, that modern things—unenumerated rights jurisprudence in *McGee*, for example—would have consequences. There were choices to make: What kind of country was Ireland going to become? In the short term, many Irish were appalled by *McGee*,[92] though perhaps as much from a lack of consensus on how contraceptives ought to be made available, as whether they should be available at all. The government of the time, led by Fine Gael's Liam Cosgrave, the son of the leader of the first Irish government, was so unenthusiastic about its legislative duty to regulate trade in now-legal contraceptives that when it permitted a free vote on its bill to license chemists to sell contraceptives, even the Taioseach worked for its defeat.

Ireland stumbled badly in the 1970s and the early 1980s. The economy was racked by its usual buggaboo, unemployment, as well as two new ones, soaring inflation and public debt. Unlike the governments of Eamon de Valera and Sean Lemass, the Fianna Fáil governments of the period lacked vision and suffered from open scandal. The "Troubles" in Northern Ireland erupted, threatening the security of the state and raising disturbing public questions about what the "Irish nation" even was: the Irish State, the aspirational nation of the entire island, or all of these plus the diaspora flung out around the globe? Members of the government were actually implicated in a scheme to send arms to Catholics in the north. These uncertainties made the complicated, but law-and-order bound, coalition government led by Fine Gael seem preferable to the too-slick Fianna Fáil leaders during the early 1970s.

Fine Gael, however, was in the midst of an internal ideological war. The "young guns," led by Garret Fitzgerald and then-attorney general Declan Costello, sought to adopt a "Great Society" ideology for their party, but Costello, at least, was unwilling to compromise traditional views on moral issues, opposing the legalization of contraceptives for use by all adults, instead of just married couples, when the government proposed legislation in response to *McGee*. Costello's and Fitzgerald's careers blossomed—Fitzgerald's as Taoiseach in the 1980s and Costello's as the president of the high court in the 1990s—but their battle to change their party was long and their success brief. The optimism of the 1960s was over.

It was an intellectually undisciplined time, a hangover of sorts from the heady 1960s, and legal observers began to wonder about the consequences of increasing legal and societal interest in notions of individual rights. Recognizing unenumerated rights from elastic constitutional language such as "prudence, justice and charity" disconcerted many experts. Particularly concerned were the group that would become the core of Ireland's future prolife activists, who recalled that just a year prior to *McGee*, the United States Supreme Court had relied in part on the seemingly analogous *Griswold* case to find that the United States did recognize a right to abortion sufficient to overturn state criminal laws banning it. They observed with alarm new activity from abortion rights groups and attitudinal changes in Irish society. If the court could overturn a section of the Criminal Law Amendment Act based on unenumerated personal rights in *McGee*, could it not overturn a portion of the Offenses Against the Person Act on the same basis?

In the short run, this was not particularly likely. Several supreme court justices had insisted in *McGee* itself as well as in other cases that the right to marital privacy was limited and did not justify overturning the criminal ban on abortion. Those justices took the right to life of the unborn very seriously and probably viewed it as an extension of either the textual right to life or an unenumerated right under Article 40.3.[93] One justice called it "a sacred trust to which all the organs of government must lend their support" in 1984.[94] Both the common law and Irish statutes reflected the principle that an unborn life has a significance separate from that of its mother,[95] though even killings of born persons are frequently justified in criminal law. Activities of the European Convention on Human Rights and in the European Community inspired concern that the statutory ban on abortion might be in jeopardy, but at least one observer's analysis of relevant European court decisions suggests that such fears were unfounded.[96]

The long run might be another story, however. Great Britain had liberalized its abortion law in 1967, making legal abortion more readily available to Irish women than ever before, though probably also limiting illegal abortions in Ireland and related pressure to change Irish law.[97] The Irish courts had overturned a decision of the censorship board banning a family planning guidebook, albeit on procedural grounds.[98] Neither prolifers nor social liberals were assuaged by the Irish Health (Family Planning) Act of 1979. The act made contraceptives available to married couples only by prescription and only to those intending to use them for bona fide family planning purposes, but it also repealed the ban on importation of contraceptives, authorized registered medical practitioners to counsel patients in their use and deleted references to contraception from censorship laws. Doctors disliked the responsibility of determining whether a patient's motives for seeking contraceptives were legally justified as well as having to provide prescriptions for contraceptives that were not medical in nature. Though the act insisted it did not change the law as to abortifacients—a subject of concern even to the Anglican Church of Ireland—or authorize crimes under the Offenses Against the Person Act (read: abortion), events did lend themselves to the conclusion that Ireland was on the proverbial slippery slope. Who knew where it all might lead?

Part II

FIVE

The 1980s and the Rise of Modern Abortion and Divorce Law

"No, I'm never having an abortion!"[1]

By the beginning of the 1980s, Ireland was a changed culture from that which had ratified the constitution of little more than forty years prior in ways far more fundamental than can be explained away merely by "sixties" influences such as television and showbands or even the particularly Irish "Troubles" and complex government relations with the church. Perhaps most significantly, emigration had begun to decline in the 1970s, and though it erupted again in the 1980s, many emigrants began returning to Ireland, implying a change in numerous underlying economic and social trends, not the least of which was an end to Irish export of "discontent" and "dissent." Marriage rates, though they continued to move up and down with the vicissitudes in the country's economic fortunes, were falling into line with those of other industrialized European countries. Numerous markers of interest in pluralism, which in Ireland became a buzzword for a desire for individualism and liberal democracy and raised notions of what Americans call "diversity," were sprouting from an intense debate among academics and opinion makers, in which particularly notable was an entire issue of the Jesuit public policy journal, *Studies*, devoted to the subject,[2] to extensive attitudinal surveys indicating that if Irish citizens had not necessarily changed their own beliefs on core moral and ethical issues, they at least appeared to have become more accepting of those with different views. In the Irish Report of the European Value Systems Study released in 1984, the Irish attitudes toward abortion, divorce and euthanasia generally were conservative outliers compared to other European countries; yet, when asked whether such activity might ever be justifiable, Irish views were softer, consistent with other Irish attitudes reflected in the survey, such as the belief that "everyone is basically good," an almost doctrinally Catholic view.[3] The influence of clerical leadership and church teaching (not the same thing) had become even more complicated and ambiguous, but the Irish Church revived when Pope John Paul II visited Ireland in 1979 and exhorted the Irish to lead the modern world to morality. One might argue they attempted to do just that.

Irish prolife activists examined the rhythms in what Americans would call their "substantive due process" jurisprudence in the late 1970s and early 1980s and were not happy with what they saw. Their first concerns were developments in the United States, already the source of inspiration to both litigant and jurist in *McGee.* Substantive due process jurisprudence related to sexual matters had taken off in the United States only a few years earlier in *Griswold* v. *Connecticut*,[4] which recognized a right of marital privacy sufficient to render unconstitutional a Connecticut law that banned the use of contraceptives between married couples, and *Roe* v. *Wade*,[5] which recognized a liberty interest in aborting a pregnancy sufficient to strike down a Texas law criminalizing abortions except where they were necessary to save the life of the mother. Admittedly, dicta in several Irish cases had discussed the relationship between abortion and the Irish constitution and found abortion to be constitutional anathema.[6] On the other hand, Irish legal observers concerned about abortion wondered whether, as *Griswold* was to *McGee*, *Roe* would be to an eventual case in Ireland. They were also concerned that as a signatory to the European Convention on Human Rights, Ireland might someday be pressured to treat abortion as a human right.

Roe contains a number of features that were likely to be extremely disconcerting to the Irish if it were ever to be used as persuasive precedent before the Irish courts. *Roe* was an attack on a Texas abortion law making it a crime to procure an abortion except by medical advice for the purpose of saving the life of the mother. As a philosophical matter, Texas had chosen to protect unborn children and mothers equally, except when the mother's life was threatened by carrying the child, in which case the mother's needs would override those of the unborn child's. By extension, Texas had decided by statute that the right to life of the mother would receive greater protection under Texas law than the right to life of the unborn child, but no lesser maternal right — such as the right to bodily integrity or the right to protect one's health —could defeat the unborn child's right to life.

The United States Supreme Court stated that it did not need to decide when life began to resolve the question of the Texas statute's constitutionality, a signal failure, because by failing to decide whether life begins at any particular point, it necessarily concluded that the unborn child did not have any right to life that the state or other born persons were bound to respect.[7] The mother had a right to privacy which would permit her to make choices to protect herself from "[s]pecific and direct harm medically diagnosable even in early pregnancy," "a distressful life and future," "psychological harm," the mental and physical exertion of "child care," "distress, for all concerned, associated with the unwanted child," and the strain on the family into which the child would otherwise be born.[8] By contrast, the state had two "important and legitimate interest[s]": (1) "in preserving and protecting the health of the pregnant woman" and (2) in "protecting the potentiality of human life."[9] The state's interests would permit regulation to the extent that those interests were "compelling," and they would become increasingly compelling at several specific times during the pregnancy.[10] The state's interest in preserving and protecting the health of the pregnant woman became compelling after the first trimester because the mortality rate of mothers in abortion before the end of the first trimester was less than in childbirth. "For the period of pregnancy prior to this 'compelling' point, the attending physician, in consultation with his patient, is free to determine, without regulation by the State, that, in his medical judgment, the patient's pregnancy should be terminated," held the Court.[11] Further, the state's interest in protecting potential life became compelling at the moment of viability, and therefore, the state "may go so far as to proscribe abortion during that period, except when it is necessary to preserve the life or health of the mother."[12] The Court made the practical implications of these decisions even clearer:

> A state criminal abortion statute of the current Texas type that excepts from criminality only a *life saving* procedure on behalf of the mother, without regard to pregnancy stage and without recognition of the other interests involved, is violative of [due process]. (a) For the stage prior to approximately the end of the first trimester, the abortion decision and its effectuation must be left to the medical judgment of the pregnant woman's attending physician. (b) For the stage subsequent to approximately the end of the first trimester, the State, in promoting its interest in the health of the mother, may, if it chooses, regulate the abortion procedure in ways that are reasonably related to maternal health. (c) For the stage subsequent to viability, the State in promoting its interest in the potentiality of human life may, if it chooses, regulate, and even proscribe, abortion except where it is necessary, in appropriate medical judgment, for the preservation of the life or health of the mother.[13]

It was a debatable point whether the U.S. Supreme Court's failure to come to a conclusion as to whether an unborn child is a "person" is justified based on the medical, philosophical and theological authorities on which it claimed to rely.[14] Nevertheless, even Justice Blackmun made the concession, on which Irish commentator William Binchy pounced in 1976, that neutrality on the moment that life begins is the "'crucial error'" of the decision — or in less judgmental language, at least the "'pivotal question'" on which the case turned.[15] By deciding that unborn children are not "persons" entitled to protection of their right to life, the rights and interests of persons far less important than the right to life might be said to take precedence, as do the mother's health and potential for distress in *Roe*.

Though the supreme court of Ireland had shown in many prior cases that it was much less shy than its American counterpart to come to conclusions based on principles it gleaned from medicine, philosophy and particularly theology, Irish law, like American law, contained no black letter rule requiring a Court to conclude that unborn children are, in fact, persons entitled to protection of their right to life. The significance of this omission, particularly in the context of the recent *McGee* decision, prompted a fascinating debate among Ireland's leading legal scholars. One side argued that justices of the Irish Supreme Court had already recognized the right to life of the unborn in *McGee*, albeit in dicta, making it highly unlikely that the court would follow *Roe* if facing its "pivotal question."[16] The other side noted that as post-*Griswold* American privacy rights cases were already being cited in Irish academic literature in support of a more comprehensive set of marital privacy rights, reliance on and perhaps ultimate acceptance of *Roe* could hardly be far off.[17]

Roe, when read in light of what the British had done in their Abortion Act of 1967, was another example of the medicalization of abortion, shifting it from a criminal matter to a medical concern. Though a doctor's substantive involvement in the actual abortion decision is no longer recognized legally, *Roe* actually left that decision to a woman's doctor, not to her directly. The same is true of the British Abortion Act, which legalizes abortion in what seems to be an almost unlimited number of circumstances but requires two medical opinions in favor of the procedure to address one of two issues before it may proceed:

> (a) that the continuance of the pregnancy would involve risk to the life of the pregnant woman, or of injury to the physical or mental health of the pregnant woman or any existing children of her family, greater than if the pregnancy were terminated; or
>
> (b) that there is a substantial risk that if the child were born it would suffer from such physical or mental abnormalities as to be seriously handicapped.[18]

Yet doctors are not law or morality enforcement officers, no matter how much politicians may wish to make them so. Despite requiring two doctors' opinions, the Abortion Act has degenerated into abortion on demand because obtaining the necessary medical opinions is no problem in practice.[19] Making abortion a medical as opposed to a legal decision might be said simply to enforce the immediate desires of the women involved. Abortion has become in Britain an almost unfettered individual right.

Therefore, the Irish prolife movement that blossomed in the late 1970s and early 1980s was primarily proactive, but there were certainly rumblings among abortion rights forces to react to as well. The leading prolife organization, the Pro-Life Amendment Campaign (PLAC), with its support from Irish doctors and formed to promote an amendment to the Irish Constitution to protect the right to life, was not engaged in "'a rubbishy academic exercise'" as Senator and future Irish President Mary Robinson charged.[20] Small groups such as Irish Women United, Contraception Action Programme, the Dublin Well Woman Centre (a clinic that would eventually become embroiled in litigation over referrals to abortion clinics in Great Britain), and the Women's Right to Choose Group arose to challenge the settled law sometimes quietly and sometimes with high-profile events such as the "pill train," which carried contraceptives illegally from Belfast to Dublin. Moreover, prolife groups were dismayed by what they characterized as the comparatively liberal Health and Family Planning Act of 1979, which permitted distribution of contraceptive devices by prescription. These developments, plus the increasing number of Irish women seeking abortions in England since the British Parliament had passed the Abortion Act, suggested that Irish law was not completely secure.

Prolife activists decided that their best strategy was to campaign for a constitutional amendment which would both "copperfasten" the legal ban on abortions in Ireland to the highest law of the land and also make a positive statement about Irish people's commitment to the right to life as well as the constitutional relationship of two classes of people, the born and the unborn. In 1982 Ireland had three different governments, so political volatility helped push the issue to center stage. As power swung back and forth between Fine Gael and Fianna Fáil during 1982 and 1983, both parties were eager to appeal to, or at least not to offend, the large prolife constituency, and therefore, they backed the effort.

Fianna Fáil managed the politics better, and its wording was the one that eventually went to the people in a referendum to amend the constitution:

> The State acknowledges the right to life of the unborn and, with due regard for the equal right to life of the mother, guarantees in its laws to respect, and, as far as practicable, by its laws to defend and vindicate that right.

The provision would appear in Article 40, the first article dealing with personal rights and the article devoted to equality of citizens before the law, within the section in which the state guarantees protection of personal rights and after the subsection in which the state guarantees to vindicate the life of its citizens. The first section of Article 40 states in part that "[a]ll citizens shall, as human persons, be held equal before the law"; therefore, the new provision's placement underscores the Irish belief that the unborn were humans with personal rights, and it confirms the status of one of those personal rights in particular — the right to life. The wording within its context indicates acceptance of three basic philosophical and political principles: (1) that the unborn are recognized as human beings under the law of Ireland; (2) that their right to life, at minimum, is equal to that of their mother's, which is in turn equal to that of other citizens; and (3) that the state is obliged to take affirmative steps to protect the right to life of the unborn.

Yet the wording and its placement in the constitution had other consequences. For example, it framed the coming debate on abortion in terms of individual rights as opposed to one about the "good" or the "family." The amendment's wording also failed to communicate an underlying sense of the individual mother's or unborn child's relationship to the groups of which each is a member or to the common good, despite the fact that the proponents of the amendment almost certainly had such a sense. Consider, for example, the words of William Binchy, an intellectual leader in the movement:

> I have argued that the notion of liberty, in the social context, carries inevitable consequences, not only for those whose conduct manifests their liberty but also for those who are the objects of that conduct. To regard the debate about the proper scope of liberty as involving simply a confrontation between the individual and the State is to ignore the vital social dimension to human conduct. The limits of liberty are not imposed from above, but rather inhere in the human being by virtue of the social character of human relationships.[21]

Nevertheless, the amendment is a provision written in individualistic "rights talk,"[22] reflecting what was as yet an unconscious shift in vocabularic fluency even on the part of those prolife supporters. It raises the inevitable question: If prolife supporters were no longer clearly advocating a common good or communitarian basis for Irish constitutional law, who would?

The wording of the abortion referendum revealed a creeping trend in Irish public discourse: the tendency to describe and treat what had previously in Irish tradition been thought of as family and community matters—such as abortion and child bearing—as matters of individual rights and decision. Even as recently as *McGee*, the supreme court, for example, had spoken of a right to marital privacy, though a key justification for that right was the notion that family groups and not the state should make decisions about family size, arguably as much a nod to Catholic social teaching's principle of subsidiarity as a victory for individual rights. By the Eighth Amendment debate, both the language and substance of "hard" rights had slipped firmly into the abortion lexicon. Abortion became an issue of comparative individual rights without clear textual reference to the interests of other groups, individuals or institutions that might mediate between them. Even the Catholic hierarchy's vocabulary changed, as it spoke openly of the "right to life" in the abortion discussion as opposed to "respect for life," a change which may have been partly an extension of the "rights" vocabulary from the Northern Ireland civil rights movement of the 1960s and which had seeped into a number of aspects of Catholic social teaching both in Ireland and elsewhere.[23] Though the state retained responsibility to vindicate those rights where practicable, the Eighth Amendment signaled a continuing shift in the way Irish people conceptualized issues about sexuality away from being primarily family matters or issues of community concern. The Irish communitarian society of groups was in the process of becoming a society of individuals and the state.

Too late, the Fine Gael leader and on-again-off-again Taioseach Garret Fitzgerald concluded presciently that this wording might permit eventual legalization of abortion, and while this may not have been the reason, given that he was on a constitutional crusade designed to make the republic seem less sectarian in order to appeal to northern unionists, his party ultimately opposed the constitutional amendment referendum that followed. Fine Gael proposed a more American-sounding amendment, limiting what the state in the form of the courts could do but directly announcing no rights or affirmative government responsibilities: "[N]othing in this Constitution shall be invoked to invalidate or to deprive of force or effect a provision of the law on the grounds that it prohibits abortion."[24] The Fine Gael government argued that the Fianna Fáil wording in the hands of the supreme court might be interpreted to mean something different from what its supporters understood it to mean in three possible ways:

1. The amendment might be interpreted to prohibit operations on women suffering from ectopic pregnancies or cancer of the womb.
2. The amendment might be read to permit abortions its supporters understood it to ban.
3. The amendment might prohibit abortifacient contraceptives.

On the other hand, the Fine Gael wording would provide no substantive guidance as to what constituted a legal abortion within the meaning of the Offenses Against the Person Act.

PLAC did not want its amendment to impede appropriate medical care for women suffering from cancer or ectopic pregnancies any more than Fine Gael's leadership, but prolife activists believed the wording was safe from such an interpretation. Though the amendment confirmed that the right to life of the unborn and the mother were theoretically equal, it did not say that judges and legislators were to treat them as equal where they clashed. The amendment says that the right to life of the unborn is to be protected "as far as practicable" with "due regard" for the equal right to life of the mother. The obvious question became "how much regard is due?"

Amendment backers liked the "due regard language" as a way of codifying the "doctrine of double effect," an important philosophical distinction between "a direct attack on the life of the unborn and [medical] treatment for the mother that results indirectly in the death of the unborn,"[25] though they were criticized for simultaneously promoting only those exceptions from an absolute ban on abortion that were endorsed by the Catholic Church.[26] The doctrine of double effect is related to the Hippocratic principle that doctors should "do no harm," and it governed Irish medical ethics on abortion.[27] Determining whether a medical act conforms with the doctrine involves application of the following analytical steps:

1. The action we choose to do which is the cause of the good and harmful effect must itself be good (or at least not morally harmful). In the case of the ectopic pregnancy the good directly sought is to bring the mother back to health, delivering her from the threat of death which her physical condition (the ectopic pregnancy) causes;
2. The good and the bad (harmful) effects must each be of an immediate or simultaneous, and causally (physically) connected result of the action which brings about both results or effects. This means that:

2a. the good effect (*e.g.* the restoration to health of the pregnant mother) is not caused by our deliberate and direct, intentional, choice of killing the embryo (*i.e.* by *our will to cause harm to it*), but rather by our will to seek the good of the mother which requires the removing of the condition of a blocked tube caused by the trapped and growing embryo. Hence:

3. The harmful effect (the death of the embryo) is permitted as a necessary and unavoidable result of our intervention to bring about good, *i.e.*, restore the health to the mother; the death of the embryo is not chosen for its own sake, nor as the means to attain the good end. We do not operate to kill the embryo; this is what is meant by "we do not intend" to kill the embryo. And, finally:
4. There must be sufficient good reason to act for permitting the harmful effect. That is, if we do not act for the good of the mother by attempting to restore her back to health, the mother is harmfully affected and could die. We have an obligation to act for her good and remove the threat to her life. The balance or proportionality of the good to be attained and the harm to be permitted justify the action.[28]

Of course, what Fitzgerald saw was that no one could be certain in the distant future that a court would limit itself to a reading which codified the doctrine of double effect and did no more.

Fine Gael's leadership urged its supporters to vote "no" on the Fianna Fáil wording in the referendum, but those directions were worth less than they might have been. The Anti-Amendment Campaign received virtually no assistance from Fine Gael Dail members, but both parliamentary and rank-and-file Fianna Fáilers worked hard in support of the amendment. The Catholic bishops weighed in late, only a few weeks before the election, by calling for a definitive "yes" vote, but emphasizing that Catholics might vote according to their consciences. Their official position was as follows:

> While some conscientiously hold a different opinion, we are convinced that a clear majority in favour of the amendment will greatly contribute to the continued protection of unborn human life in the laws of our country. This could have a significant impact in a world where abortion is often taken for granted. A decisive "Yes" to the amendment will, we believe, in the words of Pope John Paul II in Limerick, constitute a "witness before Europe and before the whole world to the dignity and sacredness of all human life, from conception until death."[29]

The church probably had no desire to alienate members who disagreed with it on this one matter,[30] but clergy in local parishes were more forceful in support of a "yes" vote. Therefore, despite the opposition of the second largest political party in Ireland, which was currently leading a coalition government, the referendum adopted the amendment with almost two-thirds of the relatively small number of voters in favor.

Despite Fine Gael's discombobulation over fine points, the amendment was a clear statement of the basic principles American law had lacked when *Roe* v. *Wade* was decided and was probably an accurate statement of the views of an overwhelming majority of the Irish people — perhaps even of many who voted against it. The amendment recognized the right to life of unborn children, and in all but the rarest of circumstances, if not always, it recognized that the right to life of the unborn was of equal constitutional weight to that of the mother. The contrast with American jurisprudence of the early 1980s could hardly be more stark. *Roe* denied that there was a right to life of unborn children, though the state did have an interest in protecting the potentiality of life after the child became viable. The state's primary concern was to be with the health and welfare of the mother only to the extent that it did not infringe on her right to privacy, which extended so far as to invalidate regulations that required notification of her spouse that she planned to have an abortion[31]; that required consent of parents in many circumstances in which minors sought abortions[32]; and that required hospitalization for the purpose of having an abortion, even in the second trimester of pregnancy,[33] during which *Roe* had said that the state had an "important and legitimate interest" in protecting the health of the mother.[34] Instead of the right to life of the unborn child being deemed equal to the right to life of the mother, in the United States the unborn child had no possibility for benevolent legal protection, let alone a right to protection of any kind until viability, and until then, almost any interest or justification of the mother was legally entitled to greater protection than the state's interest in the potentiality of life. While Irish law announced the rights of two different classes of persons and defined them as virtually equal in their interactions with each other, American law pitted an autonomous and virtually unfettered individual right against what became clear were the very minimal interests of the state in its police powers. What neither legal regime contemplated was that there might be other individuals or groups with, if not rights, at least interests in the rights to the life of others and the legality of abortion more generally.

The significant political repercussions from the 1983 abortion referendum slowly became clear. Fianna Fáil, whose history included a somewhat touch-and-go relationship with the Catholic Church, slowly completed a transformation into a socially conservative and traditionalist party and therefore, allied with the Catholic bishops, with a different character from that which it had presented under Eamon de Valera, when its image had been "radical, popular [and] anti-establishment."[35] With somewhat more difficulty, Fine Gael increasingly resolved its social policy cleavages in favor of liberal positions, though the rank and file remained split.

In 1985, the Fine Gael government proposed expanding access to contraceptives, and both parties were forced to discipline dissident members. The leading Fianna Fáil dissident even broke away to form a new, fiscally conservative but socially liberal party that probably succeeded in denying power to Fianna Fáil in more than one election since then. There can be little wonder that Irish governments have shied away from the abortion issue since then as best they could.

The abortion and contraception battles slid, without rest for the weary, into a movement from the left in 1986 for a referendum on the constitutional ban on divorce in Article 42.3.2. Marriage breakdowns, even among Catholics, were rising, and the church was annulling many more marriages that the state continued to insist were valid. Many Irish citizens' domestic relations were becoming more and more complex as persons in unsatisfactory marriages left the home, perhaps moved in with another partner, had children with different legal status than their in-wedlock children, found that their unions were recognized for some public policy purposes but not others, and were beset by complex inheritance rules.

The Fine Gael government announced a constitutional referendum for mid-1986. The proposed constitutional amendment stated the following:

> Where, and only where, such court established under this Constitution as may be prescribed by law is satisfied that—
> 1. A marriage has failed;
> 2. The failure has continued for a period of, or periods amounting to, at least 5 years;
> 3. There is no reasonable possibility of reconciliation between the parties to the marriage; and
> 4. Any other condition prescribed by law has been complied with, the court may in accordance with law, grant a dissolution of the marriage provided that the court is satisfied that adequate and proper provision having regard to the circumstances, will be made for any dependent spouse and for any child, or any child who is dependent on either spouse.[36]

The same political coalitions arose as in the 1983 abortion referendum. Fine Gael sponsored the amendment campaign under pressure from its coalition partner, Labour, but half heartedly and not unanimously. Many Fianna Fáil members enthusiastically opposed it in two philosophical factions, the first fearing greater liberalization in divorce law if the amendment passed, and the other concerned with the cost of social services that would be required when women, few of whom worked in lucrative employment outside the home, were left without sufficient economic support. The PLAC political apparatus reorganized quickly into an antidivorce campaign, with an almost completely lay leadership and William Binchy and a future Irish president, Mary McAleese, as its legal advisors.

Opinion polls led Fine Gael and Labour down the garden path to believing legalized divorce would be a big winner, and therefore the government did not prepare adequately for the intense battle it initiated. Fine Gael had not thought through questions of social welfare entitlements after divorces and inheritance rights and seemed taken by surprise when the electorate became deeply interested in those details. Government ministers and party leaders were put in the ignominious position of being unable to answer publically the most basic objections to the amendment.

By contrast, antidivorce activists were well prepared to discuss the specific disadvantages and legal challenges divorce would bring to Irish society. For example, only two years before the referendum battle, Binchy, one of the antidivorce force's chief legal advisors, had written a comprehensive book outlining the secular problems divorce would bring to Irish society such as adequate financial support for wives, child custody, degeneration of legalized divorce to legalized "quickie" divorce, and marriage stability, and providing solutions other than divorce for the problems of marriage breakdown.[37] The government was simply unprepared for the quality of this sort of response to its proposed amendment.

Worse, the government did not even have the unambiguous backing of its own supporters. It was a difficult row to hoe between Fine Gael members' belief in marriage as a lifelong commitment and the notion that divorce should, regardless of personal belief, be available to dissenters. Even Taoiseach Garret Fitzgerald told the Irish people that he personally was "committed to indissoluble monogamy," but if he and his ministers felt that way, it was not surprising that many other Irish people did so as well, and the principle was sufficiently important that allowing dissenters the freedom to act otherwise was a tough sell.[38] The government was urging that citizens differentiate in the law that would order their collective lives between what they personally believed and what would be in the common good,[39] a differentiation between public and private that the Irish were not in the habit of making.

Only days after a referendum was announced, the Market Research Bureau of Ireland revealed that 57 percent of those polled wanted to change the law, but less than two months later, after the well-organized Anti-Divorce Campaign had squared off against the feeble proamendment forces, support had slumped to only 40 percent. Women, in particular, deserted the cause, fearing the financial impact of divorce on Irish wives and anticipating a decline in the status of their traditional and constitutionally protected roles as homemakers. Given the recent Irish history of almost desperate prudence where marriage was concerned, it is somewhat amazing that the government did not anticipate that concerns about the status of the marital home and inheritance laws after a divorce, for example, would attract public attention. Journalist Mary Kenny argues persuasively that, even in the 1980s, political elites may have missed the point about Irish marriages: The real marriage "problem" of the past century had not been how to get out of unhappy marriages, but how to get into *any* marriage, marriage rates in Ireland having dropped so low during the 1940s and 1950s that even the church had begun to castigate "selfish bachelors" and "overcautious old maids" for failing to do their duty to replace the population.[40] If art is an expression of reality, then it is appropriate to note that while Irish literature does contain its share of "bad marriage" stories, such as Liam O'Flaherty's novel *The Black Soul*, the hallmark of Irish literature is the number of works about characters who desperately want to marry, but cannot, such as Patrick Kavanagh's poetic masterpiece, "The Great Hunger"; Martin McDonagh's recent hit play, *The Beauty Queen of Leenane*; and Brian Friel's autobiographical play-turned-movie starring Meryl Streep about his single mother and aunts struggling through the 1930s, *Dancing at Lughnasa*. Of course rank selfishness had little to do with male delays in marriage; understandable financial prudence rooted in agricultural communities meant that many men waited until middle age before they inherited and then married. While this conduct may have made life very lonely, the marriages that were formed under these conditions, if not full of passion, were stable.

Even as late as the mid–1980s, many Irish persons seem to have identified more with those in stable marriages who wanted to preserve them, however imperfect they may have been. Garret Fitzgerald had argued that divorce should be available to the few even though he and most Irish people would maintain their personal commitment to lifelong marriage, but anti-divorce campaigners asked, along with their attention to financial considerations, what would happen if one partner in a marriage wanted to end it while the other did not, thereby eliminating what in retrospect was somewhat unfortunately dubbed "the right to a lifelong marriage."[41] This rhetoric touched a nerve. Obviously, as both a moral and contractual arrangement given the imprimatur of the state primarily because marriage is to be "lifelong," the partners in such a marriage have a reasonable expectation and strong interest in marriage actually being a lifelong arrangement because that is what they bargained for. On the other hand, it is well established in law that contracts, which served as a foundation for the concept of a right to a lifelong marriage, may be routinely breached where the price of breach — the damages to be paid to the innocent party — are less than the price of performance, though damages did not feature in the proposed no-fault divorce scheme. Moreover, society had an interest in promoting the expectations of those who, in good faith and to gain certain types of social and financial benefits unavailable to the single, enter into a union which also promotes the public good. Prodivorce forces argued that the ban was sectarian — Catholic — but antidivorce activists criticized the operation of no-fault divorce in Great Britain for applying "the social and moral norms of the divorce legislation to all families in Britain and abroad whatever their cultural values [such as those of the Hindu or Sicilian opposing divorce] might be."[42] The obvious implication was that Irish law might do no better in protecting Catholics who opposed divorce from being forced into one against their will, with all the negative moral, social, and financial consequences that would imply, and potentially went a step further; Catholics attempting to preserve their marriage would face the pressure of a surrounding society changed by a divorce culture. Underlying the antiamendment campaign's criticisms was the notion that no-fault divorce enhanced individual freedom or rights only in the eye of the beholder, while others might be seriously disadvantaged.

Catholic moral teaching against divorce did play a role in the election, but the abortion and divorce referendum debates were not battles between the church and secularizing reformers. Laypersons, not all of whom were religiously motivated, led these campaigns. As Mary Kenny has written after an exhaustive review of numerous religious and secular newspapers and commentary journals of the period:

> The [abortion] referendum itself was depicted as an example of the Church throwing its weight around but ... the impetus and the energy for the referendum came from populist lay Catholics.... The attitude of the clergy and even the hierarchy was, overall, that they would not have chosen to engage in this battle [over the abortion amendment], but once the battle had been joined, they were obliged to support the cause of the unborn child.[43]

Similarly, the Anti-Divorce Campaign argued the case against the amendment on secular grounds, though the hierarchy made sure to indicate to their flocks that a vote against the amendment was preferred. Fine Gael leader Garret Fitzgerald argued afterward that the hierarchy had used scare tactics against the people,[44] but this sounds like sour grapes. Michele Dillon, who has documented the 1986 referendum debate comprehensively and insightfully, argues that the church's position was more ambiguous; on the one hand, it wanted to be noninterventionist if possible, but on the other, it did have a pastoral duty to address the moral implications of current events.[45] Mary Kenny made a documentary film about the divorce amendment debate and notes from her reporting that "[m]any bitter things were said about the influence of the Church, but the influence of land and of inheritance laws ran, if anything, even deeper than, or at least in conjunction with, loyalty to Catholic values."[46] This observation is also consistent with the history of Irish rural social structure since the famine—protecting land tenure by controlling marriage and procreation, with the church's moral teaching as a bulwark. In numerous forums, the antidivorce activists had argued persuasively that women's and children's economic livelihoods would be at serious risk if no-fault divorce were adopted. The lackluster support of the government parties coupled with the well-organized and substantive secular forces on the conservative side of both amendments, which responded to fundamental rhythms in Irish culture, also played an important role in dooming the amendment. Certainly, the church's moral teaching is important to religious persons in Ireland and informed the views of many voters, and poll findings indicated that among those who changed their minds between the referendum announcement and election day were those most likely to have been predisposed to be influenced by the church, but the church still permitted Catholics to vote in favor of the referendum in good conscience.[47] After all, it was not necessarily improper to permit non–Catholics the freedom to obtain a civil divorce, and civil divorce for Catholics is permissible under some conditions, though it would be a sin for Catholics to divorce and then remarry pursuant to such law in the absence of church annulment of that marriage.[48] Final vote tallies showed remarkable correlation between those who had supported the abortion amendment and those who opposed divorce amendment.[49] In the end, a people informed, but not controlled, by the institutional church and motivated by a wide variety of religious and secular concerns simply made definitive statements—after sophisticated and thorough public debates—that they wanted neither divorce nor abortion in their country.

Prolife groups quickly moved to use the new right-to-life amendment to prevent activity likely to lead to abortions. Though abortion had been essentially illegal in Great Britain pursuant to the Offenses Against the Person Act until 1967, when parliament passed the Abortion Act, even illegal abortion had always been more readily available there than in Ireland, and except during the "Emergency," as World War II was known in neutral Ireland, when travel was restricted, unmarried and pregnant Irish women often sought refuge in Britain, either to bear their illegitimate children and give them up for adoption or to obtain an illegal abortion. Maeve

Binchy's popular novel that became a big-screen movie starring Minnie Driver depicts a young woman doing just that.[50] The Society for the Protection of Unborn Children's (SPUC) legal battles targeted two groups, Open Door Counseling, Ltd., and the Dublin Well Woman Centre, which were providing pregnant women with nondirective counseling and referrals to legal British abortion providers. SPUC wanted the high court to stop this conduct, and it did so, noting that the right to life on which the constitutional provision was based "springs primarily from the natural right of every individual to life."[51]

SPUC's crusade attracted some of what were and would become some of the most illustrious names in Irish constitutional law and politics. The high court judge who decided the case later became chief justice of the Irish Supreme Court; SPUC's lead counsel, Hugh O'Flaherty, was also appointed to the supreme court; and his cocounsel is the author of a respected Irish constitutional law treatise. Perhaps most notable for the record books is the name of one of Dublin Well Woman Centre's cocounsel; Mary Robinson, who recently served as president of Ireland.

The case also raised troublesome procedural issues. The first was whether SPUC was even the proper party to bring the case. After all, SPUC had not been directly or tangibly damaged by Open Door's or the Well Woman Centre's activities. SPUC defused the issue by "relating" the attorney general, who the supreme court agreed was an "especially appropriate person" to seek such an injunction,[52] but in an action for costs, however, the High Court ultimately held that SPUC had standing absent the attorney general's involvement.[53]

The second issue was whether the courts could act to protect the right to life by enjoining private conduct in the absence of legislation implementing the Eighth Amendment. The high court, upheld by the supreme court, relied on a prior dictum that "the right to life of the unborn is a sacred trust to which all the organs of the government must lend their support," in concluding that "the judicial organ of government is obliged to lend its support to the enforcement of the right to life of the unborn, to defend and vindicate that right and, if there is a threat to that right from whatever source, to protect that right from such threat, if its support is sought."[54]

Aside from these procedural matters, the case forced the supreme court to examine the reach and meaning of the Eighth Amendment for the first time. The defendants argued that they and their clients had implied or unenumerated rights such as those found in *McGee* to impart and receive information about abortion services where those services were legal, such as, England. The unanimous supreme court held, however, that even if such rights existed, they were not situated above the right to life in the constitutional hierarchy and therefore could not justify overturning the high court's injunction against defendants' counseling activities. The high court applied similar analysis when it held that the right to life of the unborn ranked higher than "[t]he qualified right to privacy, the rights of association and freedom of expression and the right to disseminate information" and they could not "be invoked to interfere with such a fundamental right as the right to life of the unborn, which is acknowledged by the Constitution of Ireland."[55] This analysis suggests application of a canon of constitutional interpretation that enumerated rights will generally rank above unenumerated rights, reflecting perhaps that natural law interpretation was on the wane. Alternately, the defendants argued that the rights to receive and impart information were ancillary to rights under European Community law to travel and avail oneself of abortion services. The supreme court responded that the injunction did not prevent women from receiving information about the availability of abortion abroad in general; it merely restrained the defendants from providing assistance to pregnant women to travel abroad and obtain an abortion, a distinction so fine that it attracted the criticism of speciousness,[56] and thus the European Community law that would have required a reference to continental courts did not arise. The supreme court ordered that the high court enter an order declaring unlawful defendants' activities "in assisting pregnant women within the jurisdiction to travel abroad to obtain abortions by referral to a clinic; by making their travel arrangements; or by informing them of the identity and location of and method of communication with a specified clinic or clinics" and restraining defendants from that activity in future.[57] The defendants then applied to the European Court of Human Rights for relief from this injunction.

The unborn's right to life under the Eighth Amendment had clashed with generalized notions of free speech and rights of privacy in the *Open Door* opinion. The hierarchical analysis the court applied seemed inflexible, but due to the nature of the unborn's right to life as stated in the constitution, it was difficult to protect the other rights where they clashed. The case had been argued on stipulated facts, which included these:

> (b) Abortion or termination of pregnancy may be one of the options discussed [between the pregnant woman and the defendant counsellor] within that counselling.
>
> (c) If a pregnant woman wants to consider the abortion options further, this defendant will arrange to refer her to a medical clinic in Great Britain.[58]

Therefore, the counselors were assisting the mother to terminate the life of the unborn child, and the unborn child was not in a position to resist. Only a broad prophylactic reading of the Eighth Amendment would give it any meaning in such a case, given its direction that the state affirmatively vindicate the unborn's right to life, because even if the life of an unborn child was not technically at risk if the woman being counseled was not actually pregnant, it is unlikely in that case that the woman would use Open Door's or Well Woman Centre's pregnancy counseling services, and even if she did, a counselor would not necessarily be able to determine if the woman was, in fact, pregnant or not. Further, though not all women who received a referral to an abortion clinic in the United Kingdom would use it, once the nondirective counseling process that included abortion as an option for an unwed mother had gone that far, the risk to the life of the unborn child was great, while the right to impart information was still substantially protected by permitting counselors to speak in a nondirective way about abortion, even if they could not make referrals or travel arrangements.

This approach to reconciling the constitutional rights came under fire from American and British commentators, who seemed as amazed at the outcome — that the Irish courts could have placed so much stock in the right to life of the unborn that such a right could dwarf speech and privacy rights — as they were perturbed at the analytical method.[59] Some criticisms of the *Open Door* opinion simply reflect disagreement with Irish constitutional priorities. For example, American law professor James Friedman argues in response to Justice Hamilton's statement that the right to life of the unborn is a "sacred trust":

> Although [Ireland] has made an important moral judgment, questions of privacy and dignity remain when considering how such a judgment shall be enforced. One can only wish that Hamilton P. [high court judge] permitted himself to consider these competing constitutional concerns when he wrote his judgment in *SPUC.* The zeal of the High Court in the fulfillment of its 'sacred duty' made it remarkably insensitive to the values of free expression, privacy and personal dignity, values also held sacred in a just society.[60]

But this criticism begs the question the high and supreme courts needed to solve. Unlike rights to privacy and free speech, direct clashes between the right to life and other rights cannot be so easily resolved with time, place and manner restrictions and therefore lend themselves to hierarchy analysis, but this is not to say that all theoretical impositions on the unborn's right to life, however small, must necessarily be constitutionally improper. To make an imperfect comparison, a polity may permit the sale of guns in certain circumstances, and it may permit conversations about the characteristics of guns, but knowing assistance in choosing a gun that is well equipped to kill a specific person may be accessory to murder.

Moreover, prioritizing the privacy and dignity of born persons is a moral judgment no different in kind from prioritizing the right to life of the unborn. Only a few years before the *Open Door* decision, the leading expert on the history of the Irish censorship laws, Michael Adams, made a passionate argument in favor of restricting free speech with a certain amount of censorship, and those arguments demonstrate the difference that practical problems unique to one culture can have in legal analysis:

> We have all been brought up to regard freedom of speech as a basic right. But it is not the most basic right; the freedom to live, to eat, to work come before it; and the freedom to think, so that one is not sent to a camp just because one holds opinions which the State does not like. Freedom of speech is not the greatest of freedoms, nor is it an absolute one. It involves a responsibility to speak the truth as one sees it (and to speak out in certain circumstances). To protect other people against our spontaneity or our malice or our ignorance, society normally takes an interest in how we use our freedom of speech. In this country censorship of political opinion obtains—more so now than ten or twenty years ago; and the reason is that freedom of political expression is seen as leading rather immediately to public disorder due to the fact that radical ideas are being backed by physical violence.[61]

The reason Justice Hamilton viewed protecting the right to life of the unborn as a sacred trust was his acceptance of what the Eighth Amendment implied, that the unborn had a right to life equal to that of born persons. If unborn children are human beings, then permitting institutions to advise and make arrangements for others to kill them is clearly problematic.

In other words, the Irish constitution had already performed the balancing that Professor Friedman urged on Justice Hamilton. In the same way, the limits to speech in the *Open Door* case were completely different from a Hyde amendment-type "gag order" on *Open Door*'s counselors, because the two arise out of different constitutional schemes. Abortion laws are liberal in the United States and the Hyde amendment forbids only federally supported health-care providers from providing information about facilities permitting abortion. The U.S. federal government is not required, when spending money, to treat all viewpoints equally,[62] but the Hyde amendment does not, and could not, impose such a limit on completely private facilities consistent with the United States Constitution. By contrast, the Irish constitution itself imposes on the government, and with it the courts, an affirmative duty to protect the right to life of the unborn, which implies the authority to regulate private speech that threatens that right.

Fresh from its success in *Open Door*, SPUC moved to enjoin publication of University College Dublin's "Welfare Guide UCD 1988/1989," which contained phone numbers and other information to assist students interested in abortions in Britain. This was a harder case from a free speech perspective than *Open Door*. If *Open Door* could be viewed as a case about confused women needing assistance to explore a wide range of responses to unwanted parenthood, then the welfare guide case was about sophisticated young people who knew all the information they needed if they wanted an abortion except the correct London address and phone number for a clinic, which, with a little effort, they might have found in London phone books available all over Dublin. The students' real motivation appears to have been a desire to thumb their noses at the law, making their student guide a test case of sorts, which did not hold them in good stead before the courts or the court of public opinion.[63]

The high court held that absent the attorney general, SPUC lacked legal standing to challenge the students' publication, but the supreme court reversed, permitting the case to proceed. The supreme court took a broad view of who could come before the Irish courts to enforce the Eighth Amendment, holding that "a party who has a *bona fide* concern and interest for the protection of the constitutionally guaranteed right to life of the unborn" had standing to request an injunction that would vindicate and defend that right, a holding that made sense where there would otherwise be no individual person with a sufficient interest in the case to bring suit so that the court could perform its duty to vindicate the right to life of the unborn.[64] As Justice Walsh put it, "courts cannot move until powers are invoked."[65] This holding had interesting substantive and conceptual implications, highlighted by the attorney general's reluctance to join in this particular case. A father or grandparent, for example, or possibly an unrelated fellow citizen could conceivably have standing to enjoin a mother from having an abortion or engaging in activity that was particularly dangerous to the unborn child.[66] Such action might even help to protect the constitutionally protected family unit and be justifiable for that reason as well.[67] In fact, Justice Walsh, with Justice Hederman agreeing, wrote that it would:

> The right to life of each of the unborn is the private and human right of that life. *The parents or relatives of the unborn life have a private family right to seek to vindicate that right to life.* They have no right to seek to extinguish it. What is in issue in this case is the defence of the

> public interest in the preservation of that private right which has been guaranteed by the Constitution....
>
> In my view every member of the public has an interest in seeing that the fundamental law of the State is not defeated.[68]

Based on that reasoning, the positive right to life of the unborn, as well as the roles and rights of the family, mothers, and other persons in the street, underscores the concept that the bearing and rearing of children are family, community and even more generally public matters, as opposed to merely individual matters.

Perhaps anticipating these future standing issues, Justice McCarthy dissented. He differentiated between a case where the government interfered with the right to life of the unborn and one where private parties such as the Trinity students interfered with that right. In the former case, a private third party should have standing to request an injunction against the government to vindicate the unborn's right to life. This is because if the government were interfering with the right to life, it would be unlikely in a parliamentary system that one of its agents, the attorney general, would seek an injunction against that conduct, which would leave open the possibility that the government could plunder the unborn's right to life at will without the court's being able to check that conduct. That concern does not exist to the same extent where private parties were involved. On the other hand, Justice McCarthy's reasoning would also eliminate the possibility that a father acting alone might bring suit against a mother to stop the mother from going to the United Kingdom for an abortion, which would mean that the courts' ability to act as an agent of the state to vindicate the unborn's right to life would depend on a public policy decision by the attorney general, thereby rendering much of the Eighth Amendment meaningless. Along with these legal concerns, Justice McCarthy also did not seem to like SPUC very much: "I confess to a feeling of great unease at the prospect of any person or group of persons, however well intentioned, being held at law competent to maintain an action of this kind.... The implications to a free society of such a claim are alarming," he wrote,[69] without indicating why courts could not develop legal principles to limit the negative implications he feared.

On remand to determine the substantive issues in the case, the high court held that the decision in *Open Door* did not control whether the student guide could include abortion clinics' addresses and phone numbers, because the defendant counseling services in *Open Door* had been actively assisting women to obtain abortions abroad, while the student organizations were merely providing information about the availability of abortion abroad.[70] If abortion was a "service" under European Community law, Ireland might not be permitted to interfere with its citizens' attempts to procure that service in other countries, which would imply a right to receive information about those services unimpeded by the state. That right, the high court reasoned, would in turn imply a right to receive information about the availability of services, if not assistance in obtaining those services. Therefore, the high court referred three questions to the European Communities Court of Justice for preliminary ruling under Article 177 of the EEC Treaty:

1. Does the organised activity or process of carrying out an abortion or the medical termination of pregnancy come within the definition of 'services' provided for in Article 60 of the Treaty establishing the European Economic Community?
2. In the absence of any measures providing for the approximation of the laws of member states concerning the organised activity or process of carrying out an abortion or the medical termination of pregnancy, can a member state prohibit the distribution of specific information about the identity, location and means of communication with a specified clinic or clinics in another member state where abortions are performed?
3. Is there a right at Community law in a person in Member State A to distribute specific information about the identity, location and means of communication with a specified clinic or clinics in Member State B where abortions are performed, where the provision of abortion is prohibited under both the Constitution and the criminal law of Member State A but is lawful under certain conditions in Member State B?[71]

A unanimous and furious supreme court reversed to the extent it could, given that referrals to the European Court of Justice are unappealable. The court held that *Open Door*'s holding that "informing [pregnant women] of the identity and location of and method of communication with a specified clinic [is] unlawful" controlled the outcome of the Trinity students' case.[72] Therefore, the supreme court granted the requested preliminary injunction and openly rebuked the high court for failing to do so, thus postponing its duty to protect unborn life. Chief Justice Finlay warned:

> The exercise of this power to refer [a case to the European Court of Justice] does not by its nature affect the parties concerned in the sense that it does not determine any of the issues in the case. But neither does it permit the judge concerned to avoid deciding issues in a case which must be decided and the failure to decide which may be the subject of an appeal procedure or review procedure in a higher

> national court.... So far as the interlocutory application is concerned the failure to grant it amounted to a withdrawal, for a period at least, of the protection of unborn lives in being from the effects of the activities of the defendants.[73]

Even Justice McCarthy, who had expressed grave doubt that an injunction would actually save unborn lives, was perturbed:

> It is the common case that the reference would, in effect, postpone the determination of the interlocutory motion for at least 18 months. Such a result, in my view, is a breach of the constitutional guarantee and a refusal of the duty of the courts to enforce that guarantee.[74]

But particularly sharp was Justice Walsh's view:

> When the present matter came before the High Court it was clear beyond all doubt that the activities complained of were contrary to the Constitution. The decision of the High Court judge to adopt the course which she did namely, to leave the matter undecided, was in effect to suspend the provisions of the 8th Amendment of the Constitution for an indefinite period. It is not open to any judge to do anything which in effect suspends any provisions of the Constitution for any period whatsoever.[75]

Admittedly, the high court's distinction between assisting a specific person to obtain an abortion abroad and making general statements about how an abortion might be obtained abroad does have merit: It is the difference between a newspaper article describing the types of equipment one might use to burgle a home and giving specific advice on the burglary of a specific house to a person, knowing that person will attempt to break into that home by night. The former is in poor taste, perhaps, but not criminal, as the latter would be[76] (leaving aside the thorny and judicially unanswered question of whether there could be criminal liability in Ireland for obtaining an abortion in the United Kingdom[77]), and the latter also would not be protected by a free speech argument. Moreover, from a rights balancing perspective, the threat of any particular person planning a burglary based on descriptions in a newspaper article is real but low, and therefore, the threat to property rights from information in such an article may not outweigh the threat to free speech both from censoring the article and from the chilling effect that might result from defining such conduct within the range of a criminal offense. By analogy, the threat of any particular person seeking an actual abortion in the United Kingdom because of the students' publication might also seem fairly low.

Two important differences between the burglary analogy and the student welfare guide's list of abortion clinics drove the supreme court's decision, however. First, the right to life of the unborn clearly has much greater importance in the Irish constitutional scheme than publishing lists in a student guide or even the economic rights that European Community law might protect. The Eighth Amendment suggested and the court had already held that even small impositions on the unborn's right to life outweighed large impositions on other personal rights of born persons, or, in other words, the right to life is not just more important or the most important personal right; it is the most important *by a large amount*. The second difference is that even if there might be cases in which free speech rights recognized in Ireland protected publication of lists of abortion clinics in the United Kingdom, restrictions on the time, place and manner of publication would be bound to apply. After all, the unborn did not lose their right to life merely because their mother contemplated leaving Ireland; by contrast, as Justice Walsh noted, the mother's rights as a mother carried with them obligations to protect her unborn child.[78] The Trinity students' case demonstrated that the supreme court appreciated the practical "facts of international life and the practical difficulties they present for a state which adheres to a particular value relating to an aspect of human rights where surrounding states adhere to an opposing norm."[79] It was one thing to pass a constitutional amendment, but it was quite another to change behavior in volatile times.

The European Community Court of Justice, however, was not bound by the Irish constitutional scheme and the importance it placed on the right to life. Faced with the facts of the Trinity students' case, the court of justice held that provision of abortion was simply a service under European Community law. Since as a general matter, the European Economic Community Treaty prohibited restrictions on the freedom to supply services, this would normally have meant that Ireland's restriction on the students' activity was unlawful under the treaty, but in this particular case, the court of justice also found that the students were not distributing information on behalf of an economic operator in another EEC state, and so the supreme court's injunction did not constitute an unlawful restriction on freedom to supply services under the treaty. The Irish Supreme Court then decided to make its injunction against the students' publication permanent.

Categorizing abortion as a service whose provision across national lines would normally be protected from national trade restrictions raised a red flag about the impact of European law on Irish values. Irish legal scholar Diarmiud Rossa Phelan warned of "one uniform European society shaped under a single Esperanto-type legal theory of fundamental rights and a market construction of personhood," where "the rights of man are transformed into the rights of the Euro-market actor,"[80] effectively forcing less powerful, dissenting nations to compromise core national values or lose the economic and cultural benefits of European Community membership. "A fundamental right afforded by a Member State will be in the precarious position of derogation at the Court's discretion precisely because there is in reality a clash between constitutions pursuing incompatible social goals according to different theories of what is fundamental to the legal order."[81] Phelan's essential conclusion, that a multinational economic and commercial grouping should not have so much power to override core national moral and cultural values, raises but does not resolve the next question: What level of governmental authority should identify, recognize and protect human rights?

Ireland and many other European nations had more directly given up some of their national autonomy as to fundamental rights in particular by becoming parties to the European Convention on Human Rights, and the *Open Door* defendants now petitioned the entry-level decision-making entity established under the convention, the European Commission of Human Rights, to hear their case. Under the Convention for the Protection of Human Rights and Fundamental Freedoms, individuals may petition the European Commission on Human Rights if one of the "High Contracting Parties" to the convention has violated any of the rights recognized in the convention. The purpose of the commission is much like that of our own Equal Employment Opportunity Commission, that is, to work out settlements between the parties, and if it fails, the convention provides for individuals, the commission, or any of the high contracting parties to bring cases before the European Court of Human Rights. The court may then award damages to the aggrieved party.

A majority of the European commission held that Ireland's Eighth Amendment was an insufficiently precise limitation on free expression under the convention to know whether the clinics' activities were even prescribed by Irish law. The key provision of the convention was Article 10:

1. Everyone has the right to freedom of expression. This right shall include freedom to hold opinions and to receive and impart information and ideas without interference by public authority and regardless of frontiers. This Article shall not prevent States from requiring the licensing of broadcasting, television or cinema enterprises.
2. The exercise of these freedoms, since it carries with it duties and responsibilities, may be subject to such formalities, conditions, restrictions or

> penalties as are prescribed by law and are necessary in a democratic society, in the interests of national security, territorial integrity or public safety, for the prevention of disorder or crime, for the protection of health or morals, for the protection of the reputation or rights of others, for preventing the disclosure of information received in confidence, or for maintaining the authority and impartiality of the judiciary.

Therefore, all the commission members reasoned that Ireland could enjoin Open Door's activities if the injunction were prescribed by Irish law and necessary to prevent crime, to protect health and safety, or safeguard the rights of others.

The majority doubted that the Eighth Amendment truly prescribed nondirective counseling about abortion providers in other Community nations. They noted that though generally a crime in Ireland, many of the women who might have obtained an abortion in another country after counseling at Open Door would not be committing crimes in those countries and that it was not a criminal offense in Ireland to obtain an abortion elsewhere or to travel abroad for that purpose. The majority stated that "the present cases are not limited to the protection of the right to life of the unborn," which Irish law clearly required, but rather the cases addressed the "freedom to receive and impart information on a wider and more complex scale, involving not only the right to life of the unborn, but also women's health, pregnancy, family planning and abortion."[82] Given those conflicting imperatives, Open Door also could not reasonably foresee that its counseling activities would constitute a civil wrong such as a constitutional tort. "[A] law which restricts freedom of expression in such a vital area requires particular precision to enable individuals to regulate their conduct accordingly," and given the majority's conclusion that Irish law was insufficiently precise, it held that Open Door's activities were not "'prescribed by law,'" rendering the injunction against those activities improper under the convention.[83]

Several commission members diverged from the raw outlines of this reasoning. Two members believed that the injunction was, in fact, prescribed by Irish law but still found that the injunction was objectionable because it was not "necessary in a democratic society" to protect morals or the rights of others pursuant to Article 10. Five members of the commission dissented, holding that Ireland had not contravened Article 10 at all.

The five dissenting opinions implicitly recognized a variant of the principle of subsidiarity—that "[p]olitical and social tasks ought to devolve upward toward larger communities only when they cannot be performed adequately by local ones"[84]—which had indirectly received the

European Court of Human Rights' imprimatur in *Muller* v. *Switzerland*[85] and was the sleeping serpent coiled up under the proverbial table in the majority's opinion in *Open Door*. For example, two commissioners relied on the well recognized "margin of appreciation" granted to national lawmakers under the convention where important moral issues were at stake, arguing specifically that as long as no consensus existed among European countries as to the morality of abortion, individual countries were in a better position than the parties to the treaty to determine whether laws restricting abortion were necessary to protect morals and the rights of others:

> [I]t is still not possible to find in the legal and social orders of the Contracting States a uniform European conception of morals. In view of the absence of such uniformity, the national authorities are in principles in a better position than the Convention organs to judge the moral requirements of a particular society, as well as the necessity of any restrictions imposed with a view to meeting them. As far as the present cases are concerned, it is also essential not to lose sight of the fact that the Irish authorities had been in direct touch with vital public opinion in Ireland through a recent referendum on the subject.[86]

Even those commissioners who did not discuss the competence of the European commission to pass on the necessity of abortion restrictions to protect morals and the rights of others noted that it was "odd if a state were not allowed to prohibit within its frontiers acts of aid or assistance likely to incite citizens of this State to commit acts disapproved under their criminal law in countries where such acts are not illegal."[87]

This question of how large the margin of appreciation for national values should be is another way of talking about how much the convention's decision-making entities should defer to national law-making institutions and therefore how active those entities should be in determining the applicability of the convention to a particular situation.[88] The commission's majority did not have to raise the issue directly because of its conclusion that the injunction had not even been prescribed by Irish law, but to the extent that judicial activism presses the boundaries of what the law is understood to be, the increased activism of the convention's decision-making bodies signals a greater element of lawmaking in those bodies' actions. In other words, the convention's decision-making bodies are taking on the role not only of enforcing mutually agreed upon rights and principles, but also of recognizing additional such rights and principles and the relevance of all such rights and principles in new factual contexts, making it effectively a new layer of creative government and not merely a body to which national governments have delegated the responsibility to carry out certain administrative and enforcement activity. Rightly or wrongly, therefore, the evolution of this higher layer of government forces the issues of who should recognize and require enforcement of fundamental human rights.

The notion that the higher level of government ought to play that role has its initial attractions. If fundamental human rights are fundamental, they are in one sense absolute. The mere fact that some may dissent, fail to recognize them, or consent to their protection may be viewed as exactly why the largest available governing umbrella ought have the responsibility for recognizing and enforcing them in order to make sure that as many potential beneficiaries of the rights at issue have access to protection.

On the other hand, *Open Door* v. *Ireland* illustrates the pitfalls of concluding too quickly that the body with the wider umbrella ought to make the law. The commission dissenters recognized that while there was no consensus in Europe itself about abortion and the importance of the right to life of the unborn compared to other human rights values, there was such a consensus in Ireland, and the Irish had recently confirmed it through a national democratic referendum process accompanied by an exhaustive public debate. The consensus Irish view was certainly an outlier view within Europe even as early as the mid–1980s.[89] Therefore on this critical issue of constitutional magnitude within the convention's community, the Irish cannot be said to have meaningfully consented to the rule in *Open Door*.

A similar argument can be made of *Roe* v. *Wade*. The American states voluntarily delegated the power of judicial review of state court judgments[90] and the power to announce the supreme law of the land to the United States Supreme Court.[91] Nevertheless, did the states meaningful assent to state delegation of the power to determine whether there is a right to an abortion under the federal constitution, which nullifies inconsistent state laws, given that the right to an abortion does not arise plainly from the text of the constitution and only from a modern notion of the spirit of the Constitution? History and legal reasoning permit differing views on this subject.

Lack of consent in such a situation looks disturbingly like tyranny. Ireland is a small, bit player in European institutions, where France and Germany generally dominate, and therefore is rarely able to bargain for changes in the convention. If Ireland did not want to be bound to the rule, its only solution would be to withdraw from the convention, which would damage both the convention and the Irish. On the other hand, dissenting Irish citizens who have access to the information disseminated in *Open*

Door may legally leave Ireland for an abortion. The Irish people resemble one of the "discrete and insular minorities" that U.S. Supreme Court Justice Stone argued were unable to protect themselves within the political process and were at risk of having their fundamental values trampled by majority rule and therefore were entitled to have alleged violations of their rights reviewed with "a correspondingly more searching judicial inquiry."[92] A broader vision of an appropriate human rights regime might militate in favor of institutions and rules that protect the Irish people, with their outlier but consensus policies related to abortion, from majorities on the continent as much as the convention may protect dissenting Irish persons from majority law making within Ireland. At a minimum, a wider margin of appreciation is in order.

The benefit of the smaller polities—Ireland as compared to Europe—making value decisions about law related to abortion is that though some Irish may be disadvantaged by the national rule, more will be disadvantaged if the convention entities rule. Of course, if abortion is an objectively and absolutely important human right, the total imposition on the women unable to vindicate that right may be greater than the total imposition on the citizens who desire restrictions, but inevitably, as the commission's decision shows, where the higher decision maker deems the individual interest involved an important right, the temptation to protect the individual will be considerable. Who should decide whether abortion is a sufficiently objective and absolutely important human right to merit such protection and therefore be recognized as such even in light of other important competing values and then how dissenters may be best protected? Under the commission's approach, the room for dissenters might turn out to be very small indeed.

Six

The Equal Right to Life of the Mother

"I wish my baby it was born
And smiling on its daddy's knee;
And me, poor girl, to be dead and gone,
With the long green grass growing over me."[1]

Those who understood the forces propelling the development of Irish abortion law must have felt an uncanny sense of déjà vu about the tragedy that finally blew apart the fragile edifice that had been Irish abortion law. In December 1991, a forty-two-year-old man, a father of three, raped his daughter's best friend, a fourteen-year-old girl. In a tragic sense, the event might have been unremarkable; after all, the man had been sexually abusing his victim for a year and a half. On that particular day, however, the child herself conceived a child.

The girl and her parents decided she should have an abortion in England and consulted with the Irish police, the "gardai," about whether DNA tests could be done on the fetus to help confirm the father's identity. DNA profiling was a new technique in Ireland, and the gardai saw obvious constitutional and public relations concerns with using DNA from an aborted fetus in a criminal trial. The Director for Public Prosecutions confirmed the gardai's suspicions that such evidence would be inadmissible in court, and the family set off for England. But the Director of Public Prosecutions also informed the Irish attorney general's office about the family's intention to take their daughter to England for an abortion, and while en route, the family discovered that the attorney general had requested and received from High Court Justice Declan Costello an ex parte temporary injunction restraining the girl from having an abortion until he could hold a hearing on its legality. The order was technically unenforceable since the girl was already out of the country, opening Judge

Costello up to criticism for signing it at all, but the family returned to Ireland, where Judge Costello enjoined the girl from leaving the country again for the next nine months and from having an abortion.[2]

In the midst of a deafening public outcry, the supreme court heard the appeal of the defendant, X. Judge Costello had heard evidence from a number of lay and professional psychologist witnesses that X had made threats to take her own life if her pregnancy continued. He found that "there is *a risk* that the defendant may take her own life," if not permitted to have an abortion.[3] All the judges who ultimately would hear her story would agree that she was a "mental wreck," in *Rex* v. *Bourne*'s terminology. Based on this evidence, Judge Costello had agreed that the case implicated the equal rights to life of the mother and child and that the Eighth Amendment imposed on him "a duty to protect [X's] life not just from the actions of others but from actions she herself may perform."[4] Nevertheless, he also found "a real and imminent danger" to X's unborn child, and he concluded that "the risk that the defendant may take her own life … is much less and is of a different order of magnitude than the certainty that the life of the unborn will be terminated if the order is not made."[5] He further held that while X had an unenumerated right to travel, she could not exercise that right "to commit a wrong," such as going to England for an abortion.[6]

The supreme court reversed but was not outwardly critical of Judge Costello's fact finding or most of his reasoning. The attorney general argued that a mother could have an abortion only if she established that there was an inevitable or immediate risk to her life which an abortion would be necessary to avoid, but the supreme court concluded that this test did not adequately vindicate the mother's right to life, holding instead that the mother's right to life could defeat the unborn child's right if the mother could show a probability that there was a real and substantial risk to her life, as distinct from her health, that could be avoided only by an abortion.[7] Four of the five supreme court justices found that X's credible threats of suicide backed up with psychological evidence met this test. The chief justice wrote:

> In my view, it is common sense that a threat of self-destruction such as is outlined in the evidence in this case, which the psychologist clearly believes to be a very real threat, cannot be monitored in that sense and that it is almost impossible to prevent self-destruction in a young girl in the situation in which this defendant is if she were to decide to carry out her threat of suicide.[8]

On the other hand, the court also indicated that absent a threat to the mother's life, the right to travel would have to give way to the right to life of the unborn.

Only one justice dissented. "Suicide threats can be contained," Justice Hederman wrote.[9] He did not agree that fulfilling the state's duty to protect the life of the mother required that her pregnancy be aborted:

> If this young person without being pregnant had suicidal tendencies due to some other cause then nobody would doubt that the proper course would be to put her in such care and under such supervision as would counteract such tendency and do everything possible to prevent suicide.... This young girl clearly requires loving and sympathetic care and professional counselling and all the protection which the State agencies can provide or furnish.
>
> ...I do not think the word "life" in this context [as to the mother] is to be construed any differently from the word "life" in the earlier part of the same article[[10]] though the State would be obliged to do all it reasonably [and] possibly can to take steps to prevent anybody from becoming a physical or a mental wreck, short of taking innocent life to achieve it.[11]

Justice Hederman's opinion reveals two serious weaknesses in the majority's reasoning: its thin factual basis and its failure to develop a principled interpretation of the Eighth Amendment even while abandoning one — the doctrine of double effect — and thereby failing to harmonize the right to life of the mother and the unborn child so that both could be protected.

The evidence of risk to X's life was admittedly limited, but the question as the supreme court phrased it was whether there was a "real and substantial risk" that X would try to commit suicide. No psychiatrist testified before Judge Costello, though many lay witnesses and an examining clinical psychologist testified that X exhibited symptoms of serious clinical depression, including a strong sense of worthlessness and guilt, withdrawal, and suicidal ideation with concrete ideas about how to carry it out. She had disturbing physical symptoms, such as recurrent vomiting and physical pain. The psychologist who examined her for trial considered her symptoms sufficiently severe that he would not allow her to remain alone in the waiting room while he discussed his findings with her parents. He also noted that X no longer seemed depressed, though she was trancelike and vacant, but if these observations suggest that X was no longer at rock bottom, they might also suggest that she was actually at greater risk of suicide at that moment than she had been previously.[12]

Most of X's statements about her intentions were enigmatic, and by the time Judge Costello was taking evidence, the risk that she would commit suicide had declined. X had told her mother that when she had learned she was pregnant she had wanted to kill herself by throwing herself down the stairs, which may have been the sort of concrete, suicidal ideation indicative of a serious suicidal intention.[13] But that moment had passed, and many of X's later statements were not so clear. Her mother testified that when the family was returning from London for the court hearing, X had told her that she wanted to throw herself under a train for having caused her parents so much trouble.[14] This statement did indicate thoughts of suicide, but they were caused by guilt at the difficulty the pregnancy had caused her parents and not the pregnancy itself. The court's written opinions do not recount evidence about whether such guilt might be best addressed with loving reassurance from X's parents, whom all the judges praised for their care and nurture of X, or from another medical or therapeutic course. Prior to leaving for England, X apparently said to one garda, "'I wish this was all over. Sometimes I feel like throwing myself down the stairs,'"[15] which is more credible as a threat of self-induced abortion than suicide, a fact the examining psychologist implicitly noted. Another garda testified, "'[s]he did not say in my presence that she thought about killing herself, but did say she was looking at ways out of this particular situation and thought about running away'"[16]—again, a disconcerting statement, but not necessarily a suicide threat. When X's father had commented that the family's situation was worse than a death in the family, X had responded, "not if it was me,"[17] a statement indicative of significant situational depression, but not suicidal ideation. Further, X acted to get help by telling her parents about her pregnancy and the way it was making her feel. X certainly required treatment and close observation to ameliorate her pain, treat her serious situational depression, and protect her from herself in the short term, but no doctor would have prescribed an abortion.

The psychologist concluded that X was at risk of either suicide or self-induced abortion, but he was not more definitive, and many of X's statements suggest the latter was what she really hoped for. His report states, "[s]he coldly expressed a desire to solve matters by ending her life," though she did not state an intention of how she would end her life,[18] again suggesting that the most serious risk to her life had already passed.[19] He further testified,

> This is what disturbed me most of all, that she was able to talk about not wishing to put her parents through any more of this—"I thought about not putting my parents through more, it would be better to end it now than nine months more. It is hard to understand ... it is hard at fourteen to go through nine months."[20]

This again sounds as much like a threat to attempt self-induced abortion as a suicide threat, if not more, though the possibility that the attempt of self-induced abortion might itself result in the girl's death was more than minimal:

> I feel she might commit suicide or decide to terminate it herself by throwing herself down the stairs or something like that. That is the kind of thing happened in previous cases I dealt with where girls attempted to gain abortion.[21]

He noted that in his experience, however, such a risk to a young woman with an unwanted pregnancy often increases as the baby begins to move and kick, making the mother more aware of the pregnancy.

Irish legal commentators and health-care professionals on both sides of the abortion debate have agreed the psychological evidence that X's life was in "real and substantial" danger was thin given the importance of the rights involved. Gerard Hogan, coeditor of the leading Irish constitutional law treatise, finds merit in the *X* majority's real and substantial risk test, but he finds Justice Hederman more persuasive in his assessment of the high court's factual findings and the application of those facts to the law.[22] James Kingston and Anthony Whelan are disturbed that none of the defendants—X or her parents—gave oral testimony before the high court and that the only expert was a psychologist, but even though "the relative paucity of evidence adduced raises serious questions as to the ability, in the circumstances, of Costello, J., and of the Supreme Court, to judge properly the facts of the case," they assuage these concerns with the less-than-persuasive theory that the judges would have sought additional evidence had they needed it.[23] In their Annual Review of Irish law, Raymond Byrne and William Binchy cite numerous works by medical practitioners and psychologists criticizing the expert testimony and the supreme court's analysis of it.[24]

The substance of just what a woman must show to render her abortion legal under Irish law—and the supreme court's reaction to the evidence adduced at trial—reveals practical and philosophical fault lines in the law. Peter McKenna, Master of Rotunda Hospital, Ireland's leading maternity hospital, states, "I personally have never seen a patient where termination is necessary for psychiatric reasons, but I have the niggling fear that some day I might." Yet he also recognized that "the threat of suicide can be easily made and could prove to be the thin edge of the wedge" on the abortion issues, and his discussions with psychiatric colleagues had reassured him that "termination is never part of the treatment of depression."[25] These medical concerns infuriate Irish abortion rights advocates who argue that efforts to remove suicide as a legal justification for abortion stems from a belief that "women are so devious they will pretend to be suicidal in order to access abortion"[26] and that, more generally, "[w]omen, apparently, are not to be believed."[27] Yet these concerns harken all too familiarly back to British criticisms of their own infanticide act, which encouraged psychological professionals to diagnose what is necessary under the law in a merciful effort to save their patients from murder convictions. Perhaps the concern is less whether women are to be believed and more whether "the law" has any meaning divorced from the beliefs and mores of the people and how they act upon those in a crisis situation except to inform those beliefs and mores as best it can.

Justice Hederman read the doctrine of double effect into the Eighth Amendment to harmonize the apparently clashing rights at the same time the rest of the court, and surprisingly even Judge Costello, were reading it out.[28] Without specifically mentioning the doctrine, Judge Costello obliquely noted that it did not justify allowing X to travel for an abortion, because hers was not a situation in which "surgical intervention, necessary to save the life of the unborn, may involve risk to the mother's life, or in which the surgical intervention necessary to save the life of a mother may involve risk to the life of the unborn."[29] Abortion is not a treatment for a psychological condition that might cause a pregnant mother to consider suicide, and therefore the death of the unborn child from such an abortion is not simply a harm permitted to occur to bring about another good. Abortion is "deliberately *chosen* and caused."[30] Further, society would not condone killing a born person to assuage another's psychological reaction to her. Had Judge Costello and the supreme court majority concluded that the proper way to balance the clashing rights to life of the mother and unborn child was to apply the doctrine of double effect, X would have been barred both from an abortion in Ireland and from traveling to Britain to obtain one.

Nevertheless, Judge Costello believed he had an affirmative duty to protect X's life even from her own hand, which he interpreted as requiring him to assess the relative risks to both her life and that of her child's if he did or did not enjoin her from traveling to England for the abortion, and he concluded from the evidence that the risk to the unborn child's life was much greater if he did not enter an injunction than the risk would be to X's life if he did. Justice Hederman's reasoning, based on the same evidence, was similar. Gerard Hogan and Gerry Whyte have argued that evidence from prison suicide research suggests that intolerable round-the-clock supervision for months might be necessary to stop a determined person from committing suicide,[31] but no evidence suggested such extreme measures would be necessary in X's case, and normally in constitutional jurisprudence, the "least restrictive means" of protecting an interest pitted against an important right would be required to be shown to be inadequate before more intrusive means could be justified. In X's situation, treatment and monitoring should have been shown to have some unacceptable level of ineffectiveness before the extreme measure of abortion in violation of the unborn child's right to life was sanctioned. This analysis is consistent with the attorney general's proposed test, that only where the risk to the mother's life was "inevitable or immediate" and an abortion was necessary to protect her life could it be justified under the Eighth Amendment.

Justice McCarthy found the attorney general's reasoning intolerable where the rights to life of the unborn and mother clashed. Proportionality analysis is noncontroversial when an important right is pitted against mere state interests, as abortion rights are in the United States, but in X's situation, there was no "less restrictive means" to protect her unborn child other than an injunction to stop an abortion; unless the unborn child received absolute protection, an abortion was inevitable while there would never be absolute certainty that a mother in X's situation would actually take her own life. Judge Costello and Justice Hederman had essentially stopped there, but Justice McCarthy took a next step, reasoning that while the right to life of the mother and the right to life of the unborn were theoretically equal according to the terms of the Eighth Amendment, the amendment's charge to the state was merely to protect the right to life of the unborn child "as far as practicable," concluding that in some situations, it would simply not be practicable to protect the unborn child's right to life. Justice McCarthy called this a "harmonization" of the rights and needs of X and the unborn child, but it was really just a different hierarchy, this time favoring the life of the mother.

Again, even commentators who like the result shake their heads at the reasoning. Professors Kingston and Whelan take Justice McCarthy and the rest of the supreme court to task for ignoring a better analysis arising from the inevitability that if X took her own life, she would be taking the life of her unborn child as well, and therefore, "[i]t could be argued that the need to prevent the probable ending of two constitutionally protected lives outweighs the need to prevent the certain ending of one such life."[32] Yet Kingston and Whelan themselves open a Pandora's box with their probability analysis. Whether the certainty of keeping one thing in exchange for the certain loss of something else is preferable to the possibility of keeping both things at the risk of losing both depends on the specific situation and also the underlying values involved. If the mother's life is implicitly deemed more valuable than the life of the unborn, the certainty of protecting the mother's life in exchange for the unborn's life may well outweigh the utility to be gained from risking both lives in the hopes of protecting both, even where the probability of protecting both is very high. On the other hand, if the two lives truly are equal and there is merely a "real and substantial"—for "substantial" does not mean "large" in legalese—risk of death to the mother (and therefore death to both), attempting to save both lives at the risk of losing both may outweigh the certainty of losing one life and saving the other because the likelihood of protecting both is fairly high. Kingston and Whelan's probabilities analysis carried to its logical extensions might have produced wiser and sounder fruit for the supreme court majority. As Justice Hederman recognized when he announced that "suicide threats can be contained," the state could have intervened both to protect X from herself and X's child from X, dramatically decreasing the chance that neither would die, and thereby weighting the scales in favor of saving both lives. Admittedly, a good society might see limits to how much it is willing to interfere with X's autonomy or other individual rights to alter the probabilities in favor of protecting both her and her child—pregnancy tests at the Irish border or locking young women in cells would be out of the question—but no evidence even suggests X implicated the extremes, and the majority certainly did not explore them. Given the evidence, which no one thought suggested that the risk to X's life was imminent or inevitable, the majority can have concluded only that X's life mattered more than her unborn child's. There is just one problem for legal purists as well as for those who think the statements emanating from a democratic process less than ten years old matter: The plain language of the Eighth Amendment says otherwise.

The justices gave merely a bit part to the mother's or family's rights under Article 41. In what could have been an important concession, the attorney general urged the court to consider X's "'rights and duties as a mother, as a sister, as a daughter, as a parent, perhaps.'"[33] Chief Justice Finlay followed up with a question about whether X's parents' rights should be considered when balancing X's right to life against her unborn child's, and the attorney general responded that X's "right may be superior to the right to life of the unborn because of the other constitutional rights and duties."[34] If this response were correct, the Eighth Amendment, which facially equates the right to life of the unborn and the right to life of the mother, would be meaningless. Even if the list of the mother's other rights is longer than that of the unborn child, the length of the list could not render their rights to life of differing importance.[35] Nevertheless, maternal and family rights might have provided some content to what the "right to life" or the duties the additional rights of motherhood implied in this particular context. Justice Walsh, for example, had written in *SPUC*

v. *Grogan* that by virtue of becoming pregnant, a woman acquires the right to protect the life of her unborn child against those attempting to compel or persuade her to have an abortion, which might have jumpstarted a fascinating analysis—but the majority explored none of those possibilities.

Therefore, Article 41 made ubiquitous, but not particularly meaningful, appearances in the justices' various opinions. For example, Chief Justice Finlay suggested that the mother's role in various communities, such as the family and the wider society, may have an impact on how practicable it is to vindicate the unborn child's right to life:

> Such a harmonious interpretation of the Constitution carried out in accordance with concepts of prudence, justice and charity, as they have been explained in the judgment of Walsh, J., in *McGee* v. *Attorney General* leads me to the conclusion that in vindicating and defending as far as practicable the right of the unborn to life but at the same time giving due regard to the right of the mother to life, *the court must, amongst the matters to be so regarded, concern itself with the position of the mother within a family group, with persons on whom she is dependent, with, in other instances, persons who are dependent upon her and her interaction with other citizens and members of society in the areas in which her activities occur.* Having regard to that conclusion, I am satisfied that the test proposed on behalf of the Attorney General that the life of the unborn could only be terminated if it were established that an inevitable or immediate risk to the life of the mother existed, for the avoidance of which a termination of the pregnancy was necessary, insufficiently vindicates the mother's right to life.[36]

The argument is facially appealing because of its rhetorical consistency with the roots of Irish constitutional law and a sound communitarian theory of rights and duties, but what does it mean in X's specific situation? How should X's positions within the family created by her parents and the family that has been created with her unborn child affect the vindication of that child's right to life? Does X have any correlative duty arising from her preferred constitutional position as a mother to protect her unborn child? How do those relationships lead to the "real and substantial risk" test? Chief Justice Finlay never says.

In fact, the chief justice's approach to Article 41 and more general communitarian considerations might have favored the opposite holding in X's particular situation. X's position within her family was secure, and her parents were acknowledged as being very nurturing and supportive. They could be counted upon to do what it took to protect X from herself and to mitigate the psychological damage she would experience from her pregnancy, which would tend to decrease the actual risk to her life. X's broader community of neighborhood and school might or might not have affected her mental health beneficially or detrimentally, but evidence on these circumstances as well as reasonable alternatives and appropriate treatment is not apparent from the justices' opinions. Moreover, Chief Justice Finlay never considers if the unborn child's other family members, such as the father — admittedly not a character of great moral concern under the circumstances and perhaps not privy to whatever benefits Article 41 might provide, because it protects families based on marriage — his innocent other children, or other members of X's community have individual (albeit perhaps small) interests in the life X was carrying.

In many respects, Justice McCarthy's reference to Article 41 is even more abstract and obscure than Chief Justice Finlay's:

> In my view, the true construction of the amendment, bearing in mind the other provisions of Article 40 and the fundamental rights of the family guaranteed by Article 41, is that, paying due regard to the equal right to life of the mother, when there is a real and substantial risk attached to her survival not merely at the time of applications but in contemplation at least throughout the pregnancy, then it may not be practicable to vindicate the right to life of the unborn.[37]

It is unclear how Justice McCarthy envisioned Article 41 affecting his decision based on this lone reference. Perhaps he meant that X's parents' authority to make decisions about their minor daughter, implicitly respected and protected in Article 41[38] and Article 42,[39] weighed in favor of protecting X's right to life where it clashed with the right to life of her unborn child, a view echoed by Justice O'Flaherty, who called the injunction "an unwarranted interference with the authority of the family."[40] This conclusion is reminiscent of Justice Walsh's subsidiarity argument in *McGee*, but in *McGee* the court was attempting to choose the correct entity to make a decision about whether to limit family size with contraceptives, an issue specifically drawn so that it would not implicate the state's duty to protect life. Where protecting the right to life is concerned, the Eighth Amendment assigned that duty to the state, and the court did not have discretion to change it.

Neither justice probably intends the consequences of that reasoning, however. Any such application of Article 41 would imply judicial standing for fathers and grandparents opposing abortions and the potential superiority of family rights over Article 40's personal rights in nonabortion situations, both of which are unlikely to be what Justice McCarthy, who dissented from the majority decision in *SPUC* v. *Coogan* because of his hesitance to overextend the list of those with standing to protect the unborn's right to life, had in mind. Further, this reasoning lends itself to the conclusion that by virtue of being an adult mother, "when there is a real and substantial risk attached to her survival not merely at the time of application but in contemplation at least throughout the pregnancy,"[41] X also has some independent authority to decide whether her unborn child should live or die, essentially a private right to kill.[42] "If it implies that Article 41 gives a distinct legal entitlement of parents to facilitate the termination of the life of their unborn child which does not inhere in other facilitators, this is an argument that would need some further development,"[43] Byrne and Binchy note drily. This would raise disturbing questions about the mother's authority over the lives of her born children.

Only Justice Hederman integrated notions of family and maternal rights coherently into his opinion, and he confronted the problem that his colleagues ignored, that the enhanced constitutional position of mothers in return for "woman giv[ing] to the State a support without which the common good cannot be achieved,"[44] implied that the woman has duties to others which are the substance of that support to the state. A mother by virtue of being a mother might have more rights but also more duties flowing from the social condition of motherhood, which had endowed her with those rights and a protected position in society:

> The natural connection between the unborn child and the mother's life constitutes a special relationship. But one cannot consider the unborn life only as part of the maternal organism. The extinction of unborn life is not confined to the sphere of private life of the mother or family because the unborn life is an autonomous human being protected by the Constitution. Therefore, the termination of pregnancy other than a natural one has a legal and social dimension and requires a special responsibility on the part of the State. There cannot be a freedom to extinguish life side by side with a guarantee of protection of that life because the termination of pregnancy always means the destruction of an unborn life. Therefore no recognition of a mother's right of self-determination can be given priority over the protection of the unborn life. The creation of a new life, involving as it does pregnancy, birth and raising the child, necessarily involves some restriction of a mother's freedom but the alternative is the destruction of the unborn life. The termination of pregnancy is not like a visit to the doctor to cure an illness. The State must, in principle, act in accordance with the mother's duty to carry out the pregnancy and, in principle, must also outlaw the termination of pregnancy.[45]

Yet even Justice Hederman's views raise a critical question for the *X* case: Does the "natural connection" and "special relationship" between the unborn child and the mother's life give rise to "the mother's duty to carry out the pregnancy" when the unborn child is the result of the rape of a minor—a situation in which in no way can she be said to have given consent and where the mother is arguably too immature to understand what it all means? Given the right to life of the unborn, the answer may be "yes," but it too would require some development to satisfy many observers. What then of the state's responsibility to act in accordance with the mother's duty to carry the pregnancy to term? Justice Hederman does not explore whether the state or society has any specific responsibility to the mother or unborn child in such an instance other than outlawing abortion. Nevertheless, even though Eamon de Valera most certainly did not have a fourteen-year-old rendered a mother by rape in mind when he drafted Article 41, the tone of that article, which recognizes the support women generally and most emphatically this young woman specifically would give to the common good by maternal activities, taken with the less specific requirement that the unborn's right to life be vindicated as far as practicable and with regard to due observance of prudence, justice and charity, suggests that having barred her abortion, neither the state nor society at large may legally or morally sit by while X struggles alone. Just how they should help may be a matter better suited to legislatures, churches, and neighborhoods than to courts, but they must do so in order for the "common good" to be deemed "good" at all.

Justice Hederman's reasoning shows that to make any legal statement about abortion is to make a statement about public activity and the rights, duties and relationships between persons, groups and societies. Abortion forces the issue of what persons society shall recognize as entitled to individual liberties and protections of the law and what those liberties and protections will be,[46] both of which have a strong social component. As Binchy puts it:

> The task of determining how one human being should treat another is clearly a moral issue, but it also has a vital social component. One person's right to kill exposes another to the certainty of death without social protection.... To hold that murder is wrong is of course to make a judgment about an individual human act; but it is also integrally to make a judgment about social relationships—about the just society as well as the just person.[47]

Therefore, abortion is not merely an individual act or even a matter between an individual and the impersonal state; it implicates families, communities, and society at large through its recognition of who is human, how humans may and should relate to one another, and what humans or societies at large owe other humans. None of this means a lawful abortion may not exist under Articles 40 and 41, but Justice Hederman's multidimensional view of those articles, considering rights, duties and necessary protections for individuals, families and the state, better vindicates their holistic meaning than do the opinions of his colleagues in the majority. The sort of "rights talk" that characterizes all the opinions in *X*, but particularly those in the majority, isolates rights bearers in the exercise of those rights from persons, groups and considerations that might give rise to better solutions and ultimately more options, greater meaning and more fulfillment, and deemphasizes the social obligations of human conduct in determining liberty's limits and society's duties.

For the most sensitive to chinks in the right to life of all persons, born and unborn, there were other disquieting moments in the *X* opinions. Justice O'Flaherty raised the specter of *Rex v. Bourne* when he asked rhetorically, "[C]an it be that a Constitution which requires the State to look to the *economic* needs of *mothers* is unconcerned for the health and welfare and happiness of mothers?"[48] thereby blurring the distinction between life and the concept of health, welfare and happiness implicitly drawn in the specific reference to the right to life in the Eighth Amendment, and also suggesting, however obliquely, that the value of life might be measured primarily by its quality, a harbinger of things to come. Justice Egan developed a line of reasoning that the right to life of a rapist would yield to his victim's right to bodily integrity if someone killed the rapist in order to stop the rape, an arguably correct position, except that the intended analogy was plainly not well taken, for an unborn child is not the moral equivalent of a rapist. Use of such an analogy at all did not bode well for future challenges to the right to life.

One of the most alarming aspects of the published case report is another tangible aspect of the short shrift given to the state's duty to vindicate X's right to life "in the case of injustice done,"[49] which it certainly had been by her rapist: a lack of interest in whether X's medical needs were being met separate from her desire for an abortion. A high court judge had held that a minor's mental condition was such that she was a danger to herself, but neither that opinion nor the opinions of the supreme court justices (other than Justice Hederman) shows more than the most casual interest in the treatment she was receiving before or after leaving Ireland for the abortion, and no psychiatric testimony also meant no testimony about medications and other medical therapies that might have protected her life independent of an abortion. No significant discussion appears concerning possible future trauma from the abortion itself. Judge Costello's fact finding praised X's supportive family, implying that there were additional nonlegal aspects to resolving X's problems that the court could be confident would be pursued, but he discusses nothing more specific. In fact, vindication of X's right to life virtually required that she should receive the best psychiatric care and counseling needed to treat her underlying depression, which may have been what could vindicate her child's right to life as well.

Those who seem to have cared most about X in the abstract sense of being a young woman whose situation presented a vehicle for arousing support for even a small right to abortion fail to consider the individual person X. The cries in favor of X's right to an abortion are shrill; calmer voices wondering what actually needed to be done to address X's serious mental health issues—the very serious issues, normally of great concern to feminist activists, faced by a young woman forced into sexuality too early and against her will—do not rise above the cacophony if they existed at all beyond X's immediate family and doctors. One commentator has argued that protecting X's life without allowing her to have an abortion would have required "twenty-four hour supervision over a period of months" or "her involuntary incarceration," the sort of straw man that gets activists' blood boiling but without any basis in the evidence presented to the high court and which also fails to address whether the considerable mental-health-care resources X would undoubtedly have needed regardless of whether she had an abortion or not—including potential hospitalization with considerable supervision—could not be used more effectively to vindicate both the mother's and the child's rights to life to the greater good of both.[50] Attracta Ingram has characterized the high court's decision as meaning that "[t]he right to life of the mother is to physical survival while the right of the foetus is to all the nurture it needs to develop into a fully participating member of the community,"[51] an astonishing statement in light of Judge Costello's sincere compassion for the girl and her family; his actual opinion, which had virtually nothing to say about the quality of life the Eighth Amendment envisioned for the unborn child; by extension, Justice Hederman's opinion, which was the only one pleading for X to receive the medical treatment she so plainly needed; and Dr. Ingram's own failure in that article to mention X as a human being at all. X's suicide threats evinced alienation from society and constituted a cry from others around her to help her escape her situation, yet instead of support and therapy, society responded with a private right to decide to destroy her unborn child given the threat to her own life from alienation in the first place. The thoughts of another commentator ring true: that liberalized abortion law "is about finding that society does not make space for those who are in crisis, but instead allows them the wonderful privilege of sorting it all out by ending the new life in their wombs."[52]

Chief Justice Finlay went so far as to indicate that the regard that was due for the equal right to life of the mother as well as what was practicable for the state depended in part on current social attitudes, but the amendment had been understood to make direct abortion unlawful in all circumstances, which was almost certainly the intent of those who voted for it. Even though the supreme court had previously eschewed both a strict textual and an original understanding approach to analyzing the organic constitution, the Eighth Amendment was less than a decade old in a small country where the general will[53] could be understood if not empirically verified at almost all times, making it ripe for either of the latter analytical bases. As a result, the dichotomy between what the amendment was intended to do and what the supreme court ultimately interpreted it as doing raises the most critical problem in the *X* opinions. The collective will as expressed by a people after deliberation and a measure of public opinion at an emotional moment may often be at odds. Chief Justice Finlay's opinion relied on generalized notions of a living constitution informed by societal change and prevailing ideas of virtue,[54] words that try to accommodate the tensions between republicanism and democracy as well as core beliefs and changing opinions without explaining how. Anyway, had opinions, let alone the core beliefs of the Irish people, changed so much between 1983 and 1992? Polls indicated that Irish opinion had shifted toward limited, legalized abortion immediately after the high court issued its decision,[55] but that did not presage a permanent change in the core beliefs of the people or even the sort of public policy shift to which courts might give weight if actually proved. One of the supreme court's roles when faced with hard cases that temporarily and properly challenge the beliefs of a compassionate people but do not clearly reflect permanent changes in the people's collective will must be to exercise restraint and allow democratic institutions and processes, such as the constitutional amendment processes, to do their jobs. As high as the price X might pay, the price to be paid by many others in the future might be even higher. Otherwise, the rule of law may be lost to the vagaries of majority passion or, worse, to a court's mere perception of the vagaries of majority passion.

Justice Walsh himself had opened the door to the majority's reasoning in *McGee* when he wrote:

> According to the preamble, the people gave themselves the Constitution to promote the common good with due observance of prudence, justice and charity so that the dignity and freedom of the indivdual might be assured. The judges must, therefore, as best they can from their training and their experience interpret these rights in accordance with their ideas of prudence, justice and charity. It is but natural that

> from time to time the prevailing ideas of these virtues may be conditioned by the passage of time; no interpretation of the Constitution is intended to be final for all time. It is given in light of prevailing ideas and concepts.[56]

Yet, it seems unlikely that Justice Walsh, who had several times written of the supremacy of the unborn's right to life, thought natural law could be so malleable as it appeared in the *X* majority opinions.

> The idea that fundamental principles of natural law relating to human rights are to be determined by a sense of what the majority of the community at any particular time may favour is one that could very easily slip into a caricature of human rights by opinion poll.... What Walsh, J. would seem to have been rejecting was a sterile ultra-formalistic theory of original intent as a basis of constitutional interpretation. There is no reason to interpret his remarks as warranting the surrender of the judicial obligation to give effect to the authentic natural law principles that underlie the fundamental rights provisions of the Constitution.[57]

All of a sudden, however, the majority's views did not seem set in stone. From the point of view of legal predictability, events were spinning out of control. The European Court of Human Rights was hearing an appeal of the *Open Door* case.[58] The Irish government had failed to negotiate an amendment to a Maastricht Treaty protocol passed especially for the problem of Irish abortion law in order to make the protocol consistent with the *X* ruling.[59] But the government did deliver on a promised abortion referendum, giving the people of Ireland the opportunity to weigh in directly on travel, information and abortion in the face of risks to the mother's life on November 25, 1992.

They would do so in a highly charged political atmosphere On June 18, 1992, the Irish had voted on the Maastricht Treaty, which included the following Protocol 17: "Nothing in the Treaty on the European Union or in the Treaties establishing the European Communities or in the Treaties or Acts modifying or supplementing those Treaties shall affect the application in Ireland of Article 40.3.3 of the Constitution of Ireland."[60] In light of the subsequent supreme court's *X* ruling, Protocol 17 would make the already controversial treaty even more so. Did the protocol deny the right to travel to pregnant Irish women, a right that European Community law would almost certainly protect otherwise? The government did ultimately convince the Treaty's drafters to include a nonbinding "solemn declaration" at the end of Protocol 17 stating their intention "not [to] limit freedom either to travel between Member States or, in accordance with conditions which may be laid down, in conformity with Community law, by Irish legislation, to obtain or make available in Ireland, information relating to services lawfully available in Member States,"[61] but the legal force of Protocol 17 remained enigmatic. Thus, the vote on Maastricht became a preliminary de facto vote on abortion rights (though no one could be sure what a "yes" or "no" vote even meant) untidily attached to the promise of $10 billion in estimated benefits to Ireland from the treaty. It passed with almost 70 percent support despite concern that Protocol 17 would limit travel to Britain. To make matters more heated, Taoiseach Albert Reynolds's socially conservative Fianna Fáil government was headed to its downfall amid charges that the industry minister had been untruthful to a beef export industry investigation.

And no one seemed to like the wording of the referendum. The sum total of the three proposed amendments would have permitted X, for example, to receive information about abortion services in England and to go to England for the abortion, but not to have the procedure done on Irish soil. The text of the first proposed amendment stated, "There shall be no limit on freedom to travel to another country," and it would be placed within Article 40.3.3 so that it clearly modified the Eighth Amendment. The second read thus: "There shall be no limit on the freedom to obtain or make available, subject to conditions laid down by law, information on services lawfully available in another member State [of the European Community]." The most controversial would have provided the following:

> [I]t shall be unlawful to terminate the life of the unborn unless such termination is necessary to save the life, as distinct from the health of the mother where there is an illness or disorder of the mother giving rise to a real and substantial risk to her life, not being a risk of self destruction.[62]

Therefore, the proposed language on the "substantive issue" would eliminate credible threats of the mother's suicide as a justification for abortion and make it very clear that "life" meant "life" and not health, welfare or happiness.

The amount of discretionary power the "substantive" amendment implicitly ceded to doctors disconcerted many on both sides of the issue. Since Irish medical ethics considers abortion an abhorrence, abortion rights activists saw a greater short-term problem, but no one could be sure what would happen in the long run. In Britain, doctors' independent judgment as to whether an abortion meets the standards of the Abortion Act routinely conforms to the wishes of the mother. As one commentator writes:

> The amendment would no doubt have put the medical profession in the unenviable position of deciding what was and what was not an "illness or disorder" creating a substantial risk to the life of the mother. The breadth of the terms are vague, and the amendment seemed to place the decision-making process firmly in the hands of the doctors, without giving them clear legal guidelines. One could easily envisage a *Bourne*-type defence arising in situations in which the performing of an abortion might fall foul of section 58 of the Offences Against the Person Act, 1861.[63]

Doctors' role in the abortion decision process was only one of the many objections mooted by the amendment, even by its supporters. Prochoice groups condemned it as simply too restrictive, while prolife groups considered the entire package too liberal. The referendum campaign matched strange bedfellows as the most ardent prochoice and prolife adherents worked together to defeat the "substantive" amendment. Nevertheless, Reynolds's beleaguered government urged a "yes" vote on all three. The Catholic hierarchy issued a statement of milquetoast support on the theory that, while doctrinally objectionable, the amendments would serve to save lives of unborn children by preventing even more liberal laws later.

Not to be outdone, the European Court of Human Rights weighed into the discussion a month before the vote in response to Open Door Counselling's and the Dublin Well Woman Centre's appeal of the 1988 injunction against referring women to abortion providers in Britain.[64] The court concluded that the permanent injunction against the centers' counseling or assisting pregnant women from obtaining further advice on abortion or an abortion abroad (which impaired the counselors' right to free expression under Article 10 of the treaty) was proscribed by the Eighth Amendment of the Irish Constitution and that this prohibition was intended to protect morals, but that the prohibition was not necessary for that purpose and therefore was not permitted by the convention. In coming to the latter conclusion, the court was persuaded by what it characterized as Irish society's tacit acceptance of abortion under some circumstances. The court also held that neither the convention's protections for the right to life nor Articles 17 and 60 of the convention, which protect against the derogation of other rights protected under the convention or by the high contracting parties either in their own law or the law of agreements to which they are parties, justified the injunction.

The pivotal section of the court's analysis was its refusal to acknowledge Ireland's statement of the aim of the injunction. Article 10(2) of the convention limits the exercise of the right to freedom of expression as follows:

> The exercise of these freedoms, since it carries with it duties and responsibilities, may be subject to such formalities, conditions, restrictions or penalties as are prescribed by law and are necessary in a democratic society, in the interests of national security, territorial integrity or public safety, *for the protection of health or morals*, for the protection of the reputation or *rights of others*, for preventing the disclosure of information received in confidence or for maintaining the authority and impartiality of the judiciary. [emphasis added]

Ireland claimed that the injunction protected an important "right[] of others," the right to life of the unborn, but the court reasoned that since the right to life of the unborn stemmed from the Irish people's deeply felt moral values, a decision as to whether the unborn were "others" was unnecessary because the aim of the injunction could so easily be recharacterized as a protection of morals. Morals matter, but the right to life matters more, as Ireland argued to the court and several dissenters noted. The court's inexplicable choice to ignore Ireland's statement of the purpose of the injunction was the equivalent of *Roe* v. *Wade*'s concession that an unborn child could not conclusively be determined to be a person entitled to the protections of the United States Constitution. Because protection of morals is likely to be treated as of lesser importance than protection of the right to life, the inquiry as to the proportionality of the means to protect morals would be much stricter, while if life were at stake a less perfect fit between means and ends would be justified.[65] Even worse, as Judge Blayney, a former Irish Supreme Court Justice explained in his dissent, the right to life of the unborn was clearly guaranteed by the Irish Constitution, and therefore, pursuant to Article 60 of the convention, the convention should not have been construed as limiting or derogating from that right. Like *Roe*, the even more inexplicable decision to ignore the right to life of the unborn in *Open Door* drove the court's decision.

Not surprisingly, the court insisted that the "wide margin of appreciation" the convention extended to national bodies when protection of morals related to the nature of human life was concerned was not unlimited and that while national bodies could take action they considered necessary to respect the rule of law or protect constitutional rights, the means had to be consistent with the convention. Whether the means were consistent with the convention depended on "whether the restriction complained of was 'proportionate to the legitimate aim pursued.'"[66] But the importance of the aim must be a determining factor in whether the restriction was disproportionate to the aim, and the importance of the aim was a matter in which national authorities were entitled to a wide margin of appreciation where morals were concerned. Besides, the court had changed the aim from the right to life of the unborn to morals anyway. All too quickly, the reasoning was back to the conclusion that whether the means to the national aim were consistent with the convention depended on the size of the margin of appreciation. At least in theory, the court's reasoning sounded depressingly circular.

Characterization of the injunction as a protection of morals not only drove the ultimate decision, but was also a discomforting statement of the court's view of its own power. The court, and not a national governing institution, had exercised the ultimate power to recognize and rank individual rights in *Open Door* by ignoring the right to life of the unborn as a legitimate aim of Irish law when it was so clearly protected in the Irish Constitution and so was arguably within the margin of appreciation due the Irish. Several of the court's dissenters thought the margin of appreciation was sufficiently broad to protect the injunction under the convention, but they did not engage the reasoning of the commission dissenters, which was that deference to Irish authorities on what constituted an important public aim was justified pursuant to a variant of the principle of subsidiarity. The question of "who should decide" what rights or interests will be protected got swept under the carpet.

The court was persuaded that the injunction was disproportionate to the aim of protecting morals because of the *X* decision legalizing abortions in Ireland in situations where the injunction would bar the claimants' counseling and because the same information was seeping into Ireland from different sources. The court also complained that "the injunction appears to have been largely ineffective in protecting the right to life of the unborn since it did not prevent large numbers of Irish women from continuing to obtain abortions in Great Britain."[67] Several dissenters turned the majority's views upside down, arguing that

> That fact that Ireland cannot *effectively* prevent the circulation of reviews or of English telephone directories containing information on clinics in the United Kingdom, so that anyone can obtain information on abortion clinics in that country and the possibility of having an abortion in such clinics, can only, in our view, confirm the *necessity* of a specific measure such as that taken by the Irish courts. Such reviews, the directories and the persons possessing information on abortion clinics in the United Kingdom are 'passive' factors, which require a personal and spontaneous attitude on the part of the person seeking advice. The activity of agencies which organise trips and provide special services for their clients, thereby influencing the decisions of those clients, is something entirely different.
>
> The *partial* ineffectiveness of a law or a principle of case law is not a reason for deciding not to take specific measures designed to prevent

> the activities of organisations committed to seeking means of obtaining results which do not conform to the interests and values of the legal system.[68]

Another dissenter followed up in similar terms:

> I consider there to be a considerable difference between advertisements in the press, the circulation of which in a free country it is virtually impossible to prohibit, and the setting up of specific advice and information services (together with the organisation of trips to and stays in appropriate clinics in the United Kingdom which carry out abortions), so that the contested interference cannot be regarded as ineffective. Indeed it constitutes an entirely appropriate means—although evidently not 100 per cent effective—to attain the (legitimate) aim pursued; in any event, without such a measure there was a risk that the aim in question would not be attained.[69]

Could the relatively low abortion rate for Irish women compared to that for women in other European countries stem from the injunction? Was the injunction effective in protecting the lives of the unborn at the margin? Was the injunction all the government could reasonably do to vindicate the right to life of the unborn, and was it necessary for what it achieves? Byrne and Binchy predict that more intrusive means of meeting the aim of protecting the right to life of the unborn, such as "[a] policy of wide-ranging day-to-day controls on the first state's borders would undoubtedly be stigmatised as oppressive and would certainly not meet with the approval of the Court of Human Rights."[70] The dissenters had a point.

Having also heard from the European Court of Justice in the *Grogan* case, the high court heard SPUC's request that it make permanent the injunction against publishing addresses of abortion clinics in the student guide.[71] The ink was barely dry on *Attorney General* v. *X*, but Judge Morris's opinion made clear that *X* did not change the law as to the provision of abortion information as long as the information was being given to women who were not facing a real and substantial risk to their lives as a result of a pregnancy.[72] Judge Morris entered the permanent injunction.

When the Irish finally voted on their three referenda, the right to travel and information amendments passed easily, but the final amendment, which delineated when abortions would be legal in Ireland, was defeated 34.6 percent to 65.4 percent. Paul Ward, an Irish barrister and University College Dublin lecturer, warns that "it would be unwise to read too much into the figures and from what quarter the votes were cast"[73] and that strategic voting probably masks the implications of the vote. More than one study suggests, however, that most voters were divided into three groups of roughly equal size and another small group: liberals who thought the substantive amendment wording was too restrictive; conservatives who thought it too liberal and therefore worth voting against; centrists who found it acceptable; and a very small group of conservatives who thought the wording too liberal, but preferable to the supreme court's ruling.[74] That analysis indicates continuing strong support for the right to life of the unborn because the total supporting the proposed language and those rejecting it because it was too liberal were still a clear majority. If anything, the Irish people remained more conservative than their law.

Despite these informed speculations, the odd coalition working for the substantive amendment's defeat provides little indication of precisely what alternate amendment might have cobbled together a majority. Had there been many votes to be won on the back of a much more liberal proposal, likely one of the political parties would have taken advantage of the opportunity, but Irish politicians shied away from the issue. The 2002 referendum, held only after immense political and factual research, with its complex balancing of interests such that it cannot be clearly characterized as more liberal or more conservative, failed to garner a majority. On the other hand, the outcry over the *X* case, the huge majority favoring the Maastricht Treaty, and the passage of the travel and information amendments do not lend themselves to the interpretation that a radically more restrictive third amendment would have found substantial favor with voters. Perhaps the Irish were simply willing to accept the law as outlined by the supreme court for lack of a better solution; particularly where the proposed alternative asked more questions than it answered, they would have none of it.

Seven

The Lone Irish Rights Bearer of the 1990s[1]

"In Ireland, when you marry someone, you marry them for life."[2]

The year 1995 marked a turning point in Irish family law. First, the Oireachtas passed and the supreme court gave its imprimatur to the Regulation of Information (Services outside the State for Termination of Pregnancies) Act, the legislative response to the Fourteenth Amendment. A few months later, the supreme court held that courts could consent on behalf of a ward of the state to have artificial feeding and hydration tubes withdrawn and those processes terminated, so that the ward would die. At the end of 1995, the Irish finally approved a constitutional amendment by a slim margin to permit certain divorces. These three legal events, along with another disturbing *X*-like abortion case two years later, further defined and changed the contours of the nature of the family, the relationship and legal standing of its constituent members, and its relationship to the state. Women increasingly took on the character of "lone rights bearers,"[3] making sometimes life-and-death decisions "isolated in [their] privacy,"[4] with few limits in sight.

Regulation of Information Bill

The Regulation of Information Act outlawed most public advertising and dissemination of information concerning abortion services available abroad except for truthful and unbiased nondirective information and counseling about services that were legal in the place where they were offered. The act restated much of what was understood to be the constitutional law related to abortion information: that counselors were not allowed to make travel arrangements or appointments at abortion clinics in other countries for pregnant Irish women and that advocating abortion to a pregnant woman was illegal. It also sought to limit financial incentives or profit motives for providing abortion information. In no way did the act purport to liberalize the law by making lawful acts directly affecting the life of the unborn that were not lawful prior to passage of the Fourteenth Amendment related to abortion information.

Before signing the bill, President Mary Robinson invoked special constitutional procedures to obtain a supreme court ruling on its constitutionality before it came into effect. These Article 26 "reference" procedures were among the most creative innovations in the de Valera constitution, having no roots in prior Irish law and being unknown to the American, which eschews such advisory opinions from judges in the absence of the necessary concrete factual development of the conflict. One of the very few, substantive presidential powers in Irish politics, reference procedures are rarely invoked but can be profound because they insulate the referred legislation from future constitutional attack. In evaluating the information bill, the supreme court justices were required to presume it was constitutional and issue only one written opinion. They could take no factual evidence. The court appointed two groups of counsel to argue against the bill, one to make arguments based on the right to life of the unborn and the other to argue the mother's right to life.

The bottom line for the court was whether a woman could lawfully obtain information about abortion services abroad even if there was no "real and substantial" risk to her life from a pregnancy. Prior to the enactment of the Fourteenth Amendment, supreme court precedent had indicated a woman had the right to travel and receive abortion information only if she would otherwise have been entitled to an abortion on Irish soil because of a real and substantial risk to her life from the pregnancy. The purpose of the Fourteenth Amendment was to "remove the inhibition placed on the granting of information with regard to these services relating to the termination of pregnancies"[5] even if the contemplated abortion would be illegal in Ireland. By using the reference procedure, President Robinson was forcing the court to confirm the legality of both the information bill specifically and the Fourteenth Amendment itself.

To do so, the court first had to wrestle with foundational questions about constitutional interpretation: whether natural law, which the attorneys for unborn children argued conflicted with the Fourteenth Amendment, could override the will of the people as expressed in the Fourteenth Amendment. Since the Fourteenth Amendment was a product of democratic action and the natural law represented a substantive notion of the good, the natural law versus Fourteenth Amendment battle drove to the heart of the constitution's compromise between liberal and Christian democracy, the democratic rule of all versus the republican "general will." What authority gave mothers and unborn children whatever rights they had?

The court drew a fine line on this foundational issue. On the surface, the court plumped for the liberal democratic rule of all: Natural law could not override the will of the people as expressed in the constitution, and therefore, the Fourteenth Amendment was not unconstitutional even though it arguably conflicted with natural law. On the other hand, reports of the death of natural law after the decision were exaggerated. In a revisionist version of constitutional history, the court insisted that past precedent had not relied on natural law to identify the unenumerated rights the constitution protected but instead had looked only to which rights "could be reasonably implied from and w[ere] guaranteed by the provisions of the Constitution"[6]—such as the preamble's reference to prudence, justice and charity—in determining which rights were implied in the constitution. The justices ignored the inevitable rejoinder that "prudence, justice and charity" had been frequent rhetorical entrees for natural law thinking in Irish constitutional jurisprudence, such as Justice Walsh's natural law tome in *McGee*.[7] The court concluded that natural law's role was simply to determine whether the information bill was a "fair and reasonable balancing" of the conflicting rights at stake and "is not so contrary to reason and fairness as to constitute an unjust attack" on any party's constitutional rights.[8] Therefore, the court consigned natural law's role as an interpretive tool to the interstices of constitutional law: fleshing out textually recognized rights and otherwise recognizing new ones consistent with the text. It was a victory for the primacy of liberal democratic decision making.

The court rejected all of the arguments against the bill made by counsel for mothers. The court first held that the bill's various limitations on the type of information given—that the information not advocate or promote abortions and that no giver of information may make appointments at abortion clinics or make travel arrangements for that purpose—were "fair and reasonable" legislative efforts to respect and vindicate the right to life of the unborn while also having regard for the equal right to life of the mother.[9] The court was unconvinced that the bill would stifle physicians from speaking either to abortion providers about their patients once appointments for abortions had been made or to their patients about their health and the various options available to them in circumstances that would seriously impair health care. Nor did the court agree that the act's ban on information providers' accepting any form of remuneration or voluntary donations from either abortion providers or women receiving information was so overly broad that it would create a chilling effect on the provision of such information.

Counsel advocating the rights of unborn children were no more successful in undermining the constitutionality of the act. Their primary arguments had focused on the use of natural law in constitutional law, but they also raised concerns about the protection of parental and spousal rights. First, they argued that by defining a "woman" to whom act information might be given as "a female person," the bill permitted minors to obtain abortion information without anyone's informing their parents, which would violate their parents' rights. Second, they claimed that providing abortion information to a woman without the knowledge and consent of her husband would violate his rights if he were the father of the unborn child. The court held that the mere fact that the bill did not require notification to parents of minors or to husbands of wives did not make it unconstitutional because the court presumed that the provision of such information would be done in accordance with principles of constitutional justice, which required that the giver of abortion information have regard for the rights of third parties likely to be affected. Therefore, the decision left open the possibility that parents or husbands might have rights entitling them to notification or other involvement if a child or wife obtained act information.

A Ward of Court

Only a few months after the information bill case, the supreme court faced more immediate life issues in a case referred to as "A Ward of Court."[10] In the mid–1970s, a young woman had undergone a minor gynecological operation under a general anesthetic and was left with serious brain damage. Two decades later, after no significant improvement in her condition, the ward's family petitioned the court to permit them to terminate feeding by tube and to cease any minor medical treatment the ward had or would receive.

The facts painted a tragic picture. According to High Court Judge Lynch:

> Since that catastrophe the ward has been completely dependent on others, requiring total nursing care. She is spastic as a result of the brain damage. Both arms and hands are contracted. Both legs and feet are extended. Her jaws are clenched and because she had a tendency to bite the insides of her cheeks and her tongue, her back teeth have been capped to prevent the front teeth from fully closing. She cannot swallow. She cannot speak. She is incontinent.

> ...For some twenty years she was fed through a nasogastric tube. Generally, but especially in the later years, she seemed to find this distressing and it was replaced by a gastrostomy tube in April, 1992, which required the administration of a general anaesthetic. Since then she has been fed through the gastrostomy tube with much greater ease and success. This tube became detached in December, 1993, and a new tube was inserted which came out the next day and had to be reinserted the following day under general anaesthetic.
>
> The ward is, of course, bedridden. She is in a condition which is nearly, but not quite, what in modern times has become known as persistent or permanent vegetative state (P.V.S.).[11]

That the ward was not actually in a permanent vegetative state was the fact onto which those opposed to the family's petition latched, but there was virtually no chance her condition would ever improve. She had minimal capacity to recognize familiar faces, such as her family and the health-care professionals at the hospital where she lived. She showed distress when strangers entered her room and reacted to other stimuli. The trial judge found that if the ward continued to be fed by tube and was treated for whatever minor ailments she might catch, she could live for many years. All agreed that if the petition to terminate feeding and medical care were granted, the ward would die.

The caregivers and the institution where the ward was living, along with the attorney general, and the *guardian ad litem* (someone who is appointed by the court to represent the ward's interests), opposed the family's petition in varying degrees, and the trial judge split the difference between them. He held that the court, not the family, should decide whether feeding by tube and other minor medical treatment would cease under the court's *parens patriae* jurisdiction. The family appealed, arguing that as the "natural primary and fundamental unit group of Society" according to Article 41, the family and not the court should make the decision, but the supreme court held that since the family had invoked the high court's jurisdiction when it petitioned the court to make the woman a ward of the court two decades previously, the judiciary had become responsible for her. The trial judge also decided that the woman's best interests demanded that feeding by tube and all other than palliative medical care should cease, and though the supreme court agreed, the five justices produced five opinions with different reasoning, mirroring in miniature the fissures developing in Irish national philosophy on the continuum of sacred to secular values.[12]

The attorney general, guardian ad litem and the institution where the ward resided all argued that the high court's order should be overturned based on the right to life. Article 40.3 of the Irish Constitution requires that the state vindicate the right to life of born persons "as far as practicable," and they argued that withdrawing nutrition, hydration and medical care from a person who had cognitive ability and was only chronically but not terminally ill violated the ward's right to life. They added that the high court's decision, which had been partly based on an assessment of the ward's "quality of life," was impermissible under Article 40.3 and Article 40.1, which state that "[a]ll citizens shall, as human persons, be held equal before the law."[13]

Of all the justices in the majority, Justice Hamilton's decision was the narrowest and most informed by a religious understanding of the sanctity of human life.[14] He reasoned that the right to life in Ireland takes precedence over all rights that cannot be harmonized with it, and other "natural" rights may be implied from it. The right to have nature take its course, to die a natural death, and not to have life artificially maintained if the person involved so chooses are such rights. Since feeding with a tube interferes with the integrity of the ward's body, the right to bodily integrity, recognized in 1965 in *Ryan* v. *Attorney General*,[15] would also justify the ward in having the tube withdrawn, even if so doing would cause her death. The right to die a natural death, made by a competent adult, also arose from the qualified right to individual privacy. Therefore, the ward would have the right to choose not to have her life artificially maintained if she were competent to make that choice.

The problem with this reasoning was simple. The ward was not able to "have the tube withdrawn," nor was she a "competent adult" able to exercise any rights. Yet as the court concluded, to ignore her rights due to her incompetence would further deny her right to be held equal with other citizens under the law. Her rights to die naturally, to bodily integrity and to privacy did not simply disappear because she was incompetent, and the responsibility to vindicate them fell to the high court. After all, someone had to consent to or reject the continuation of feeding and treatment if the ward's rights were to be protected.

Therefore, in an effort to protect the ward's right to personal autonomy, the court took that personal autonomy from her. As one commentator argued, "it is *self-contradictory* to assert that a proxy *not chosen* by the patient herself can exercise her rights of autonomy.... Furthermore, if autonomy lies in the free exercise of will and choice, it is at the very least *paradoxical* to say that our autonomy would licence an act that put autonomy permanently out of business."[16] The court's decision to withdraw nourishment or treatment "cannot be justified as an exercise of the patient's right to die but must be recognised as an exercise of the surrogate decision maker's right to end the life of the patient."[17]

A majority of the supreme court justices held that taking into account all the constitutional rights involved, including those of the ward, the family and the state, the proper test to apply when exercising the court's jurisdiction in such a case was to determine from the standpoint of a "prudent, good and loving parent"[18] whether it was in the ward's best interests to have her life prolonged by medical treatment with clear and convincing proof of all relevant factual matters, a higher standard than usually required in most civil litigation, but not as high as the "beyond a reasonable doubt" standard applied to criminal fact finding. Because the high court judge had found that termination of nourishment would be in the ward's best interest under the test, the supreme court upheld the order. "The true cause of the ward's death will not be the withdrawal of such nourishment but the injuries which she sustained on the 26th day of April 1972" during her operation, wrote Chief Justice Hamilton.[19]

Irish commentators met the court's decision with strong skepticism when applied to the more philosophically adventurous opinions of the justices. For example, both the chief justice and Justice O'Flaherty tried to distinguish the ward's situation from a case about euthanasia, which was still anathema, because euthanasia is termination of life by a positive act, while withholding food, water and medical care are not positive acts. The distinction breaks down almost immediately, however. Eating, for example, is a positive act, but people who refuse to do so if they have cognition are not letting "nature take its course"[20]; they are killing themselves.[21] Gerry Whyte challenged the court's reasoning by comparing the example of an otherwise mentally competent quadriplegic who is unable to feed herself. Such a person would be similarly situated to the ward, except that she has normal cognitive capacity while the ward's is extremely limited. "Yet to permit the quadriplegic to refuse all nourishment seems to fly in the face of the Chief Justice's earlier statement that '[n]o person has the right to terminate or to have terminated his or her life or to accelerate or have accelerated his or her death.'"[22] As another commentator argued, "[w]hether withdrawal of feeding by a carer is treated as an act or omission does not affect the basic *actus reus* of homicide — to cause death."[23] Neither Chief Justice Hamilton nor Justice O'Flaherty explained why not.

In fact, "A Ward of Court" sounded *a lot* like a euthanasia case. Counsel for the institution made much of the fact that the ward did have cognitive capacity and was not fully PVS, and the court almost grudgingly agreed this was true. Several justices relied on a conclusion that provision of nutrition and hydration was "medical treatment," which Irish doctors disputed, calling food and water basic necessities of life though they were to be given in an artificial way,[24] and American "right to die" jurisprudence does agree with the Irish court on this principle. Further, the court characterized the ward as "terminally ill," even though the ward's medical condition was not progressive and would not ultimately result in death. By contrast, Catholic moral teaching permits removing extraordinary, life-saving treatment from a ward who is terminally ill, but not from a merely chronically ill ward.[25] As Pope John Paul II states in *The Gospel of Life*:

> [W]hen death is clearly imminent and inevitable, one can in conscience 'refuse forms of treatment that would only secure a precarious and burdensome prolongation of life, so long as the normal care due to the sick person in similar cases is not interrupted'.
>
> ...It needs to be determined whether the means of treatment available are objectively proportionate to the prospects for improvement.[26]

Despite the justices' characterizations of the facts, the wardship case did not justify withdrawing medical treatment from a terminally ill patient, but instead, it justified withdrawing nutrition and hydration — thirsting and starving to death — a chronically ill person with cognition who might otherwise live for many years and just might recover more cognition.

Can it be in a person's best interests to starve or thirst to death? Even if dying can be said to be in a person's best interests, those are particularly gruesome ways to die. And if so, what is the principled way to determine where wards' "best interests" end and pure involuntary euthanasia begins?[27] The institution had argued that the high court had been improperly influenced by the fact that the ward's quality of life seemed so low: "[L]ife is a light, [and] her life may not have the same luminosity as other people's but ... we are not entitled to say just because it is not so luminous that her light is not sufficient."[28] Legal scholar and medical ethicist Dermot Feenan believes the court relied too heavily on the ward's mother's testimony that her daughter just stared and that there was nothing in this "'unless it be please let me go'" and that it was too quick to accept the description "near-persistent vegetative state" for the ward's condition instead of insisting on a neurologically accepted diagnosis.[29] While Chief Justice Hamilton tried to limit the right to refuse life-sustaining treatment to cases of terminal illness, despite the fact that the ward was not terminally ill, Justice Blayney did not make the distinction clear and Justices O'Flaherty and Denham did not consider the distinction relevant at all.[30] Justice Blayney stated that the trial judge had protected the ward's right to life by "addressing very fully the question of whether or not it was *of any benefit* to the ward to prolong her life given the burdens on the ward involved in doing so."[31] Justice O'Flaherty was even more blunt: "The ward may be alive but she has no life at all," adding later that the ward's life lacked "purpose, meaning or dignity."[32]

To wonder whether someone's life has quality or is of benefit to that person is to wonder why one lives in the first place. In the wake of the decision, one Irish commentator argued that the primary reason to live is "to love and be loved."[33] Put in a different way about persons with Down's Syndrome, "[t]he children who suffered from this handicap would never be among the elite of the world, but they could lead lives harmless to others and even pleasing to themselves and to those who came to love them."[34] The ward was not in the happy situation of being able to love or to live a life particularly pleasing to herself, but all the evidence suggested she received great quantities of love from others and not just from her family. "[I]n and through her helplessness, she draws forth responsive love and care from those in whose charge she is. In that way, she is, unknown to herself, a great educator."[35]

The best interests test is not concerned with whether the ward is a great educator. What the ward gives to others, even if it provides her with benefits, does not count at all; it is only what she gains directly and with awareness that must be taken into account, and she cannot directly gain the benefits of giving to others or of receiving love when she lacks awareness. American courts apply a "substituted judgment test" in which the court determines and then effectuates what the ward would have wanted; under such a test, a ward may be generous and exercise moral judgment or appreciate the limited life she has regardless of an objective or professional determination of her "best interests."[36] Nevertheless, in the absence of judicial recognition that a near-PVS patient can give something of value to others, who perhaps return something of value to the patient, no other result would be possible.

Though the wardship case implicates the right to life at its end, many of the justices' comments could eventually bear on life's protection at its beginning. In a speech at Fordham University School of Law, Chief Justice Hamilton explained that the "central issue" facing the Irish Supreme Court in *In re Ward of Court* was "[i]n speaking of the 'right to life,' what do we mean? What constitutes 'life' in this context?"[37] Would the quality of life issues Justices Blayney and O'Flaherty raised have any relevance, for example, to the protection of either an unborn child's or a mother's right to life when they clashed? What did "life" mean in the abortion context? *Roe* v. *Wade*, for example, justified a right to an abortion so that women could avoid "a distressful life and future."[38] By contrast, the Irish Supreme Court was clear in *X* that only a threat to the "life, as distinct from the health of the mother,"[39] should justify an abortion, but all of a sudden, increased reference to notions of quality of life and "purpose, meaning or dignity" when discussing the right to life (and death) raised an uncertain specter of just what the Eighth Amendment might be held to protect in the future.

Only Justice Egan dissented. If no party had argued that "a degree of cognitive function, however minimal, ought to preclude the Court from consenting to withdrawal of the tube," Justice Egan would have joined his colleagues in holding that the court could consent to its removal as long as the intrusive feeding method was painful and burdensome. He insisted, however, that no such finding was permissible on the evidence.[40] He also rejected the notion that the ward was "terminally ill."[41] The issue therefore became stark:

> The inevitable result of removal would be to kill a human being. In view of the Constitutional guarantees it would require (and I deem the right to life to be the highest in the hierarchy of rights) a strong and cogent reason to justify the taking of a life.[42]

From that point, Justice Egan committed himself to the line in the sand his colleagues had avoided. "[T]his is not a case of no cognitive function," he wrote.

> Such function is present, however minimal and however close to P.V.S. If slightly more cognitive function existed, would a right to withdraw sustenance still be claimed to be permissible? Where would the line be drawn? Cognition in a human being is something which is either present or absent and should, in my opinion, be so recognised and treated. Any effort to measure its value would be dangerous.[43]

Justice Egan expressed considerable sympathy for the ward's family but would not have allowed them or anyone else to withdraw treatment.

But that is exactly what the court did. The institution, a Catholic one, as are most medical facilities in Ireland, had argued that removal of the feeding tube would require it to violate its ethical obligations to the ward, but no one wanted a showdown over whether the courts could order a religious institution to violate such beliefs. The high court's order simply permitted removal of the tube but did not require anyone in particular to do so, and the institution's personnel refused to remove the tube. As it had done after the *X* case, the Irish Medical Council criticized the decision, and both the council and the An Bord Altranis (the Irish nursing board) indicated that it was not ethical for a doctor or nurse to withdraw artificial hydration and nutrition from a patient who was not dying.[44] "Things can be legal and not ethical," the chairman of the medical council's ethics committee explained.[45] Some wondered if incompetent PVS patients seeking death would have to go to England to exercise the right to withdraw nutrition and hydration in light of the doctors' and nurses' positions.[46] The ward, at least, did not; her family arranged for her to die at a hospice.

It is a cliché to say that hard cases make bad law. The wardship case was hard, the ward's situation pathetic and her family's pain deserving of sympathy, and the law, or at least the indicators of future law that the court left behind, were diverse and analytically unsatisfactory. Justice Denham's opinion, for example, reviewed a wide range of abstract matters, such as "Spiritual Aspect," "Bodily Integrity," "Sanctity of Life," "Common Good," "Dignity," "the Family," "Causation," and various rights including the right to life, the right of privacy, and the right of "choice" before latching on to the "best interests test" and a list of twenty factors to consider in evaluating a ward's best interests. The case raised more questions than it answered. Is there a religious understanding of the sanctity of life remaining in Irish law? Will involuntary euthanasia find, either through jurisprudence or shading of fact, legal protection in Ireland? What is the basis for protecting life at all in Ireland? Who should make those decisions? And what did it mean for the right to life of the unborn or mothers? No matter what answers one prefers to those questions, the wardship case provides little comfort.

The Right to Remarry versus the Right to a Lifelong Marriage

Less than ten years after legalized divorce had received a drubbing in the last referendum battle on the subject, another coalition government decided to try again. Marriage breakdown in Ireland was still extremely low compared to the numbers in other European countries, but it had increased significantly in the prior decade, and much had changed on the legal front. Careful legislative tilling in the law related to recognition of foreign divorces[47] and judicial separation[48] and even an effort to protect wives' interests in marital homes that was ultimately found unconstitutional[49] had prepared the country for what legitimization of modern marital breakdown might mean. The Judicial Separation Act of 1989, in particular, is essentially a comprehensive, fault-based divorce regime, except that it does not grant courts the authority to enter a decree ending the marriage. Otherwise, the act provides for judicial separation based either on fault or an extended period of separation and the entry of orders related to protection, child custody and visitation, temporary and permanent property settlements, temporary and permanent maintenance and child support, and adjustments to the parties' succession rights. The act was unsuccessfully challenged in an unreported decision as violating the rights of the family under Article 41, but the Irish Supreme Court held that the constitution permitted the Oireachtas to provide for legal separation where marriages had deteriorated sufficiently that the common good called for separation.[50]

The government had learned tough lessons from the 1986 experience and did not make the same mistakes twice. It carefully prepared responses to inevitable concerns related to succession, the marital home, pension division and other property rights it had missed in 1986. Then it packaged its proposals into a referendum and legislative campaign for what it called "the right to remarry"[51] and proceeded to spend $500,000 in public funds in support of its position, an expenditure the Irish Supreme Court later found to be unconstitutional.[52]

As a result, the antidivorce forces faced a much tougher opponent with less substantive ammunition than they had enjoyed in 1986. The proposed wording of the 1995 constitutional amendment would permit divorce only after four years of separation:

> A court designated by law may grant a dissolution of marriage where, but only where, it is satisfied that
> i. at the date of the institution of the proceedings, the spouses have lived apart from one another for a period of, or periods amounting to, at least four years during the previous five years,
> ii. There is no reasonable prospect of a reconciliation between the spouses,
> iii. Such provision as the court considers proper having regard to the circumstances exists or will be made for the spouses, any children of either or both of them and any other person prescribed by law, and
> iv. any further conditions prescribed by law are complied with.[53]

Further, the government published the specifics of the divorce legislation it planned to introduce after the referendum was adopted, which turned out to be very similar to the Judicial Separation Act regime with which the Irish were already familiar.[54] These government efforts narrowed the range of arguments available to antidivorce forces, even though all the government's legislative proposals gave courts wide latitude in crafting temporary and permanent orders, sometimes with disconcerting results. One judicial separation case, for example, held that a woman was not entitled to a judicial separation on the grounds that she had been physically abused by her husband "on a few occasions" but did hold that a separation was appropriate because the parties were no longer participating in sexual intercourse together.[55]

The antidivorce position started out twenty points behind in the polls. A series of dismal sex scandals had weakened the church, with fresh allegations coming out a week before election day. The leader of usually socially conservative Fianna Fáil, where the 1986 Anti-Divorce Campaign had found much of its organizational muscle and whose backbenchers were displeased with its leaders' decision to support the referendum, had left his wife and was himself living with another woman.

But the antidivorce campaign was by no means out of intellectual muscle; it countered the proposed amendment with a concept William Binchy dubbed "the right to a permanent marriage."[56] In one formulation, those opposing the amendment characterized marriage as a special form of contract in which the length of performance — the "lifelong" quality of marriage — was of the essence and could not be breached. This concept was not unique to the divorce debate; it appears in *Gaudium et Spes*[57] and had broader legal roots in Irish constitutional law:

> [T]he Constitution makes clear that the concept and nature of marriage, which it enshrines, are derived from the Christian notion of a partnership based on an irrevocable personal consent, given by both spouses which establishes a unique and very special life-long relationship.... "Family" is a word which in every day use has many different meanings. The Constitution does not attempt to define it but instead describes it as the "natural primary and fundamental unit group of Society," as a "moral institution," as the "basis of the social order," and as being "indispensable to the welfare of the Nation and the State.... A married couple without children can properly be described as a "unit group" of society such as is referred to in Article 41 and the life-long relationship to which each married person is committed is certainly a "moral institution."[58]

Antidivorce forces argued that introducing the mere possibility of divorce into that relationship would rob all marriages of the "same substance or commitment."[59] All married persons, even those who wanted nothing to do with divorce, would be materially damaged:

> The remedy of divorce is not a medicine administered only to the suffering: all of us have to swallow the cure and live with the side-effects. Those in the Divorce Action group who want second and subsequent marriages to have the same high moral and social status as the first marriage do not seem to realize how contradictory their goal is: the high status of marriage is directly dependent on its indissolubility.[60]

The campaign bolstered this position by arguing that while Article 41 gave special state protection to the family, both the first and second families could not be protected equally after a divorce, so that the first family would come out the inevitable loser. Divorce provided a "right to remarry," but it also took away rights from the identifiable first family members as a collective left behind.[61] The antidivorce forces added meat to these abstract concerns by pointing out the proposed legislation's broad judicial discretion to divide property and award maintenance and support as well as the specter of higher taxes to maintain divorced wives with children.

"The right to remarry" and "the right to a permanent marriage": The juxtaposition of these two concepts could not say more about the philosophical visions for Irish society butting heads in the mid–1990s; "[t]he two positions represent an inherent societal conflict to what extent may one retain individual freedoms without creating a non-functioning individualistic society."[62] The result — a victory for proamendment forces by only a few tenths of a percentage point — demonstrated that the fight was a real one. None of the heady rights language really applied, but gone were the days when, only a few short years before, Michele Dillon had argued that the Irish did not understand how to describe their aspirations in terms of rights[63]; it now appeared that the *only* aspirations on the Irish radar screen were individual "rights."

The two sides had really just set up the old conflict between the notion of purely private rights and the rights of sociality. The right to remarry was a vision of the marital relationship as a private one, arising from individual autonomy and freely created and terminated at will.[64] The right to a permanent marriage protected a distinctive way autonomous persons may exercise individual freedom — to make a commitment to another person for life and give up the freedom of future options[65] — and in so doing create a social unit with greater moral content and impact on the society around them. "A couple who marry are not simply giving expression to a present feeling or to a hope about the future," Binchy explains; "they are engaging in a morally transformative human act which has implications for them for the rest of their mutual lives."[66] Though Binchy describes the institution of marriage in secular terms, for an overwhelmingly Catholic people, marriage also created a covenant between two persons, "integrated into God's covenant with man" and based on the free consent of two individuals[67]:

> The intimate partnership of life and the love which constitutes the married state has been established by the creator and endowed by him with its own proper laws: it is rooted in the contract of its partners, that is, in their irrevocable personal consent. It is an institution confirmed by the divine law and receiving its stability even in the eyes of society, from the human act by which the partners mutually surrender

> themselves to each other; for the good of the partners, of the children, and of society this sacred bond no longer depends on human decision alone. For God himself is the author of marriage and has endowed it with various benefits and with various ends in view:[] all of these have a very important bearing on the continuation of the human race, on the personal development and eternal destiny of every member of the family, on the dignity, stability, peace and prosperity of the family and of the whole human race.[68]

Therefore, the consequence of divorce was to drain marriage — even the marriages of those who absolutely intended at the time they took their vows to marry for life — of the broader moral, social and religious content its unique lifelong commitment gave it so that no Irish person, even one who wanted it for moral, religious or fulfillment reasons, would ever be able to experience it again. This was the direct and tangible result of divorce: By permitting one spouse the individual freedom to end the marriage, the other spouse is robbed of the freedom to enter into that sort of commitment and therefore gain fulfillment from it. It was something serious to lose.

The 1995 divorce referendum was a philosophical choice between the demands of an individualistic view of autonomy and a more holistic, communitarian notion of freedom. Permitting one spouse on a humanitarian basis to terminate a marriage to which society has given its imprimatur and then remarry directly and concretely damages the most intimate commitments and expectations of another specific individual, the other spouse, regardless of anything that spouse had done. It further damages the expectations and opportunities available to every other person for now and for as long as divorce remains legal. The opposing cases had been communicated clearly and articulately by activists and commentators; therefore, the fact that the referendum was adopted by only three-tenths of one percent of the vote, which may have been manipulated by the government's improper public spending in support of the amendment, reflected that the Irish people were at a crossroads in the development of their public philosophy. As Taoiseach John Bruton acknowledged after the vote, the government "must reflect on why there was such a large 'no' vote.... It wasn't all because of negative campaigning."[69]

The State versus Parental Rights

From the perspective of those who support the right to life of unborn children in Ireland, the ground on which they have fought their legal battles has been as bad as that which the Confederate army occupied at Gettysburg.

Who knows what might have happened if the Irish abortion cases had been about, say, married professional women seeking to choose the sex of their children? Instead, both *X* and the second major Irish abortion case, *A and B* v. *Eastern Health Board*[70] (referred to hereafter as "*C*") involved rapes of young teenagers. The factual setting of *C* was even more horrible, if that is possible, than *X*; it arose when a thirteen-year-old member of Ireland's detested traveling community was raped by an adult neighbor in the community and conceived a child. Travelers are a frequent target of discrimination in Ireland; they lack fixed homes, move from community to community and are alleged to bring crime wherever they go. "*C*" and her nine brothers and sisters had "lived in particularly squalid conditions which were quite unlike the conditions in which most travelling people lived."[71] The girl was "severely traumatized"[72] by the rape and, because her parents, A and B, had not been appropriately supportive of her situation, C was taken into state foster care.

C wanted an abortion. At first, C's parents agreed to allow her foster mother to take her to England for that purpose. Eventually, however, C's mother became "absolutely opposed" to an abortion, and her father opposed it unless C would otherwise commit suicide. Unlike in the *X* case, the district judge heard extensive evidence from one psychiatrist as to C's mental health and another as to her competence, and C's statements that she would commit suicide if she did not have an abortion were more unambiguous than X's. The district judge did not definitively hold that there was a "real and substantial risk" to C's life, which would allow her to obtain an abortion in Ireland. Instead, the district judge, exercising a juvenile jurisdiction pursuant to the Child Care Act, 1991, simply decided that C could obtain medical treatment in the form of termination of her pregnancy by traveling to another jurisdiction.

Prolifers' worst nightmare became reality. Binchy amassed a considerable array of evidence challenging the X court's analysis of the threat to X's life on medical grounds,[73] and now here was the consulting psychiatrist who routinely gave testimony in family court cases in Ireland testifying that because of the "very significant risk" that C would commit suicide, C should have therapy and "termination of pregnancy should take place as soon as possible," using virtually the exact words the X holding required.[74] A district judge exercising jurisdiction over a child pursuant to the Child Care Act may enter orders related only to specific matters, one of which is the child's medical or psychiatric treatment. Therefore, the high court went on to hold that based on the psychiatrist's evidence, abortion in response to a real and substantial risk of suicide due to the pregnancy *was* medical treatment, so that an order permitting the abortion was within the district court's jurisdiction.

The high court did provide additional shape to the travel amendment from 1992. The district judge had not actually ruled that there was a real and substantial risk to C's life in the form of suicide if she carried the child to term, but C argued that did not matter: Whether she was suicidal or not, the travel amendment gave her the right to travel under her parents' authority to England for the abortion regardless of whether it would be legal in Ireland, and her right to travel should not be impeded simply because she was in foster care. But this argument went farther than the high court was willing to go. It was one thing for an adult woman to go to England for an abortion; another for the parents of a minor to take her to England; but *quite* another for an Irish court to put its imprimatur on an abortion in the form of a travel order for a foster parent or a government health board to take a child out of the jurisdiction for an abortion otherwise illegal in Ireland:

> A court of law, in considering the welfare of an Irish minor in Ireland and considering whether on health grounds a termination of pregnancy was necessary, must, I believe, be confined to considering the grounds of termination which would be lawful under the Irish Constitution and cannot enter a direction authorising travel to another jurisdiction for a different kind of abortion. The amended Constitution does not now confer a right to abortion outside of Ireland. It merely prevents injunctions against travelling for that purpose.
>
> . . .
>
> [T]he fact that there may be different views as to the importance of the constitutional right to travel does not in my view affect the issue of whether the District Court under the Child Care Act 1991 can actually exercise a jurisdiction authorising travel for a particular purpose, namely, for an abortion in circumstances where the proposed abortion would not be allowed under Irish law. I think that the court would be prevented from doing so by the terms of the right to life of the unborn expressed in the Constitution and as the Supreme Court has held, unaffected by 'the travel amendment.'[75]

Unlike many Irish constitutional law cases, particularly *X*, the high court looked to the historical context in which the Irish people passed the travel amendment, which, after all, was only five years old. The high court judge held that the purpose of the travel amendment had been to avoid a repeat of the *X* case and to prevent injunctions against travel to have an abortion abroad. It did not give C an entitlement to an abortion abroad and therefore authorize the district court to enter an order for the Eastern Health Board, through C's foster mother, to take C to England if she did not otherwise have a right to an abortion under Irish law. C could go to England because the high court interpreted the district court as having held that there was a real and substantial risk of her committing suicide, but not otherwise.

So only fifteen years after the Eighth Amendment announced that the state must protect the right to life of the unborn to the extent practicable, with due regard for the right to life of the mother, the Irish state, through the Eastern Health Board, paid for a young mother to have an abortion in England after having what some considered overly aggressively fought for the authority to do so. What crisis will be next? If parents of a potentially suicidal pregnant girl refuse to take her to England for an abortion, will a regional health board consider that fact a sufficient ground to remove the child from its parents and place her in foster care, from which the state could provide an abortion?[76] The district court had defined abortion to be "medical treatment" where there was a real and substantial risk of the minor mother's committing suicide and had given little weight to A's and B's objection to C's abortion plans because it had determined that they were neglectful and had therefore lost some of their legal authority regarding their daughter. Would a state that provides funds for a minor to receive an abortion do the same for an indigent adult woman if she presented with a real and substantial risk to her life from suicide?[77] Even if her husband objected? The *Information Bill* case insisted that information could be given to a woman only when consistent with constitutional justice, implicating that fathers had a role in the abortion decision, but went no farther. More obviously than in the *Information Bill* reference or the *Wardship* case, *C* renders the role of the state in vindicating the right to life ever more obscure and both the imperatives and mutual duties of family and community increasingly uncertain.

Part III

EIGHT

On Tara Road: *Women and Flourishing*

> "You know, Ria, you must know that I'm seeing someone, and well, we've just discovered she's pregnant. I am going to be a father again. She's going to have a baby and we are very happy about it. I was going to tell you next weekend. I thought suddenly that you must have known."
>
> —Maeve Binchy, *Tara Road*[1]

"Ria lived on Tara Road in Dublin with her dashing husband, Danny, and their two children. She fully believed she was happily married, right up until the day Danny told her he was leaving her to be with his young, pregnant girlfriend." Thus the publisher of Maeve Binchy's bestselling novel *Tara Road* describes the crisis facing the not-quite-forty Ria Lynch, who created a community headquartered in her huge kitchen of family and friends from Dublin's Tara Road neighborhood. The neighborhood is a milieu of the well-to-do and modest, the trendy and traditional, the commercial and residential, the urban and rural, the law-abiding and more sinister, all anchored by Ria and Danny's restored-from-scratch dream mansion.

In Number 16 Tara Road, Ria is queen, however much she may be taken for granted or underappreciated. Daily roaming in and out of the kitchen, where she both presides and provides, are her intelligent teenaged daughter Annie, her faux pas waiting-to-happen son Brian, her penny-pinching sister Hilary, her glamorous businesswoman friend Rosemary, her busybody mother, her former work friend turned cleaner who begs for advances to keep her abusive husband in drink, a local recovering alcoholic who transforms himself into a trendy restauranteur relying on vegetables he raises in Ria's garden, a "fast" teenaged friend of Annie's, Danny's boss and his "fancy woman," and many more. Ria's days are overfilled raising her children, keeping Annie away from temptation, tidying up after her son, providing lunches for her mother, sister and half the neighborhood, dinner for her family, evening drinks and hors d'oeuvres for Rosemary, make-work for Gertie the cleaner, space for Colm the restauranteur, lush and sentimental comforts for her family, "alibis" for her husband's cheating boss, support and solutions for everyone she knows—providing, providing, providing. Ria provides so much that even when she and Danny face financial challenges, he insists she stay home providing there. Later, however, the whirlwind that surrounds Ria becomes so intense that at the same time she is considering adding to it by having another child, Danny is choosing peaceful privacy with the twenty-two-year-old waif Bernadette over the dream home of his youth. With no warning Ria can stop long enough to recognize, Danny announces he is leaving and that they must sell Number 16 Tara Road to survive financially.

Tara Road is the story of what Ria, whose very self is intimately defined by the communities—family, circles of friends, neighborhood—of which she is a member and the leader, does when the foundation for those communities starts to crumble. At her lowest ebb and on a whim, Ria enters into a "house trade" for a few months with an American woman, Marilyn Vine, who is separated from her husband and friends due to grief over the accidental death of her son. All of a sudden, an outsider's view of Ria's character and life is informed by juxtoposition to that of this quintessential American woman. Ria prepares for Marilyn's arrival by making her home even more homey and making sure Gertie will be available to let Marilyn in and give her a tour. Gertie ultimately falls down on the job — as usual, her husband is on a dangerous drinking binge — but Colm, also intimately familiar with the Lynch residence, easily fills in. By contrast, Ria meets up with Marilyn's friend Carlotta in Carlotta's Connecticut beauty salon, and Carlotta offers her an aromatherapy and massage treatment — as well as a bill when it is over, "generously" discounted by fifteen percent. Ria may be considered "rich" in her circle in Ireland, but she gulps when she sees amount she owes. More surprisingly, Carlotta later admits that she has never been inside Marilyn's home, despite the fact that they are apparently close friends.

It is the first of many insightful contrasts. On her first day in the United States, Ria invites Carlotta and another of Marilyn's friends for an evening of wine drinking and experience sharing, the latter a normal course of events on Tara Road but not in Stoneyfield, Connecticut. Later, the Americans, who Ria expects from cultural lore to be so "friendly," are disconcerted by the intimacy of that evening. In Ireland, Ria's friends and children are under orders to call on Marilyn early in her residence there, so that she will be surrounded by company that, unbeknownst to Ria,

Marilyn has come to Ireland to avoid. Slowly but surely, to Marilyn's horror, they take up residence again in the kitchen, where Marilyn reveals herself as far less than Ria's equal at the same time Ria is winning a part-time job in a bakery for her talents. Luckily for Marilyn, Colm provides her with regular leftovers from the restaurant, so the remaining of Ria's saucepans survive unharmed, but it is a sharp contrast to the reaction of one of Marilyn's in-laws, who shocks Ria with his attentions and is himself shocked that Ria makes her shortcake from scratch. The American Marilyn, in the self-imposed isolation her culture facilitates, has lost her ability to nurture, but the Irish Ria, with genuine pleasure and fulfillment, seems almost incapable of not giving of herself to nurture everything around her.

Binchy does not let the reader forget the cost of Ria's nurturing. Marilyn hesitantly accepts an invitation for a dinner out with Rosemary only to be confronted by an ugly incident, in which one of Danny's cast-off mistresses publicly reveals the embarrassing secrets of Colm's patrons—including Danny and the mother of his child to come—and Marilyn's companions indulge their culturally Irish tendency to gossip about Ria's tragedy. Marilyn is disgusted:

> Marilyn could not take in the degree of involvement and indeed interference that these people felt confident to have in everyone else's life. They thought nothing of discussing the motives and private sorrows of their friend to Marilyn who was after all a complete stranger, here purely because of an accidental home exchange. While she felt sympathy for Ria and all that happened to her, she also felt a sense of annoyance.
>
> Why had [Ria] not kept her dignity, and refused to allow all these people into her life? The only way to cope with tragedy and grief was to refuse to permit it to be articulated and acknowledged. Deny its existence and you had some hope of survival. Marilyn got out of bed and looked down on the messy garden and the other large redbrick houses in the neighborhood. She felt very lost and alone in this place where garrulous people wanted to know everything about you and expected you to need the details of their lives too.
>
> She ached for the cool house and beautiful garden in Stoneyfield. If she were there now she could go and swim laps in her pool, safe in the knowledge that no one would call and burden her with postmortems about last night.

It is a turning point for both Marilyn and Ria. As the two women learn from each others' secrets and from taking over each others' lives, each in turn confronts the limits of her own experience—relatedness on the one hand and isolation on the other. Ria and her neighborhood are caricatures of traditional Irish women's lives translated into a present-day context, but like caricatures that work, they ring true and illustrate both values from the past as well as what is both fulfilling and dangerous when those traditional values are translated into modernity. Ria's recognition that by focusing on nurturing the world around her, she failed to nurture the private things between her and Danny and that by opening her life and her self to the world, she allowed those closest to her to walk off with the things that mattered most to her, is painful. They are the risks and downsides not just to a life such as Ria's but also to relatedness and community generally. *Tara Road* ends when Ria learns to limit those risks without losing the fulfillment from her kind of life, but with an undercurrent of caution that if it is possible to limit such risks, it is not possible to eliminate them entirely. Marilyn's situation is not universal, but her response to her grief exacerbates her culturally modern American tendencies to individual reliance and its less attractive form, isolation, showing just how threatening the risks of relationship and relatedness can be. Through her relationships with Ria's friends and family, Marilyn recognizes that the cost of isolation is the joy she misses from relatedness, and she opens her life again to relationships with her husband, friends, and even mere acquaintances.

Tara Road was an international bestseller and a choice of Oprah Winfrey's book club, which gave the book a high profile, both in Ireland in the United States. It is a Maeve Binchy novel — Maeve Binchy the sister but not ideological soulmate of William Binchy, the Irish prolife activist — so Marilyn eventually works through her grief, and Ria develops modern-woman ambitions as a caterer with a ready-made colleague and potential love interest, Colm, awaiting her return. It is a "happily-ever-after" kind of story. Real life sometimes is not.

The primarily American internet discussion of *Tara Road* on Oprah Winfrey's website revealed a curious response to this tale of two cultures. Many readers liked Ria and even identified with her, but the strength of the opposite response was telling. "Naive," "infuriating," "made me angry" and "weak" were persistent themes in the reactions to Ria's character, particularly in her pining for her husband, even among those who did like the book more generally. One reader was angry at Ria for thinking her life was perfect because "her life was never perfect.... She was too self-absorbed to catch on." One reader who still had not finished the book asked, "Will someone tell me if Ria gets some gumption and starts acting like a real woman?" Though readers certainly felt for Ria, and many revealed similar experiences, what was more surprising was the belligerence with which many announced they lacked any pity for her. A substantial group of readers seemed to have joined a chorus crying, "Get a life!"

But Ria already had a life, an important and valuable life. We all know women like Ria. Perhaps they are our mothers or grandmothers. Perhaps they are even our friends, siblings or selves. They are women that society once taught us to admire. Now, we are not so sure.

Developments in foundational, Irish constitutional law of the past century arose from continual deliberate efforts to find the right balance between the communitarian and liberal values that its culture and politics share. It has been a challenge; the two are not necessarily antithetical, but as interests competing in a political arena, they inevitably clash. At one extreme, the inherent tendency to majoritarianism in communitarianism can leave dissenting individuals and minorities at risk, but liberalism also threatens communitarianism's focus on the common good. Irish political philosopher Iseult Honohan highlights this threat by comparing the benefits of individual shareholders in dividends from mining or salmon-farming companies with the interests of the common good or the community generally in preserving wilderness areas, sites of historical or religious significance, or cultural heritage. The dividends from mining or salmon farming are more tangible, and they actually will be distributed to shareholders. Small groups of environmental or religious activists also have competing tangible and distributable interests; more is at stake. A wider group also has an interest in preservation of ecological or culturally sensitive sites:

> There is a real social benefit to a wider group; the wider benefit is *not easily distributed* or assignable across individuals; even identifying the beneficiaries in question may be difficult because they may not yet be born. The urgency of environmental and heritage issues derives from the danger that certain options may be shut off for ever for future members of our society.... [F]or public harm to be experienced, it is not necessary that each member of society suffer a specific harm or loss, but that positive possibilities are shut off, and negative ones become more likely.[2]

A similar analysis applies to abortion rights. For women who would face severe consequences from an unplanned pregnancy — or for women like X or C facing crisis pregnancies "right now" — a right to an abortion is a tangible benefit that may not be immediately distributed but will be at identifiable times in the future. But abortion rights have a corresponding negative effect on other groups, even aside from the unborn. Because abortion is such a foundational issue, recognition of a right to an abortion may change a society, and the shared good of the type of society in which citizens live may be lost or irreparably changed. No longer will those citizens live in the kind of society where no right to abortion is recognized or protected.

Citizens really do have an interest in what kind of country they live in. Intangible shared goods such as a shared national language, a culture that supports marriage, or a shared belief in the sanctity of the life of unborn children adds to individual citizens' flourishing. Individual flourishing and fulfillment are not merely about individual activity; they are about interests in even very intangible and abstract shared goods such as these:

> Self-expression through a common culture is often held to be one of the central common goods. It is not just a matter of speaking one's own language, knowing one's own history, holding one's own religious beliefs, *but living among people and within institutions that recognise these.*[3]

The Catholic Church philosophers are not the only ones who recognize that people are social beings—Aristotle and Cicero said the same thing—and membership in communities of shared values and history is "essential to human happiness."[4] A healthy balance between liberalism and communitarianism, particularly as a means to a proper balancing of individual interests and the common good is therefore imperative for human flourishing and fulfillment.

The United States has also balanced the interests of communitarianism and liberalism, but the modern American balancing is almost exclusively weighted on the liberalism side. Many hoped liberalism in the form of individualism in many guises, including rights to abortion and liberalized divorce, would benefit women, leading to greater human flourishing and fulfillment that way. Have women at large been so significantly advantaged by abortion rights and liberalized divorce laws in the United States as to outweigh the others' loss of correlative shared goods? If increased individualism and rights consciousness damages the fabric of community and sociality in which so many women flourish and find fulfillment, can their icons, such as abortion rights and liberal divorce laws, be justified?

In 1987, Mary Ann Glendon asked the intriguing question, why did the United States develop a legal regime of abortion and divorce so far outside the mainstream of those of most western nations?[5] In comparing the law of the United States, Canada and numerous western European countries, she found that only the United States permitted abortion freely until the unborn child's viability, and after viability, abortion was still permitted, though potentially subject to regulation. She also identifies two explanations arising from differences between the cultures involved: tendencies to individualism in American society and law and a lack of connectedness and group association within the United States.[6] In the United States, Glendon concludes, liberty has become the equivalent of individual autonomy.

For those reared to believe that the great genius of America's nation building was the citizenry's loyalty to various schools of citizenship[7] or the little platoons that were the first link to a love of country and mankind,[8] and also that Americans had created a series of mediating institutions between citizens and the state grounding political and social activity in groups[9] that would eliminate the horrors of factions and the effects of more universal vices such as greed, selfishness and ambition,[10] Glendon's findings come as a profound indictment.[11] But her concerns are not new. Almost as soon as the United States and the first French republic were born, observers were warning about the fragility of the interlocking communities on which republican society could be based, and history has proved them right.[12] "While social historians have had to look hard to find little islands of individualism there in the Middle Ages," *Habits of the Heart* observes, "social scientists have to strain to discover latent networks of community and kinship in contemporary America."[13]

Liberty was not always so closely associated with individual autonomy in U.S. law or public philosophy. The early process of applying the Bill of Rights and other individual rights to the states via incorporation in the Fourteenth Amendment's guarantee of substantive due process after the Civil War recognized that individual rights are also rights to sociality and to participate in communities unfettered by government interference. The standard early articulation defined substantive due process rights as

> denot[ing] not merely freedom from bodily restraint but also the right of the individual to contract, to engage in any of the common occupations of life, to acquire useful knowledge, to marry, establish a home and bring up children, to worship God according to the dictates of his own conscience, and generally to enjoy those privileges long recognized at common law as essential to the orderly pursuit of happiness by free men.[14]

Each of those rights is social in nature. They facilitate interaction with other individuals, groups, and communities. They are "rights of men and women exercised in partnership with other men and women," speaking "fundamentally, to values of sociality and solidarity."[15] Further, they are limited in the public interest by what is a essentially a formulation of the common good, "the orderly pursuit of happiness by free men."[16] Such a notion of a mutually reinforcing relationship between a human's individuality and her inherently social nature as the basis for democratic government and a philosophy of the common good has roots in the Catholic social and intellectual tradition as well,[17] which is why American commentator John Courtney Murray could correctly posit in 1960 that American Catholics were particularly comfortable within the American political tradition. It was their tradition, too.[18]

In fact, through the United States Supreme Court's 1965 decision in *Griswold* v. *Connecticut*,[19] which holds that married persons have a right of privacy to make decisions concerning that relationship that reached far enough to invalidate a law forbidding them to use contraceptives, sociality remained an important part of substantive due process jurisprudence, but soon afterward, the Court reached a fork in the road of individual rights and chose the one leading to individual autonomy.[20] In *Eisenstat* v. *Baird*,[21] the Court held that "[i]f the right of privacy means anything, it is the right of the *individual*, married or single, to be free from unwarranted governmental intrusion into matters so fundamentally affecting a person as the decision whether to bear or beget a child,"[22] a divergence both from *Griswold*, which roots the right to privacy in marriage and community and the history of substantive rights jurisprudence that defines so many of the substantive due process rights in terms of sociality and participation. The holding of *Roe* v. *Wade* that the "attending physician, in consultation with his patient, is free to determine, without regulation by the State, that, in his medical judgment, the patient's pregnancy should be terminated"[23] to varying degrees at varying times during the pregnancy, started out sounding like a right of sociality. The U.S. Supreme Court even relied on *Rex* v. *Bourne*'s interpretation of statutory language protecting the life of the mother as also protecting her from significant risks to her health as well,[24] which is notable because the Court later criticized the Texas statute for permitting abortions solely where the life of the mother is at stake from the pregnancy.[25] But *Roe* was quickly and quietly reinterpreted to stand for a woman's individual right to choose an abortion, regardless of any consultation with a doctor, balanced against what was defined as the state's very limited interests in both the mother's and the unborn child's health at various stages of a pregnancy. Despite the Supreme Court's insistence otherwise, after *Roe*, pregnant women were isolated in their privacy,[26] their liberty having been defined strictly in terms of their individual autonomy.[27]

Almost immediately, the United States Supreme Court began rethinking the definition of liberty as "autonomy." Justice Powell in particular questioned the extent of a teenaged mother's autonomy in cases challenging the validity of state laws requiring that parents give their consent or be notified prior to their minor child's receiving an abortion.[28] With his eye to these cases, Donald Kommers argued in the mid–1980s that the Supreme Court was struggling with the "right balance between liberty and sociality" in abortion law.[29]

Justice O'Connor's 1992 opinion in *Planned Parenthood* v. *Casey* suggests that the struggle continues:

> Some guiding principles should emerge. What is at stake is the woman's right to make the ultimate decision, not a right to be insulated from all others in doing so. Regulations which do no more than create a structural mechanism by which the State, or the parent or guardian of a minor, may express profound respect for the life of the unborn are permitted, if they are not a substantial obstacle to the woman's exercise of the right to choose. Unless it has that effect on her right of choice, a state measure designed to persuade her to choose childbirth over abortion will be upheld if reasonably related to that goal. Regulations designed to foster the health of a woman seeking an abortion are valid if they do not constitute an undue burden.[30]

Reference to "state measure[s] designed to persuade [the mother] to choose childbirth over abortion"[31] sounds as though Justice O'Connor envisions a role for the community in the abortion decision, but as *Casey* mades plain, not many such state measures are likely to pass constitutional muster. On the one hand, Pennsylvania's carefully crafted requirements that women receiving abortions be provided with information about the risks and consequences of abortion ("informed consent requirements") are constitutional, and a required twenty-four-hour waiting period between consent and the abortion procedure is "a closer question"[32] but still constitutional. On the other hand, requirements that spouses be notified of planned abortions are not. In other words, Pennsylvania's two efforts to discourage abortion through interaction between the individual and the state are constitutional, but the one provision respecting sociality and the social realities of sexual interaction, family, and a parent's interest in his unborn child are not.[33]

Those hoping *Casey* might shift the balancing between autonomy and sociality more toward sociality were disappointed. Despite her initial rhetorical concern for sociality, Justice O'Connor went on to say, in support of the spousal notification holding, that a "husband's interest in the life of [his] child [does] not permit the State to empower him with this *troubling* degree of authority over his wife."[34] But it has not been that troubling to the French, who even with their liberal abortion regime, have required women to participate in *counseling* prior to making the decision to abort, ideally with the father of the unborn child.[35] Justice Blackmun, the author of *Roe*, argued that "*Roe*'s trimester framework does not ignore the State's interest in prenatal life,"[36] but it does ignore other interests of many individual citizens in the shared good of a society without abortion. Justice Stevens acknowledged many of the ingredients a shared good in his *Casey* concurrence, such as a desire for such a society based on religious motivations, based on philosophies of respect for human life, based on the value of the lives that will ultimately be born in the form of future Mozarts or Curies, but he went on to argue that these are either impermissible justifications for abortion restrictions under U.S. law or they just are not very important.[37] From an individualism perspective, an intangible state interest compared to the crisis of a very tangible individual woman, he might be right. But the argument ignores the significance of the aggregate of all the individual interests of all people in a particular kind of community or lifestyle for all time. After *Casey*, individual autonomy of a few is virtually the only value driving American abortion jurisprudence, and defending abortion rights American style as virtual abortion on demand simply means the needs and desires of some societal "winners" trump those of all the others all the time.

Mary Ann Glendon wrote little about Ireland, the country on the other end of the abortion law spectrum from the United States, but other American writers have produced a string of indictments of Irish family law. Their primary criticism is that the Irish protections for individual rights—such as to travel, to engage in expression and exchange information, and to maintain bodily integrity and individual autonomy—have been less definitive than the American, particularly in the context of abortion. These critics characterize most of the Irish family law battles of the past twenty-five years as battles between medieval authoritarianism in the form of the church and brave women who are up from Catholicism. American observers find it difficult to believe that Irish people would freely choose this legal regime.

The voices that emanate from each nation explain why. While Americans place ever-increasing emphasis on individualism and individual voices, from the rise of the Republican movement until the present day, the national voice has dominated Irish public life, along with other strong community voices, such as those of the Catholic Church, families, neighborhoods and villages. Group voices are strong in Ireland, while in the United States they are comparatively weak. Those group voices and the stories they tell have shaped the lives and characters of generations of Irish people and have provided a universal vocabulary of cultural connectedness that adds to the individual fulfillment of Irish citizens. The Irish remain what *Habits of the Heart* calls a "community of memory," informed by "a context of meaning that can allow [them] to connect [their] aspirations for [them]selves and those closest to [them] with the aspirations of a larger good and see [their] own efforts as being in part contributions to a common good."[38] Any sense of individual rights is likely to be mildly tempered in such a context.

Not surprisingly, individual Irish voices have been slow to increase in volume and range. The U.S. Constitution refers to our most cherished values as "freedoms" held by the people, but the modern vocabulary is to speak of individual "rights." The Irish, by comparison, are new to rights discourse; in her analysis of the 1986 divorce referendum, Michele Dillon argues that as late as 1986, the Irish lacked fluency with the vocabulary of individual rights.[39] In Ireland, individual voices have tended to provide a harmony to the collective melody, and only recently has the balance between the two been noticeably fine tuned.

During the last decade of the twentieth century, Irish constitutional law and culture generally, and Irish abortion law specifically, have become more and more individualistic and rights based, but Irish law is still easily distinguished from the American. First, the foundation of Irish abortion law is a constitutional "given" that an unborn child is a human life deserving of essentially equal protection as that of the born mother, though the moment at which an unborn child becomes fully human for purposes of constitutional protection — the moment of fertilization, which has been the tacit position of Irish criminal law and prosecutions versus the moment of conception, which is the position of the Catholic Church — is a subject for debate. As a result, virtually all abortions are illegal, and at the margins of legality, the Irish abortion "problem" is always about clashing rights to life of fully human persons. By contrast, U.S. law denies that the unborn have rights, and therefore, important individual rights do not directly clash. The second difference is that the Irish Constitution defines a proactive role for the state in protecting unborn children — a constitutional responsibility not to remain neutral in the abortion conversation — while the American states' roles are purely discretionary.

Whatever legal regime a society chooses, the legal and cultural attitudes toward abortion and also to some extent divorce are the most essential issues that society must face. In the first place, they speak most directly to the foundational principles upon which citizens in a community will hazard their fortunes together. They *matter* deeply. "Who is a person?" "Who is fully human?" "What protections do we owe other persons or humans?" "How do we value the life of a human, born or unborn?" "What is the value of the life of a human, and how do we measure it?" "What circumstances require choices between human lives, and how should such choices be made?" "What responsibilities do humans have to each other?"

These are first questions, the answers to which are first principles for any community and become part of that community's shared goods. Kristin Luker argues that the abortion debate in the United States is important because it is the "most visible ... place for ordinary Americans to grapple with the philosophical issue of personhood,"[40] and while that is apparent in the context of the personhood of the unborn child, in some respects it is true of women as well. Women confront lived existence from a position that is different from that of men, for example, which raises questions not so different in kind from those raised by unborn children about the value of their lives and the full personhood and citizenship of women in society. Moreover, in a world where use of the phrase "quality of life" is waxing as a substitute for "value of life," these concerns become even more urgent for both women and the unborn.

Second, abortion encapsulates at this fundamental and foundational level decisions about what constitutes a "good society" or what people consider "sacred and important."[41] William Binchy describes the stakes from the perspective of the unborn as follows: "At a ... basic level, the unborn force us to consider what the demands of a humane society are. At the heart of a humane society is an almost instinctive response to dependency, weakness, immaturity and small size."[42] Yet women, especially women in crisis, make demands of the humane society as well. "There is a tremendous sadness and loneliness in the cry, 'A woman's right to choose,'" American commentator Frederica Mathews-Greene has observed. "No one wants an abortion as she wants an ice-cream cone or a Porsche. She wants an abortion as an animal, caught in a trap, wants to gnaw off its own leg."[43] Or as Catharine MacKinnon puts it, the "right to an abortion" arising from a right to privacy "is an instance of liberalism applied to women as if we *are* persons, gender neutral" and means "a woman's decision to abort would have no claim on public support and would genuinely not be seen as burdened by that deprivation,"[44] even if some of that public support might translate into tangible tools to provide for the child after birth. The discussion therefore comes full circle, giving rise to the question of whether women and unborn children both might be better off with fewer rights that meant more.

Finally, legal and cultural attitudes about abortion, and again to some extent about divorce as well, are not only an expression of what people believe about fundamental issues of the soul, but they also educate the soul in turn. Writes Mary Ann Glendon:

> Law for better or worse, now penetrates deeply into every aspect of life. Government, whether pursuant to a constitutional obligation or

> not, plays an ever greater role in the lives of individuals as a source of support and security. Under these conditions, law becomes increasingly identified with legitimacy in the minds of the citizens.[45]

Therefore, the fact that a supreme court or a constitution has declared some conduct to be a matter of right or to be constitutional entrenches its status as such and adds the fact of apparent constitutionality to its more general legitimacy, which in turn lends credence to the sense that it *should* be constitutional, or vice versa. Hence the origin of "slippery slope" arguments.

The irony of the battle between the winners and losers in the American abortion debate is that so much has been lost by so many to provide so little benefit to so few. What is surreal about American notions of a right to an abortion is that deep down, abortion rights are not what many people who claim to support them really care about; what they care about is improving women's well-being. Supporters advocate from a sincere belief that legal abortion substantially improves women's well-being[46]—it gives women reproductive freedom—but the conclusions that reproductive freedom arises from legalized abortion and that such a legal regime really contributes more than other possible regimes to any individual woman's well-being are not facially evident. In the first place, reproductive freedom for women has increased since *Roe*, independently of abortion rights. Second, any increase to women's well-being, defined as flourishing or fulfillment, from abortion rights is very indirect. For one thing, what women want in order to increase their flourishing and fulfillment is not easy to characterize. After all, as Simone de Beauvoir argues, women have a wide variety of political and social priorities. The challenge to those who justify abortion rights as a benefit to women is that, especially given the possibility that an abortion ends a human life, what justification for abortion rights can there be if they do little or nothing to help women flourish or find fulfillment?

Feminist theory, which might be expected to have a good response to that question, never proves that abortion is a very important part of what women want. Since the modern feminist movement began in earnest in the 1960s, modern society has recognized three basic models of womanhood: "traditional woman," "liberal woman," and "radical woman," each differentiated by the very different philosophies of "what women want," on which each is based. Of course, the categories are deceiving—few women fit so completely in one category or another, and many women pick and choose values from all three. Ria Lynch, for example, is a quintessential traditional woman, who flourishes through her family and community interaction and sociality generally. The liberal woman insists on terms of equality with men both in her career and in her bedroom, much like Ria's friend Rosemary Ryan. Analogous to the principles of racial equality espoused by Dr. Martin Luther King, Jr., during the American civil rights movement, the liberal woman demands equal rights with men in law, seeing those rights as a vehicle for empowerment. The hybrids of the liberal woman model are numerous; some liberal women, for example, "have it all"—career, husband, children, and community life—while others feel compelled to try, even in the face of varying degrees of success. The radical woman, on the other hand, questions whether equality with men under the circumstances of male hegemony in society is possible or desirable and may even resort to lesbianism both for sexual fulfillment and political expression. Who are men to be equal to? the radical woman wonders, thus making herself the "Malcolm X" of feminism.

The respective approaches of liberal and radical women to abortion rights are as different from each other as they are to those of traditional women. Liberal women embraced the sexual revolution and concluded that heterosexual sex was good and that they wanted more of it without the risk of potential pregnancy, though many liberal women also married, had children, and enjoyed happy family lives along with their careers. Abortion rights were the key to sexual freedom on the same terms as men by disconnecting sex from fertility and childbearing so those potential consequences of sex would not interfere with the liberal woman's career, the planning of her family or other lifestyle choices. Liberal women were the ones who seemed to benefit most from abortion rights. When abortion rights actually became part of U.S. constitutional law, however, they were based not on the theory of equality between the sexes, but on notions of privacy.[47]

Radical women recognized the disadvantages of the privacy theory first. They saw women's sexuality as "a social construct of male power: defined by men, forced on women, and constitutive of the meaning of gender,"[48] and they sought freedom of a different kind, "the ability *not* to have sex with men, and therefore not to get pregnant."[49] By basing abortion rights on privacy rights, radical women saw American leaders making all-too-convenient assumptions radical women contest: that women control sex and meaningfully consent to it, despite male hegemony in the private sphere. Therefore, radical women concluded that abortion rights simply increased women's sexual availability to men, and while the right was necessary, it was disappointingly flawed because it did nothing to change the balance of power between men and women or provide women with meaningful freedom or choices.

The relevance of abortion rights to traditional women is unclear. From one perspective, they are completely irrelevant; traditional women doubt their moral propriety and do not need them anyway since the caricature of the traditional woman finds her fulfillment in bearing and rearing her children, as many "as God sends," without a clear demarcation between that number and any independent set of desires. This sort of attitude, rare as it is undiluted in real life, starts liberal women screaming at their traditional sisters to "get a life!" just as so many of Oprah's readers did to the fictional Ria Lynch. Radical women, on the other hand, take a more maternalistic (as opposed to paternalistic) approach, sighing that if only such traditional women could have their consciousness of the "lived knowing of the social reality of being female" raised, they might come to a better understanding of how to fulfill their "authentic selves." In both versions, feminism assumes what constitutes women's well-being, further assumes that those assumptions are universal to all women, and then goes even one step farther, assuming the women who do not live according to those assumptions are doing it wrong.

As the experiences of more and more modern American women are informed by some aspects of feminist theory, at least of the version which has seeped into the popular culture, and therefore experience at least a consciousness-raising light, the cop-out that traditional woman "just doesn't get it" is increasingly inadequate to explain her conduct. As feminist, Tulane law professor Ruth Colker has noted, feminism is subject to the criticism that it is unable to explain or accept the views of women who evaluate their best interests differently from feminists—women who genuinely enjoy participating in pornography, take pride and pleasure in being whistled at in the street, or knowingly choose apparent subservience to men — except to marginalize them as lacking consciousness about their own situations, or as Colker does, to discount the value of their individual fulfillment because it does not contribute to the good of the team.[50] On the one hand, Colker assumes the woman who enjoys men's whistling does so in full consciousness (admittedly, a position many feminists would deny). On the other, she argues that the woman has still been sexually objectified because women generally would feel objectified, and a compassionate man "who respected women would not whistle at any individual woman and take the risk of inflicting pain and fear on her."[51] Even at the risk of triviality — and echoes of "doesn't the man have the right to free expression?" are already wafting in from stage left — it is worth asking, "so after all that, what *of* the pleasure of the woman who likes men's whistling?" Are the only two alternatives feminism offers for coping with the unreconstructed that they are not living in the real world, or worse, that they do not matter anyway?

Even for those doing it "right," the extreme presentation of liberal women's roles in the popular media can be sufficiently daunting as to call unbridled liberalism into question. That presentation tends to ignore the way many women actually live, respond to liberalism or would make lifestyle choices based on a deeper understanding of feminism. One of those extremes is that of the powerful liberal career woman who bests men in a man's world, though she too is often depicted in the popular media doing so while wearing modern women's power costume: a short, tight skirt or a low-cut blouse — Clinton confidante and University of Southern California law professor Susan Estrich has written of being slightly shocked at her female students trooping off to law firm interviews looking like they are "dressed for a date"[52] — or worse, dressed and coiffed so as to be indistinguishable from the men around her. At this extreme, Kathy Rudy argues that the poverty of this modern conception of womanhood is that it defines women's aspirations as abstractly and one-dimensionally as prefeminist philosophies:

> The liberal subject is available to work long hours, to relocate, to make a complete commitment to the career that will eventually define identity. In such a climate, anything that restricts the individual's ability to compete — such as a pregnancy — can only be understood as a drawback, as something to be overcome. The abstract right to abortion offers the pregnant woman the option of regaining her nonpregnant status in order to fully and competitively participate in the public sphere. Abortion thus functions as an equalizer; any woman who does not want a pregnancy can simply have it removed and thus immediately return herself to the Ur-position of the abstracted liberal self. The idea that pregnant women might desire more choices than "being pregnant" or "not being pregnant" — such as more adequate childcare or larger systems of kinship, in which the cost and burden of raising a child is spread among many — is beyond the limits of the liberal imagination.
>
> In my thinking, it is not a coincidence that the abstracted competitive, nonpregnant person of the public sphere most resembles men.[53]

Of course, many actual liberal women aspire to and have husbands, children, families and a rewardingly balanced life, though the popular conception all too often either relegates those aspects of a liberal woman's life either to second place or paints her as an almost fantasy superwoman. For others, the modern popular conception is a grinding reality in which no other path is acceptable and family goals must be fit in around her career, which has been ingrained in her to be of primary importance, just as husbands and children were to women of an earlier era. The modern liberal woman is certainly no long imprisoned in her house, but a workplace prison may not provide significantly more fulfillment than the house prison. Many women find the liberal workplace rewarding, especially those who achieve a balance with family and other priorities which stem from the community and society that is also critical to flourishing and fulfillment. But many women in an earlier age were fulfilled in the house prison. Workplace demands—the same demands men experience but without the expectations that they will also primarily care for family and community—can make that balance elusive. Those who fail to find it carry the weight of expectations that they can and should "do it all." A few will marry men who happily wear the nurturing, stay-at-home hat, though these exceptions may actually succeed in proving Rudy's point that the women who succeed most are those who most resemble men.

Distilled to its essence, the liberal-woman role fits the radical feminist critique of male-dominated society: using men's standards to judge women, except that this time, the male standards in vogue are the same standards men apply to themselves. Those women who struggle to find a balance in community and sociality may better carry the mantle of true feminism, but regardless, their needs deserve respect in both culture and law. While abortion rights may facilitate the harder core, liberal-woman lifestyle, if broad-based abortion rights impede the liberal women seeking balance as well as the traditional women whose opportunities for flourishing also arise from community and sociality, they materially limit the total flourishing in society that recognizing and protecting such rights permits its members.

Women can also scarcely be criticized for rejecting the popular media's latest, heavy-handed presentation of the liberal-woman "extreme," the "girl power" lifestyle. Women espousing "girl power"—or rather, "girls espousing girl power," because the tragedy of "girl power" is that all too often those who adopt this lifestyle are truly girls—seem enticing in the sexual liberation their skimpy clothes and overt behavior suggest, until that apparent power is revealed as nothing more than acquiescence to purely male standards of sexuality and eroticism and then a trade of the sex she thus attracts for other benefits. The lifestyle appears to justify abortion rights because they increase a woman's ability to have sex without consequences, but in practice, the girl power justification for abortion rights is really about benefiting men. True, girl power assumes the woman's ability to withhold sex—after all, there is no "trade" without that power—but such power declines when abortion is widely available and cannot be withheld forever if women are to benefit from trading. Rather, the power to withhold sex is granted by men, and it may not be granted on very generous terms. As Germaine Greer has observed, the content of even preteen, British girl power magazines is so obsessed with getting and keeping men that "[a]ny boy who dipped into this literature would get an immediate and vivid impression that girls are abject in their need for the most casual and uncommitted male attention and think of very little else."[54] Girl power, therefore, is nothing new; women have been doing it in discrete and bizarre ways since time immemorial, and in no way is it empowering or liberating. It is only a form of sexual subservience and male dominance that uses the powerful tools of the popular culture and young people's need to conform to exploit the youngest and most vulnerable, who are unable to see it for what it is. It is the male domination form of what freebase is to cocaine — the purest form of all.

Most women reject these and other extremes of liberal feminism, for good reason and perhaps with considerable consciousness. Mere observation suggests that most women pick and choose, cafeteria style, from the modern options offered, including a few liberal ideals here and a few traditional-style community and social ideals there. In effect, they balance individualism and community, much as Irish law does, in a modern American culture that is increasingly hostile to the community side. Feminism and its justification of abortion rights may not have explanations for such women who pick and choose more eclectically from the cornucopia of opportunities for women, including those that involve traditional motherhood and whistling in the street, but even if feminism denies the validity of such choices, wider society should not. In asking the questions "what is good for women?" and "what do women want?" the deep-rooted concerns of the capable women who seek a balance between liberalism and community and whose work lives are secondary to their family and community lives but necessary to achieve financial goals deserve as much if not more attention as those of the go-getter liberal career women at the top of the social and economic scale. Therefore, if women's interests are the key concern, what is good for community and sociality deserves special attention in an increasingly liberal and individualistic world.

The modern American understanding of what women want has also been limited by the vocabulary chosen to describe it. In Marshall McLuhan's prophetic words, "the medium is the message,"[55] meaning that the medium, or in this case, the vocabulary, of a discourse can determine its substantive outcome. In the political and legal arena, Americans translate their values and aspirations into the individualistic language of rights; we package together a complex set of legal and cultural values, interests, trade-offs— things we want — in a mental box and slap the label "right to whatever" on the top. The fact that something is labeled a "right," with the constitutional and philosophical imprimatur that implies, can very quickly legitimize it as something that *should be* desired. Therefore, when the questions "what do women want?" or "what should women want?" come up, the answers quickly degenerate into "more rights!" In a language dominated by a rights-based vocabulary, it is easy to lose in the shuffle the fact that "rights" were the way we chose to talk about values and aspirations, not the values and aspirations themselves. A rich sense of women's most essential needs and deepest desires— or to coin a phrase, a thick theory of the female good—gets lost in the translation to a rights-based vocabulary.

If abortion was necessary to achieve liberal women's goals that alone might justify legality even if it did not justify its recognition as a right, but if anything, abortion is even less necessary today than it was thirty years ago, when the Supreme Court handed down *Roe*. Even for those who place high value on reproductive freedom, abortion as a right de jure may actually add very little of practical value to women's aspirations de facto. Medical technology and advances in public health now mean that only the most marginalized women truly *need* abortion to avoid pregnancy. Many women may avoid pregnancy by using artificial contraceptives, following natural family planning techniques or not having heterosexual relations at all. We now live in a world where condoms are openly stocked on supermarket shelves and where both women and men encounter new incentives to use them: from the risk of HIV to a hardened legal attitude expressed in souped-up, child support enforcement requirements[56]; corresponding nondischargeability rules in bankruptcy for child support debts[57]; and rules maxing out earned income tax credits, child tax credits and temporary assistance to needy families benefits at two children. Though many fathers may not have realized the consequences when they made their sexual decisions, their sons will. Very different conversations about very different values are going on around kitchen tables with sons and brothers and on street corners with friends.[58] Meanwhile, efforts to increase both male and female awareness of issues that cut to the heart of "consent" such as date and marriage rape and respect for partners have not been wholly successful, but they have been partially so, and women have at least had the opportunity for increased awareness, if nothing else. Therefore, where women have access to appropriate family planning methods, both natural and artificial, and if our society emphasizes the importance of careful decision making and respect for women in sexual relationships, a "right to an abortion" could become irrelevant to a woman's ability to control her fertility in all but the rarest situations. Given these circumstances, "[t]he right to a safe and legal abortion" *actually can* "be disengaged from a woman's right to reproductive freedom."[59]

Questioning abortion rights as tangibly assisting women to avoid pregnancy relies on the assumption that there is a deliberative process related to whether sex will occur and whether contraception will be used. That assumption is not always correct. Presex contraceptive conversations and decisions can be impossible for poor and vulnerable women,[60] especially teenagers, whose sexual encounters may be the least consensual and for whom asserting enough dominance, self-esteem, and knowledge in a sexual relationship to insist on using contraception may simply be unrealistic.[61] Conversations about using condoms, the form of contraception most readily available in a pinch with a good record of success, become bound up with issues of trust, commitment and the status of the relationship at precisely the times when they are most likely to lead to rejection or humiliation, which necessarily has a substantial impact on whether those conversations will occur at all.[62] Circumstances of sexual encounters among the poor and vulnerable may not even give rise to opportunities for deliberation about contraception:

> In some urban poor communities ... sexual activity begins as young as age 11 or 12 for girls and a few years older for boys. The role of sex in these children's lives is neither an erotic expression nor a response to romantic love, but rather a happening — a part of the "warm body syndrome" or the search for comfort. For many urban poor there is neither privacy nor time for loving sexual encounters and many of those which lead to pregnancy (and perhaps to HIV transmission) occur in hallways with both partners fully dressed.[63]

Haunting as these stories are, the role a privacy right to an abortion can play to ameliorate them is minimal at best. Abortion can terminate the pregnancies made under these circumstances, but it cannot solve the real problems, such as violent or oppressive conduct, poverty, and hopelessness. Moreover, society prone to well-she-could-have-just-had-an-abortion sort of thinking may lack incentive to address the roots of those problems. If the risk of pregnancy can play any role in mediating conduct in these situations, and it may not — research shows both that even the risk of HIV infection plays a limited role in discouraging unprotected sexual activity among the poor and vulnerable and that pregnancy may actually be an attractive outcome of sex to many such women — the right to an abortion eliminates it. The most vulnerable are also less likely than many to respond to unplanned pregnancy by having an abortion,[64] and so the right to an abortion for these poor and otherwise vulnerable women may carry with it no more practical meaning than it does to the middle-class suburban woman who meticulously uses the pill or natural family planning or the orthodox Catholic woman who already has five children and is unconcerned with the prospect of more. Clearly, the situation of these most vulnerable women cries out for attention, and perhaps the next great contribution of the feminist movement will be what many have been attempting for some time: to eliminate the perceived need for abortion through social work and awareness, helping such women find self-esteem and self-worth and thereby empower them to make hard moral and personal decisions even under very difficult circumstances.[65] The point is that the perceived need for a right to abortion in these situations may really be just that — perceived — and such an insignificant response to the complexities from which they arise as to be dwarfed into irrelevance.

Worse, a privacy right to abortion impedes progress in ameliorating the "serious, lifeshaping costs"[66] of childbearing and rearing both for poor and middle-class women struggling to make ends meet and higher income earners facing an unrelenting ethic of career development. The abortion right starts by telling the woman that her sacrifices to bear the child will not be substantially valued by wider society, when what many really want to hear is how much those sacrifices do matter. When the decision to bear a child is completely private, society treats the consequences of that decision the same way and tends to deny special financial or moral responsibility for the child to come — the ring of "well, she could have had an abortion" is all too shrill. Evidence suggests that men in particular may feel this way, diminishing their sense of responsibility for the pregnancy and therefore decreasing their likelihood of marrying the mother.[67] Public, private and intermediate institutions can take the rough edges off the consequences of childbearing and rearing for both women of many socioeconomic backgrounds through medical support, adoption services, information and parenting classes, support and therapy groups, ever-improving, child support enforcement, public benefits for dependent children, quality daycare, support for employers who hire and promote mothers with families, and enriching afterschool programs, among others, and if the decision to bear and rear a child were not quite so private, these forms of assistance might be a higher societal priority.[68]

So back we come, full circle, to the most enthusiastic champion of abortion rights, the liberal woman, thirty years after *Roe*. Is she satisfied with her success? Some such women certainly are. Abortion rights were the keystone of a list of policy changes, legal developments and cultural shifts liberal women believed would allow them to function in the public world on terms of equality with men, safe from the consequences of private sexual conduct and decisions. To a considerable degree in the United States, the policies changed; the law developed; and the culture shifted.

Many women now choose paid work outside the home and make it their top priority. Society has relegated other priorities to positions of individual choice — though it can hardly be said that whether a church is strong or whether a neighborhood is full of healthy, community-oriented families is ever a matter of individual choice — and the policy prescriptions of radical women, interesting and often insightful though they are, have never been considered a serious option to increase women's well-being. The opportunity for flourishing in the workplace has never been more available, and it is hard to find any commentator who does not acknowledge the increased emphasis on individualism in American culture. Abortion rights as part of the obsessive modern American emphasis on individualism undermine community and sociality, at the cost of other opportunities for fulfillment and flourishing. Moreover, it is unclear that liberal women even needed abortion to achieve those goals. Women who rely on career and individual pursuits primarily for fulfillment may have been advantaged. Others, however, have been greatly disadvantaged. After thirty years, the total number of truly flourishing women may not have increased as much as it could have, because in the American balance between individualism and community, the pendulum has become stuck on individualism.

Legal changes may not have caused these powerful social and cultural revolutions, but there can be little doubt that they both reinforced them and made them more extreme. Before clucking that liberal women should have expected to reap what they sowed, imagine someone who never signed on to these liberalizing changes in the society around her, an innocent bystander as it were. Imagine Ria Lynch. Maeve Binchy works hard in *Tara Road* to describe a marriage that would have broken down regardless of the law, for example, but marriages go through good and bad times. In Ria's case, she will be divorced against her will in considerable part because she had the rotten luck to run into a particularly bad moment in her marriage at the same time Ireland reformed marriage law to permit no-fault divorce based on a virtual right to a divorce and after Irish culture had become more forgiving about marriage breakdown.

If Ria were American, however, her position would be no more enviable. Under the law of most American states, divorce is effectively available upon demand. If Danny and Ria Lynch had resided for the past 180 days in a representative state such as Kentucky, they could be divorced 60 days after the date of their separation.[69] In Kentucky, on the request of one of the parties or the court's own motion, a judge may adjourn a hearing for 30 to 60 days to give the parties an opportunity to seek counseling or may even order a conciliation conference, but such procedures are not the norm, and they cannot stop a divorce if one party is determined to obtain it.[70] No grounds other than Danny's testimony that the marriage is "irretrivably broken" would be required to obtain a divorce decree, so any delay would simply be a delay of the inevitable.[71] The real fighting in an American divorce is over division of property and debts, claims for maintenance by one of the spouses and custody of children. Is this "easy divorce"? The decision to pursue a divorce and the economic and social hardships arising from that decision are anything but easy, but obtaining the actual decree itself is a walk in the park. In Kentucky, it is not even absolutely necessary that the other spouse know a divorce petition has been filed.

The economic consequences of divorce differ, but they tend to be most severe on women. Women are rarely the primary wage earners during the marriage, and even in this world of liberalization, many fail to hone their labor force marketability during marriage, when family concerns and children compete with jobs and career for attention and energy, and they can expect very little support from their exhusbands under U.S. law. Child support enforcement improved after the passage of the federal Family Support Act of 1988, but the standards for calculating child support assume that the custodial parent, usually the woman, will pay a proportional share of a statutorially determined cost of raising the children that anecdotal evidence suggests is smaller than the true cost to begin with. Another traditional source of postdivorce spousal support, alimony or "maintenance," is usually available on a permanent basis in Kentucky only if the marriage has lasted more than fifteen to twenty years. Spouses are eligible for maintenance if they do not have or did not receive sufficient property to provide for their "reasonable needs" in a property award; they are unable to support themselves through appropriate employment; or they are the custodians of children whose circumstances are such that it is appropriate that the spouse not seek employment outside the home.[72] Moreover, even if one spouse can show facial entitlement to maintenance based on these criteria, the amount of maintenance payable depends on a variety of factors, not the least of which is the other spouse's ability to pay. Not surprisingly, permanent maintenance awards are rare.

A savvy American woman entering marriage at the dawn of the twenty-first century and realistic about the modern prospects for new marriages may conclude that she must continue to work after marriage, particularly if she has a career that is likely to develop her skills and marketability in the labor force, and *especially* if she has children. Marriages are most likely to end in the early years — 40 to 50 percent, depending on the study, within the first fifteen years of marriage — before entitlement to maintenance kicks in, but after the first children are born and while they are still in their minority. Most women hope to gain custody of their children after divorce, but a property settlement plus child support is unlikely to allow a woman to support herself and her children because few marriages end with the couple having significant assets other than retirement programs, if they even have those. An otherwise young, able-bodied woman will be considered able to work for maintenance purposes, and few divorcing couples on the verge of maintaining two households on the same income with which they probably struggled to maintain one will have the luxury of one spouse not working to raise children. A woman's economic survival after marriage — that is, economic survival without welfare, bankruptcy, crime or support from family —can be a desperate struggle and will in most cases depend on a woman's ability to draw as large a paycheck as possible. The facially liberalizing near "right" to a divorce creates practical economic consequences that limit the range of many women's life choices.

The message any wise American parents would give their daughter is simple: Wise women become working women in modern American life, and therefore, *wise women become liberal women.* Thus, liberalism in law begets liberalism in culture, but it is a trend that speaks more to fear than to fulfillment. The role of "stay-at-home-mom" is one fewer and fewer women can afford, thereby dressing even the unwilling "traditional woman" in liberal garb. The extent of a woman's ability to "be more like a man," as Professor Higgins put it in *My Fair Lady*, is likely to bring her the greatest success on the terms under which she joined the liberal world — money, stability and security — but not necessarily fulfillment.

For these women, it is unfair simply to cluck that liberal women have reaped what they have sown in family law. Liberal women, men, and corporations may have sown, but *every* woman reaped —for many, there was very little freedom or individual choice about it — including many otherwise traditional women and those who sympathized but did not adopt liberal thinking as a whole, who picked and chose from the attitudes and philosophies more carefully, who confronted the rough-and-tumble, sex-blind workplace equality with greater vulnerability, and whose opportunities for flourishing were more fragile. Many of the strategies to ameliorate the effects of these huge changes in foundational family law — more generous child care benefits, for example — arguably make matters worse, leaving the children many mothers would prefer to raise themselves with strangers while lowering the cost of care and therefore increasing the marginal benefit of work. Yet in an almost haplessly snowballing sort of effect, they seem almost necessary for a humane society in the face of modern realities. All of these immense forces had their further inevitable role to play in altering the varying communities—family, neighborhood, church and other shared goods— that provided so much meaning to the lives of those most unwillingly caught up in the maelstrom. For them, a very important shared good has been lost. The American fascination with rights, the adoption of a constitutional right to an abortion, and the effective right to divorce in the United States have not increased women's options, opportunities and potential for flourishing and fulfillment as much as one might expect, but they have certainly picked a different set of winners and losers among women and justified the choice.

Demystifying the right to an abortion opens the door to a deeper understanding of what policies, protections and agreements among citizens might help create a society where women, men and even unborn children have their best chance of flourishing and finding fulfillment. Rights talk by even the most sophisticated thinkers within the liberal democratic tradition has degenerated into a method of avoiding the most foundational problems of community life; it limits and closes off conversations about what is good and what people should want, instead of inviting all citizens to the sort of educative and community building dialogue and mutual inquiry that is itself both just and fulfilling and that the Irish have hesitantly undertaken.[73] By setting aside the right to an abortion or looking critically at the fallout from easy divorce, a community, as opposed to a set of individuals, frees itself to give attention to how it might show respect for women, their unique creative capacity, and their many complex and fulfilling aspirations. The community can identify and take the necessary steps to enhance every member's place in the society, instead of allowing the rights construct to isolate some members of the community from others and to eliminate the community's responsibilities toward those members.

A comparison even with the way the Irish have tended to talk about rights reveals a different way of thinking about people's aspirations. Where U.S. law emphasizes a set of civil rights related to individual activity or activity of a pair in privacy to describe aspirations, such as the right to marry,[74] the right to raise one's own children as one chooses,[75] the right to pursue a calling,[76] the right to procreate,[77] the right to privacy,[78] the right to an abortion,[79] and free exercise of religion, Irish law and commentary reveals potentially different ways of thinking about rights: rights that facilitate sociality and imply corresponding obligations.[80] The right to life of both the born and unborn are rights calling on the state and therefore society generally, to fulfill duties to other members of society. Irish children are entitled at least to a free primary education, thereby facilitating sociality and the provision of education. Family rights entitle families to State (and societal) protection and therefore protection for a form of social activity. A social institution, that of marriage, is still rhetorically protected, though time will tell what this means in light of the removal of the provision barring dissolution of marriage. The religious freedom provisions guarantee free profession and practice of religion, but only after "[t]he State acknowledges that the homage of public worship is due to Almighty God" and pledges to "respect and honour religion." William Binchy draws on this tradition when he speaks of the "right to a permanent marriage" or public protection for a form of relationship and sociality that facilitates human flourishing.[81]

Perhaps what many women want has more to do with shared goods, that is, with the kind of family, community and society in which each lives. The Catholic and secular teaching that humans realize themselves and flourish in families and social groups speaks to some extent to all humans, but it may speak with particular intensity to some. Watching children grow and develop their personalities, meeting other women with strollers on the street and comparing notes, gossiping around the coffee machine, interacting in Bible study and prayer groups, establishing a neighborhood watch program, working together on local disaster relief, watching the sun go down holding hands—these can have as much to do with fulfillment and flourishing as career and individual achievement. Perhaps what some want instead of individual rights are shared goods: to live in a particular type of town, city or other society, such as one where religious associations are strong, where societal supports for marriages are such that they are free within their family unit to do things (such as stay at home and raise children) that might make them vulnerable outside marriage, and where there are no abortion clinics to tempt and undermine their values. Perhaps what many want is the opportunity to live in an interlocking community of fairly like-minded persons who have hazarded their fortunes together for better or worse. There may be no right to such a lifestyle, but sometimes what makes life worth living is the freedom to give up freedom in order to live in harmony with others.[82] A better law would honor that principle.

Imagine, for example, a woman whose primary fulfillment comes not from a career (though she may have one), but from her family, her church and the community of shared values—the community of memory—around her. She has raised fine children, provided a comfortable home and touched many lives. She is in every way a citizen we should and do value. But if she becomes pregnant with one child too many; if her husband strays during a midlife crisis; if she must choose between satisfying her children's material desires and providing the presence of a nurturing parent; or if she is simply a more desperate and more realistic version of Ria Lynch, our modern notions of protection for women such as legal divorce, the right to an abortion, tougher child support laws and equal pay for equal work offer almost nothing to support her aspirations and provide fulfillment, and worse, abortion and divorce rights may primarily undermine the foundations of their lives.[83] The same is true of many less traditional women; even the apparently most liberal woman in theory becomes more traditional in fact when the baby is on the way or her vulnerability in her relationship is exposed, as the example of young career women who marry, leave their careers for at least a time to raise children, and ultimately never get back on the fast track, prove. Modern notions of rights—particularly in abortion and divorce—do much to undermine many women's aspirations and serve as barriers to their fulfillment because they alter and destroy the communities—families, neighborhoods, circles of friends, villages and towns, and churches—from which for many that fulfillment arises.

NINE

Keeping Their Rough Edges: Constitutional Consent in Ireland

> If I wasn't from Ireland, I think I'd look at everything in an entirely different and much more bland way. In a way, I almost enjoy the completely buggered up psyche of Ireland. At least it's interesting. Everybody in Britain and America, they're always trying to smooth everything over and make it all nice and palatable for everyone, multiculturally. But that tends to dilute the rougher edges. I think it's important to keep your rough edges.
>
> — Neil Hannon [1]

The landscape left in the wake of the legal rights battlefield in the women's liberation movement is obscure. The promises of real liberation and genuine life choices were so intoxicating that the actual results from the abortion and divorce law aspects of the movement do not live up to expectations. The challenge of honoring *all* women's aspirations has not been met. For women whose aspirations and needs are bound up with relationship, interaction, community, mutual support, duty and other complex intangibles without solid foundations in modern U.S. constitutional law, the extreme consequences of abortion rights and liberalized divorce have had significant disadvantages and may have been counterproductive. Rights alone do not address those women's needs or give voice to their aspirations.

The foundations of Irish abortion and divorce law contain seeds for U.S. legal foliage that would enhance these women's potential for fulfillment and flourishing while also honoring other aspirations and needs. Of course, Ireland's communitarian lessons will be academic only until Americans abandon the limiting intellectual shackles of national abortion rights, but as discussed in chapter eight, women might not miss much if they did. The Irish have also been shackled — by small size, peripheralism, and the colonial experience — but those handicaps also created a comparatively homogeneous society of shared history and values nurtured at home. The process was not pretty; for example, poverty and materialism justified the Irish diaspora which scattered those most likely to dissent around the globe. Nevertheless, the twenty-first-century Ireland that emerged in the wake of these challenges is a society enriched by shared values and a willingness to compromise; support for favored values without converting dissenters into societal losers; and true liberty that arises from a balance between new individual rights and a longstanding, overlapping network of communities and associations within which individuals flourish. There is much to admire in such a culture, but the American experience of vast size, cultural heterogeneity and independent spirit is so different that lessons from the Irish experience may initially seem irrelevant. On second glance, however, the United States is also a patchwork of many smaller and more homogeneous "communities of memory" — states, cities and towns — similar to modern Ireland and its municipalities. Legal principles that respect a healthier balance between community and individualism could reinvigorate U.S. law and society through their constituent parts. Yes, the Irish do have things to share.

Perhaps the most significant insight to be gleaned from Irish abortion law is the process that made it, which produced a set of foundational principles crafted with negotiation and compromise. Both Ireland and the various American states had statutory criminal bans on abortion prior to the constitutionalization of the law, though in the United States, several state statutes were on their way to repeal or amendment by popular demand. Modern Irish abortion law has developed through democratic constitutional referenda within the context of a national debate that seeped through to discussion on an individual scale over a period of twenty years. The process of crafting the law occurred through individual citizens, both as activists in prolife and prochoice groups and as referendum voters. The judiciary participated but did not lead in interpreting the products of those referenda. The legislature ultimately formulated the referenda language and the information bill. President Robinson used her constitutional powers to bring the judiciary back to the table in the information bill reference. Since the information bill, an all-party Oireachtas committee engaged in an extensive study of abortion over several years, including lengthy hearings and numerous expert and lay submissions.[2] A government committee released another comprehensive "green paper" on the subject.[3] Armed with this background, the government approached the people again in 2002 with another complex and highly nuanced referendum and supporting legislation. The process has not always been pretty, but it has been democratic, with numerous opportunities for Irish in all walks of life to participate and have a real impact on the outcome. *Roe* v. *Wade*,[4] on the other hand, made a nationwide change in U.S. law which effectively closed off democratic input to that law, even in jurisdictions that strongly opposed it. The rare opportunity to confront questions of personhood in public policy, as Kristen Luker described it, is lost to American citizens.

Because the Irish made their foundational constitutional decision about the right to life through the democratic process as opposed to judicial fiat, their law has greater authority with the people whose lives it shapes. Americans have high respect for Supreme Court decisions, but judicial authority is not limitless. It can get used up, and it stands on both the quality and popular acceptance of the reasoning of judicial decisions. Losing breeds discontent:

> For the winner, a victory in a constitutional case represents a satisfying confirmation of the winner's understanding of American society and its values, and a strengthening of the bonds between the winner's community and the larger society. For the loser, however, the result is something else. To lose a lawsuit in this way—to be told authoritatively that one's understanding of the nation's fundamental values, on a matter of great personal significance, is flawed—can only be a deeply socially alienating experience, both for the individual loser and for the community of which he or she is a member and for whom he or she may indirectly speak. The rejection of a constitutional claim sends a distinctly unpleasant message to the unsuccessful claimant: It says that the claimant was ignorant of the true nature of American fundamental values, and that the nation is not quite what the claimant thought it to be. In serious cases, where the position advocated by the claimant is deeply felt and the object of a strong personal or communal commitment, an adjudicatory rejection can not implausibly be understood to reveal significant differences between the values, and hence the identities of the loser's community and the dominant society.[5]

By contrast, democratic processes, as long as they are seen to be fair, belong to the people who made them and draw authority from the opportunity to participate. Not surprisingly, many Americans continue to deny the authority of *Roe* v. *Wade*, while the opposite is true of the Eighth Amendment, however much dissenters may disagree with it as a policy decision. *X*, *C*, and the information cases also make better claims to the respect of the Irish people because they arise directly from a recent constitutional text. By contrast, the reasoning of *Roe* v. *Wade* and its progeny is cut loose from the constitutional text, which lends credence to the criticism that they are mere "legislation from the bench."

The distinction between winners and losers in Irish abortion law is also not so stark as in the United States. Prolife activists in Ireland are concerned that the *practical effect* of Irish abortion law is little different from that of U.S. law, which they see as allowing abortion on demand, because national and European protections for the right to travel to England effectively give Irish women access to abortion on demand as long as they can afford what is an ever-less-expensive trip, while in large swathes of the United States, abortion is sufficiently disfavored culturally that there may be neither an abortion provider nor information on how to find one for hundreds of miles.[6] The biggest practical difference between Irish and U.S. law may be the set of messages they both send about societal values and membership in society.

Those messages are profound. "What is troublesome about American constitutional policy," writes Donald Kommers, "is that it gives tremendous support to certain kinds or classes of people, but hardly any support—community support—to those persons who have chosen other values."[7] American law endorses abortion by labeling it a right, and there is little room in it to honor the views and concerns of dissenters or to permit their meaningful participation in the law-making process. By contrast, the Irish exalt the right to life of the unborn, but the right to travel and to information acknowledge those who do not agree, and the flexible constitutional amendment process and judicial invitations to legislative activity offer Irish citizens substantive opportunities to participate directly and meaningfully in crafting the boundaries of their abortion law. The law tangibly belongs in some way to every Irish person, while many Americans have been told in their law that their deeply held values do not count.

The missed opportunity to participate in abortion-related law-making has wider implications for American society. A democratic decision-making process related to such a foundational matter is like graduate education in citizenship, further equipping the Irish to cope with other public challenges. No society can ignore decisions about what a just society is; to avoid the choice is a choice in itself. Labeling the greatest challenges social relationships create as "private" and then sweeping them off the public agenda as beyond the pale is a cop-out for a mature democracy. Making core judgments as a society about the duties and obligations of foundational social relationships is hard work, requiring immense civic skill not simply innate in human persons; it is a social resource that must be raised, tended and jealously protected:

> [C]itizens cannot be factory-built or found in electronic villages. They must be raised at home. That rearing takes place in real polities: places

> where community and politics meet, where individuals learn the *habit* of democracy face to face, where decision making takes place in the context of communal interdependence.[8]

There are risks to excessive majoritarianism in the law; to be sure, the *X* case did much to help average Irish persons understand what it meant to walk around in dissenters' shoes, and therefore the subsequent travel and information amendments were less about the Irish protecting dissenters than they were about the Irish fearing that they might one day be numbered among the dissenters. Yet looking in one's neighbor's eyes and seeing oneself is the stuff of which some of the best compromises and the best foundations for stable societies are made, a valuable education in citizenship and the risks and responsibilities of democracy Americans miss.

The comparative messages Irish and U.S. law communicates about societal values become especially urgent when a baby is on the way and decisions about carrying it to term must be made. The practical effect of Irish abortion law may not actually be much different from that of the U.S. law, but Ireland tells a pregnant mother that the unborn child she is carrying and her act of carrying it to term are valued highly in Irish society, a message that reaches not just women in crisis pregnancies, but *all* mothers, even while the rights to travel and to information send a quieter liberal message about the importance of individuals and autonomy. U.S. law sends an equally powerful but more absolute message. "When a country's law states that abortion is a 'right' which can be exercised without having to give any reason, it sends out a powerful message about the value of human life into society, a message that has potentially far-reaching implications," Mary Ann Glendon has said.[9] Ignoring the possible humanity of the unborn child and transforming a woman's pregnancy into a disposable matter of personal choice denigrates the choice to bear the child and casts doubt on the security of others whose status as humans may be obscured by uncertainties, exigencies or ideologies of a given time.

Ironically, the Irish legal regime, criticized by so many commentators for interfering with women's rights that are supposed to be empowering, itself actually empowers women in their dealings with boyfriends, husbands, family and friends over the abortion decision, particularly if they want to keep their children.[10] When a behavior is illegal, it is easier to say "no," even under pressure and especially when that would have been the decision maker's inclination anyway. Irish law reminds all the participants what the socially preferred decision is and holds a woman's support circle and society at large partially responsible to help her carry the child to term. By contrast, a behavior's status as not only legal but also as a cherished right, also becomes a "linchpin of a structure of values" that transforms the thinking and conduct the decision maker, the support structure around her, and society at large.[11]

Admittedly, the Oireachtas could do more to help mothers with unplanned pregnancies. An early goal of the new Irish crisis pregnancy center program is to determine what practical supports women need to carry such a pregnancy to term and then provide them,[12] but the program is still in its infancy. Irish statutory law has honed a counseling framework that already existed in women's health and advice centers, which could be exploited to materially help women facing tough decisions. Many who support abortion rights recognize that informed consent and counseling requirements that could not currently pass constitutional muster in the United States often benefit women in crisis and are not necessarily efforts to talk vulnerable women in crisis out of abortions. Several European jurisdictions with laws allowing abortions in numerous circumstances also wax eloquent about the value of unborn life in their written law and require waiting periods of a week or more before proceeding with abortions and extensive counseling by American standards.[13] Academic research shows both that the pressures of crisis pregnancy can overwhelm attempts at a reflective process about the abortion decision and particularly that pressure from male partners or those partners' failures to be available for material and emotional support may tip the scales in favor of abortion when even slightly different circumstances might have produced a different decision. Feminist Ruth Colker urges that jurisdictions be permitted to develop "mechanisms to encourage women to consult other people" and to "improve a woman's deliberative process about abortion," such as group counseling and consciousness-raising groups[14] so that the woman does not face the decision effectively "isolated in her privacy."[15] In the United States, such mechanisms have generally met with Supreme Court disapproval; the twenty-four-hour waiting period barely survived constitutional muster in *Casey* as an undue burden on the privacy right to abortion, but Colker's proposals would find fertile soil in Irish law, to the great advantage of Irish women.

One disadvantage of allowing virtually no abortions at home but not limiting Irish women's access to abortion abroad is that it is more difficult for the Irish state to shape the decision making process or otherwise regulate abortion provision. The supreme court suggested in the *Information Bill* case that constitutional justice might require that husbands or other interested parties be informed about a woman's decision to seek abortion information, and the information amendment subjected the freedom to obtain information to "conditions laid down by law." Among the conditions to receipt of information could be notification requirements, counseling, or other services, as long as the Irish Supreme Court does not decide that they are unconstitutionally burdensome to the freedom to obtain information. Of course, even if constitutional, additional requirements for the receipt of information might keep women away from access to such information, limiting both dissemination of information and opportunities for regulation. Therefore, using the point of access to abortion information to regulate the decision-making process and provide services would require careful planning.

Other countries navigate the trade-offs between abortion and carrying a child to term by permitting the abortion but using either carrots or sticks to discourage it. For example, several European countries require that the medical grounds for an abortion be certified by multiple doctors, whatever the medical standard may be in those countries. Dr. Peter McKenna, master of the leading maternity facility in Ireland, Rotunda Hospital, criticizes the proposed legislation that accompanied the 2002 constitutional referendum in Ireland for its failure to require multiple medical opinions that a mother's life is in danger prior to an abortion because "[t]he reality is that no practitioner when dealing with a sick woman would ever undertake such a decision [to perform an abortion to save her life] without consulting widely."[16] Involving multiple doctors does not necessarily limit access to abortions, as Great Britain, with its two-doctor rule and virtual abortion on demand prove, but it might make medical sense if used in good faith, thereby protecting the health of both mother and child. On the carrot side, Sweden, for example, permits abortion on demand early in the pregnancy, and abortion is usually legal until the twenty-fourth week, but Sweden also provides generous social benefits far above subsistence level for mothers to encourage them to carry the child to term and raise it themselves.[17]

As a practical matter, financial support for Irish women in crisis pregnancies and long-term aid prospects for Irish single-parent families will not soon reach the Swedish level because despite the Celtic Tiger, Ireland remains a comparatively poor country with fewer resources to spend. The welfare state came late and grudgingly to Ireland in 1946, when Eamon de Valera opened poorly funded health and social welfare departments. Today, health and welfare programs are well funded given the country's level of prosperity, though the country has the church to thank for its comparatively high-quality maternal health care. Key planks of what some Americans think of as necessary services for young children, however, such as institutionalized child care and nursery schools, are much less available than in the United States, reflecting the societal view that young children should be home with their mothers and the practical fact that money is probably not available to fund them anyway.

Public and private financial support impact the abortion decision in the way they compare to economic prospects if the child is aborted. A poor country with strong respect for motherhood may need to provide less economic support than wealthier countries to mothers in crisis pregnancies to shift the decision in favor of bearing the child, because in the subtle negotiations that occur with male partners, families and friends about how the children of crisis pregnancies will be provided and cared for, even small amounts of support in a comparatively poor society where prospects were modest anyway can meaningfully empower women who want to keep their children. Roddy's Doyle's comic novel, *The Snapper*, about the fictional experience of Sharon Rabbitte, who at age twenty is still living in her working-class parents' three-bedroom home with four brothers and sisters and finds she is pregnant, illustrates these sorts of negotiations. Of course, Sharon's parents are shocked and embarrassed when Sharon breaks the news of the fact of but not the circumstances that gave rise to the pregnancy, a less-than-consensual encounter with a friend's father. In a voice barely raised above a whisper, her father, Jimmie, asks "d'yeh want to keep it?"[18] Sharon initially does not even understand him, but once her mother derisively translates, "[h]e wants to know if you want to have an abortion," Sharon insists, "[t]here's no way I'd have an abortion.... Abortion's murder."[19] "It is o'course," her father agrees.[20] Later, however, Jimmie's mates at the local pub point out that the person buying "food for it, an' nappies, an' little f------- tracksuits" is going to be Jimmie.[21] Of course, "she'll have her allowance," one points out, referring to the Irish children's allowance paid to the parents of all minors, and even though Jimmie insists repeatedly "I don't care," by now the novel makes it clear that he cares very much.[22] The Rabbittes are the caricature of Irish families used to cramped, multigenerational living conditions with children spilling out of every nook and cranny, suggesting that one more child will hardly be noticed. In Sharon's happy case, when she threatens to move into a flat from the comfortable family home if Jimmie does not treat her with more respect, her father finally realizes she is "the only civilized human being in the whole f------- house,"[23] unwed mother and all, and begs her to stay. Yet even small public benefits make a difference when otherwise benevolent fathers of young mothers feel increasingly "hard done by."[24]

The Irish might do well to tear a page out of the American playbook when they start fine tuning social welfare programs, and interestingly, the most modern developments in U.S. welfare policy are infused with communitarian principles. Before the end of the twentieth century, the bulk of public support for the nonelderly and nondisabled poor in the United States focused on cash payments and other in-kind benefits to nonworking single mothers with children. What both experts and the general public came to understand was that nonwork (and to some extent, nonmarriage) *caused* poverty in the United States and that "gett[ing] a job and keep[ing] it" and "get[ing] married and stay[ing] married" were not only consistent with basic American values but also played an important role in lifting people out of poverty.[25]

Therefore, during the 1980s and 1990s, American policymakers began focusing less on cash payments as a basis for welfare and more on the mutual obligations among citizens. In 1989, among the questions posed to New York's mayoral candidates by Joe Klein of *New York* magazine and later *Primary Colors* fame were "What does the community owe a fifteen-year-old mother on welfare?" and in a break with the past, "What does a fifteen-year-old mother on welfare owe the community?"[26] A few years earlier, New York University, Lawrence Mead identified something called "the civic conception," which required "linking welfare benefits to obligations like work," and he argued the wisdom of work and related requirements for welfare receipt "to ensure, for their own benefit and others', that recipients do in fact discharge the common obligations of citizenship."[27] Communitarian thinking, championed by Amitai Etzioni George Washington University, was in the ascendance.

It was the beginning of the end for welfare-as-we-knew-it. During the late 1980s, state governors requested and received waivers from the stringent requirements federal welfare laws imposed on states so that those states could implement creative local programs to discourage conduct that tended to promote poverty — such as unwed motherhood and nonwork — through the welfare system itself. In 1991, a group of Republicans in the House of Representatives, who ultimately played instrumental roles in the comprehensive welfare reform later in the decade, called for "a new social covenant" between national, state and local leaders who would provide appropriate assistance for human investment programs shown to work, would promote the moral and educational development of youth, and would stop making excuses for "unacceptable behavior" by the poor who the lawmakers in turn called on to "follow the rules" of responsible conduct.[28] By 1992, Michigan Governor John Engler and presidential candidate Bill Clinton were promoting welfare reform that required work for able-bodied recipients under the banner of a "new social contract" and a "New Covenant," respectively.[29]

In 1996, President Clinton and the Republican majority in Congress crossed the proverbial Rubicon of antipoverty and welfare reform with the Personal Responsibility and Work Opportunity Reconciliation Act of 1996, or the "Welfare Reform Act of 1996," which eliminated the cash payment for nonworking single mothers and time-limited those benefits. Such a major change in the social safety net was possible because of the strength of the work support system of the minimum wage, the Earned Income Tax Credit ("EITC"), the child tax credit, state income supplements and EITCs, Medicaid, the child health insurance program ("CHIP"), various child care programs, and child support enforcement.[30] Taken together, these programs reflect a public commitment to poor parents that if they work and try to pull themselves up by their own bootstraps, the rest of American society will give them a boost by pouring cash and in-kind benefits into their wallets. A mother working full time at minimum wage can expect benefits from work support programs that may lift her income to as much as $15,000 per year,[31] much more than within the prior cash-payment welfare system. Therefore an American single woman in a crisis pregnancy of limited means but some ability to work will be able to afford to bear her child. The size of the credit increases if the family has two children, *but not if more children arrive*, reflecting the basic policy of a number of work support and welfare reform programs. Their effects on future abortion rates remain to be seen.

Ireland provides a similar smorgasbord of programs, but with slightly differing provisions reflecting different values. Every family with a child in Ireland may receive the monthly Child Benefit (the "allowance" referred to in *The Snapper*) in the amount of I£34.50 for the first two children and even more per child for subsequent children, I£46.00, in 1999. Ireland also provides income supplements for working poor families through its social security programs, paying sixty percent of the difference between a family's income and an applicable income threshold, which depends on the number of children in the family. During 1998, more than thirteen thousand families received an average of almost I£40.00 per week, an amount comparable to the benefits available from the Earned Income Tax Credit, the flagship of the American work support programs. Ireland also provides a one-parent family payment, similar to the old American Aid to Families with Dependent Children in that the amount of the benefit is determined by adding a base payment to increases for each additional child, though it is not limited to nonworking parents.

Some income support and relief for working families with children is also available through Ireland's tax provisions. Ireland's one parent family tax credit is worth €1,520 for tax year 2002, and when added to the equal single person's tax credit, the total of both credits is equal to the married person's credit, which means that while the credit does not actively discourage marriage, it certainly does not encourage it. A single person who qualifies for one parent family tax credit is taxed at the lowest tax rate for a larger portion of income than single persons without dependent children, and income spent on maternity care may also be entitled to favorable tax treatment. None of these credits are means tested. On the other hand, while the amounts sound extremely generous and exciting at first in a country where the poverty line is approximately €8,580 according to the CORI Justice Commission and the average income twice that, they are not refundable and therefore lack the maximum value for those most likely to be driven in their abortion decision making by purely financial concerns.

The compromises of Irish marriage law also acknowledge the aspirations and needs of Irish women better than the American regime does for American women. Irish law respects marriage as a public act, a public commitment from one party to another, starting with the constitutional statement "The State pledges itself to guard with special care the institution of Marriage, on which the Family is founded, and to protect it against attack."[32] Even though a marriage may now be legally dissolved, Irish law still makes getting that a final decree a chore. Both Ireland and most American jurisdictions have no-fault divorce, but while in the United States a "quickie" divorce is possible with the grounds proved in only a few sentences of testimony, Irish law requires separation of households for at least four years before a decree may be entered. Proving the separation may turn out to be a challenge. Commentators expect that courts will usually require the parties to show expensive separation of households, while in many other Anglo jurisdictions, including the United States, mere physical separation is sufficient to permit entry of a decree.[33] Further, since the constitution requires courts to protect the institution of marriage, courts may require outside evidence to ensure that the parties' collusion does not undermine the meaning of the statutory requirements for a decree.[34]

Irish respect for marriage does not leave those in unsatisfactory marriages completely out of luck, even if eligibility for a divorce decree will be long out of reach. Parties who can live with a lesser level of finality may opt instead for judicial separations, which may be granted after only one year of separation but require a showing of either fault or consent of both spouses.[35] Judicial separation procedures may leave a damper on the number of Irish divorces because for many, separation will constitute a sufficiently meaningful compromise between maintaining the unhappy marriage and complete divorce, particularly where religious considerations intervene. Many American jurisdictions also provide for formal legal separations that divide assets and debts; determine child custody, visitation and support; and award maintenance, but it is rarely used when a decree is so easy to obtain. By contrast, judicial separation for cause and informal separations is becoming even more common in Ireland, while the finality of divorce still remains rare.[36]

Finality may continue to be rare if the potentially cost-prohibitive, four-year separation requirement remains. Like most swords, the long separation requirement cuts both ways for women. The cost of household separation may frighten married women who are still more likely not to work outside the home in Ireland and discourage them from initiating either separations or divorces they may need even for their physical safety.[37] On the other hand, where marital and family status remains an important component of a woman's self- and community esteem, many women benefit from rigorous grounds that leave open greater possibility for reconciliation and communicate the subconscious message that divorce is strongly disfavored and intended to be used only in extreme situations.[38] The separation requirement's impact on the number of decrees entered will depend on how judges exercise their discretion to award what Americans know as *pendente lite*, or temporary maintenance and child support orders. If Irish courts make generous awards to women, particularly those who relied on their husbands' support during marriage, the separation process will be less hostile to women and discourage men from initiating them lightly.

Like the differences between U.S. and Irish abortion law, many of the key distinctions between U.S. and Irish marriage law boil down to each society's respective view of the institution as either public or private. In fact, it is really both. Except for the common law marriages still recognized in some American states, marriage starts with a public act, the state's civil solemnization of the union. Solemnization is not trivial; other unions exist, such as living together, which may be very committed and also involve financial partnership, or merely dating, which is looser, but neither receives special state recognition or benefits. U.S. law focuses on resolving difficulties resulting from individual marriages, treating marriage breakdown as a private matter, while Irish law pays comparatively more attention to *the institution of marriage* as fundamentally public.[39]

Concern for the institution of marriage means extra focus on the external sources of breakdown: preferring an alternate partner or life course, the costs and rewards of separation or divorce, social pressures such as the advice of friends or professionals based on what "reasonable" persons would do, as well as the individual partner's own values, all of which are informed by the societal response to divorce.[40] As the ring of the frustrated expletive "I want a divorce" dies down, external influences go to work determining the future of marriages in crisis— and Irish law starts by giving divorce seekers a long time to ponder them. Then, the Family Law (Divorce) Act of 1996 requires that attorneys for both the applicant and respondent discuss the possibility of reconciliation; provide the parties with contact information for persons qualified to help effect such a reconciliation; and counsel the parties about the alternative of judicial separation as opposed to divorce. The government also subsidizes voluntary marriage counseling services for the express purpose of "prevent[ing], as far as possible, the final breakdown of marriages."[41] The divorce option is available in Ireland, but the law prefers marriage.

Rhetorical support for the institution of marriage partly makes up the loss of the right to a lifelong marriage. The tragedy of Ria Lynch's divorce in *Tara Road* is that there was never a woman for whom an affirmative right to a lifelong marriage seemed so compelling because she symbolizes the hope and expectation that marriages in which men and women make pledges they promise to keep "'til death do us part" really will last that long. Legalized, no-fault divorce based solely on separation and breakdown requirements destroys lifelong marriage because what divorce gives with one hand in freedom, it steals with the other the assurance that the marital union is one for life. Even the mere availability of divorce terminates for all the certainty that marriage is lifelong,[42] regardless of the will, the beliefs, and the religion of the parties:

> When people marry, they commit themselves *not to remarry during their mutual lives.* In a divorce regime, the legal system professes to mishear the commitment that marriage involves and it treats those who have committed themselves not to remarry as if they had made a commitment encompassing remarriage during their partner's life. It is important that the legal system would recognise and underpin people's right to make such a commitment.[43]

Both society and every marriage are materially damaged every time governing authorities delegitimize an institution, such as marriage, that it originally legitimized as a union for life. The message legalized divorce sends to those who struggle desperately through the sometimes cruel challenges of marriage is that their neighbors do not appreciate their struggles even though they contribute to the common good. A society in which the expectation that marriage is a union for life is almost always a reality is fulfilling in itself for its members. Many want their own marriages to last, but they may also want to live in the type of society where marriages generally last because that type of society contributes significantly to their fulfillment and happiness. As Irish political philosopher Isealt Honohan puts it, "[y]ou cannot be a monogamist in a polygamist society, you are just someone with one wife so far."[44] Likewise, you do not have a lifelong marriage in a society with easy divorce; you are just "still together." For many, the latter is simply unacceptable.

Does a right to a divorce or to an abortion have no meaning in the face of women's deepest and most burning needs and desires? Of course not. What makes these trade-offs hard is that some women and perhaps many women — particularly gut-wrenching examples are women with serious marital problems and women who face significant constraints of many kinds on their ability to bear and raise a child — do find such laws a godsend, at least in addressing their immediate problems. Those short-run crises may mask longer-term aspirations, however: The woman who needs a domestic violence order (or "barring" order in Ireland) or even a divorce or an abortion might really aspire to a supportive and stable marriage, circumstances in which a child could be born and raised, and a comforting community of like-minded neighbors where those aspirations can be pursued to their full, and not simply to get out of marriages or avoid births. Addressing those immediate concerns with tools that do greater damage to citizens' underlying life aspirations will not create the kind of country so many of its citizens truly want.[45]

What kind of country a society becomes also depends on the rules by which the society makes that decision. For many years, a school of American economists has studied the dynamics of group political decision making and shaped what is known as "public choice" theory. Their studies critique many aspects of simple majority decision making and conclude instead that supermajority decision rules and decision rules approaching unanimity, decentralized decision making in large polities better promotes liberty and protects against tyranny.[46] The American assumption is that abortion rights as announced in *Roe* v. *Wade* increase women's liberty, but public choice theory demonstrates the irony that while Irish law does not recognize a right to an abortion, it better promotes liberty and minimizes tyranny against women. Application of public choice principles to the Irish experience also shows that decentralized decision making on a state-by-state or community-by-community basis about abortion regulation would be more likely to facilitate individual fulfillment than *Roe* v. *Wade* regime that protected a recognized individual right to an abortion on a national basis.

Economists Richard Wagner and James Gwartney argue that as a result of the growth of government and the changing locus of what is considered acceptable government activity, the American view of what government is for has changed from a "*consensual arrangement* designed for the *mutual betterment* of all" to "an agency through which we pursue objectives *favored by a legislative majority*."[47] The difference between the two is simple: Consensus means everyone wins, while majority rule means that some win — those sufficient to create a legislative majority, which may not be a majority themselves — but some lose, maybe those who care most about the issue. "Most Americans are virtually oblivious to the inherent conflict between majoritarian government and the liberty of individuals,"[48] which is that the minority find themselves almost wholly out of luck, possibly required to endure a legal regime antithetical to their most cherished values, goals, and hopes, precisely the opposite of liberty and fulfillment.

A decision rule requiring a supermajority or unanimity to regulate citizens' activities requires that the interests and concerns of potential dissenters to the proposed regulation be placated or that their other needs be addressed by the polity in the form of a "trade" in order to cobble together a sufficiently large coalition of votes in order to regulate. Decision making of this type is constitutional order: "a complex network of trades based on consent — that is, mutual agreements between parties" — that produces unanimous consent for public activities.[49] Though information decision making by unanimity in many church and civic groups is common in practice, most Americans are wedded in theory to simple majority rule and are unaware that the United States Senate, for example, operates roughly by unanimity. Senate rules allow individual senators to put "holds" or temporary vetoes on disfavored bills and to filibuster, speaking indefinitely on a piece of legislation so that it may never be brought to a vote. The Senate's formal procedural rules are so cumbersome that it routinely acts by unanimous consent to bypass them. To obtain unanimous consent for all these purposes, Senators trade votes on one matter for another, insist on amendments to legislation, and obtain promises of other more important benefits for their districts. Even if some senators disagree in principle with a measure, all necessarily consent to its passage because without unanimous consent of all one hundred senators, few matters could even be brought to a vote at all.[50] Even matters passed by a bare majority final vote have been acquiesced in by virtually all senators. Therefore, unanimity rules are not more theoretical niceties; in many institutions familiar to Americans, they are the norm.

Critics of supermajority or unanimous decision rules argue that they are really rule by the minority, but that argument is a fallacy, as James Buchanan and Gordon Tullock explain in their classic, *The Calculus of Consent*:

> This line of reasoning seems quite plausible until one confronts ordinary economic exchange. Note that in such an exchange, the interests

> of the two contracting parties clearly conflict. Yet unanimity is reached. Contracts are made: bargains are struck without the introduction of explicit or implicit coercion. In this case, no interest prevails over the other; both interests are furthered. *When parties trade, both benefit.*[51]

It is true that in a polity with a rule requiring a 75-percent majority to regulate, if only 74 percent can be mustered, it may appear that the other 26 percent have thwarted majority rule. On the other hand, taken individually, the 26 percent would have been thwarted had the regulation been enacted with only 74 percent support, just as each member of the 74 percent is without the regulation. Perhaps trading efforts did not succeed in reaching a 75-percent majority because it is very important to the 26 percent to avoid regulation in this situation while it is less important to the 74 percent that regulation occur. In other words, the 74 percent were not willing to give enough in return for even one more percent of the total vote. Utility to the entire society has been optimized in this situation, despite the fact that 50 percent plus one would have enacted the regulation under simple majority rule.

Regulation of abortion may mean either limitations or increases in its legality. In nature, abortion occurs in the absence of public approval or sanction; therefore, laws that make abortion illegal appear to be forms of regulation that economic public choice theory argues should occur only where supermajority or unanimous support is present. On the other hand, at the most foundational level, when rules to govern future rule making are being made, few citizens would consent to rules that allow the taking of their lives without giving them a veto over that decision; instead, most of us would demand that such rules could not be enacted without near unanimous or unanimous support even if the costs of reaching those decisions were very high.[52] Therefore, a rule liberalizing abortion laws can be regulation as well.

An initial decision on whether the unborn are fully human beings and citizens becomes imperative in foundational decision making about how abortion will be regulated and what regulation will even mean. As the Irish Supreme Court noted in the *Wardship* case, the mere fact that people may be physically unable to exercise their rights does not divest these people of those rights or citizenship, and therefore, if the unborn are fully human beings and citizens, they should have some voice in the foundational decision about how abortion regulation should be crafted. They would be expected to demand a rule of unanimity or virtual unanimity before any law permitting abortions was enacted and other protections for their right to life, given that they have no other way to protect it. Of course, born persons may find it in their interest to restrict abortion even if unborn persons are not recognized as fully human, because some societies will find "benefits" of legalized abortion to be so small that they outweigh the disadvantages to others or that trading adequately addresses the concerns of dissenters, but if the born do not choose to recognize the humanity of the unborn and make rules in their interests, abortion law in that jurisdiction may be significantly affected. Not surprisingly, in Ireland, where the unborn are accepted as fully human, the constitutional "rules of the game" mean that decisions to permit abortions are regulation and the law has remained stable only when a supermajority agrees to liberalize the law.

In the United States, on the other hand, because abortion is a right protected by the Constitution, one person may challenge a regulation — a legal limitation on abortion — and such burdens on the right to an abortion are regulations that will be deemed improper without at least a supermajority in support of a constitutional amendment on the subject, a Herculean task. From the perspective of public choice theory, the constitutional-level decision rule, that is, the decision rule that governs how future decisions to regulate will be made — that a constitutional amendment or supermajority is needed to regulate — was not made by even a majority of Americans; the Supreme Court made that decision. Immediately, *Roe* v. *Wade* raises a red flag warning of impropriety. Yet the important point of comparison between the American and Irish experiences is that while U.S. law teaches that a very high degree of agreement should be necessary to regulate abortion, the Irish experience shows that there is nothing remarkable about requiring a very high degree of agreement before *permitting* abortion.

Irish abortion law is an example of law and regulation in a constitutional order where mutually beneficial trades leave everyone better off. The Irish recognize the humanity of the unborn in the Eighth Amendment, a consensus principle enacted by a supermajority of the Irish people, and many of the voters who opposed the Eighth Amendment referendum probably just favored a different antiabortion wording.[53] Over a short period of time and using very direct means, the Irish people made more trades among themselves— maintaining right to life for the unborn in return for rights to information and travel and tacit agreement that suicide threats are a justification for an abortion — to produce a comprehensive law of abortion that is unlikely to change soon. The 2002 referendum was a particularly complex set of potential trades, but even it could not garner majority support. Further, the travel and information amendments are special trades because they ensure that no dissenter is damaged more than rhetorically; Irish women can, in fact, obtain abortions virtually on demand elsewhere while not overburdening those in Ireland who do not want legalized abortion to be part of local life. Irish law is a consensus law, and if consensus regulation is a bellwether of liberty, Irish abortion law can be said to promote it.

For one of the few times in their history, size and homogeneity may be on the Irish side because it is easier to bring a small group to consensus or a near-unanimous decision, and consensus politics protects liberty and promotes fulfillment. "Near" consensus may exist anyway, decreasing the number of trades necessary to reach consensus in smaller and more homogeneous communities. Compare trying to amend the United States Constitution, with its two-thirds decision rule and the massive investment of resources required to meet that requirement, to the relatively brief, Irish referendum campaigns over and over again tinkering with the precise contours of abortion law. Small communities where general consensus on foundational principles exists can "afford" rules that restrict individual activity because those rules will impose on relatively few members of the community.[54]

Perhaps the most important distinction between U.S. and Irish abortion law challenges American acquiescence in nationalizing that law: the ability to travel or move to find a more desirable legal regime. If several political units are available to an individual person, the external cost to that person of a decision in one political unit is minimized because that person can simply move to another political unit, the equivalent of moving from town or state to another for a lifestyle more conducive to the individual's flourishing,[55] creating another criterion for application of the principle of subsidiarity. Judge Frank Easterbrook of the United States Court of Appeals for the Seventh Circuit explains the phenomenon as follows:

> Competition depends on movement: consumers can turn to other vendors, producers can turn to new sources of supply or build new plants in different places. Inputs into production move, finished goods move, capital and labor move. The role of private ownership in this process is widely understood. What is less recognized, but no less vital, is that laws themselves can move — or, what is the same thing, money, goods, and people can move to the laws. A corporation dissatisfied with one state's law can reincorporate in another, effectively choosing the rules of law that govern its operations but leaving the operations themselves unaffected.[56]

Mobility of peoples or "voting with your feet" also keeps polities honest. If a polity regulates such that too many people are disadvantaged, too many may move, creating disincentives to regulate further.[57] The United States has a history of migrations of peoples searching for more advantageous legal and cultural conditions; it is, after all, what the Pilgrims did.

Other examples abound: Just a few include the great migration of black Americans from the South to the North; the movement of Mormons to Utah and other western states; and the gravitation of gays to San Francisco and more liberal communities. In this way minority groups may be empowered; they have more impact on the law and culture of a small community where they are a comparatively large portion of the population than they would in the entire United States, for example. This sort of analysis may also aid federal polities in determining how to apply the principle of subsidiarity.

Ireland offers two opportunities for movement to decrease the costs of abortion regulation to dissenters from that law. First, Irish persons may leave the country temporarily to obtain an abortion legally elsewhere, at some cost, but perhaps at less cost than other Irish persons would experience if abortion were widely available in Ireland. For Americans living in jurisdictions where abortion is legal but just not readily available, travel for an abortion is also unimpeded but often necessary. In this sense, Irish women who seek abortions are no more disadvantaged under their constitutional scheme than many American women who have a right to abortion.

Second, for antiabortion adherents in jurisdictions where abortion is legal, widely available, and openly part of the culture, or for those living in Ireland but preferring the former type of culture, the modern European Union offers significantly greater freedom to relocate permanently to more advantageous regimes. The Irish have a long and checkered history of emigration, particularly to Britain, where abortion is available virtually on demand, so resorting to emigration solutions in the Irish context no doubt leaves a bad taste. On the other hand, it is also not difficult to imagine an Irish person satisfied with the current state of abortion law scratching her head wondering why Ireland should have to change and she be disadvantaged when so many other countries offer the lifestyle options dissenters prefer. For those most burdened by Irish abortion law — and Irish law is now such that only a few can be said to be so burdened — the option is available and may even be desirable, especially since in such a situation, it is unlikely that abortion is the only bone of contention between the actor and wider Irish society. This analysis supports the views of the dissenters from the European Court of Human Rights' decision in *Open Door* v. *Ireland* that a wide margin of appreciation should be granted the high contracting parties for regulation of morals; dissenters, after all, can take national legal regimes into account when making locational decisions, and again, everyone benefits.

By contrast, permanent relocation does not help Americans who dislike the abortion law under which they live, because that law is national.

At first glance, U.S. and Irish abortion law appears to have been made at the same level of government, but Ireland, with its small size, more resembles an American state. In a federal system such as the United States', the states are actually sovereign just as Ireland is sovereign, and at least theoretically, the American states have simply delegated limited powers to the federal government, perhaps not completely different in kind from the relationship between members of the European Union and the European Convention on Human Rights and their governing bodies. While Europeans can move from member state to member state and find radically different laws of abortion, Americans moving from state to state are confronted with virtually the same law, despite the fact that if left to their own devices, several American states—Louisiana, Kentucky and Utah are likely to be among them—would likely restrict abortion's legality if given the opportunity. In fact, strong, but not necessarily majority interest groups are benefitted from winning the battle for federal regulation in lieu of state regulation in the United States because federal regulation changes the law everywhere in one fell swoop and makes those regulations difficult to escape, effectively forcing those who disagree from the economic marketplace or even the marketplace of ideas.[58]

Along with constitutional order, another form of public decision making is "Hobbesian anarchy." The examples of Irish abortion law and the United States Senate make constitutional order look messy, but Hobbesian anarchy really is messy. In Hobbesian anarchy, "anything goes."[59] Trading may occur, but so does violence or "plunder," in which some members of society enrich themselves at the expense of others, also called "rent seeking." Plunder takes from the minority without their consent or compensation[60] and may even result in minority rule over the majority as a result of agenda control and strategic voting.[61] Using game theory, Wagner and Gwartney have analyzed public decisions made through trading and plunder and conclude that while individual citizens may benefit from plunder, trading maximizes utility for society as a whole; everyone gets at least something they want, and plunder is absent.[62]

Roe v. *Wade* and its progeny are products of Hobbesian anarchy in that they establish a decision rule that legalized abortion and abortion rights are the constitutional baseline and that "regulation" or making some abortions illegal required unanimous (thereby avoiding constitutional litigation) or supermajority (thereby permitting constitutional amendment) support, without considering the natural position of those most likely to dissent or attempting to win the consent of the born American people. This rule was established and maintained in the face of widespread discontent without any efforts to trade with or compensate the dissenters, the definition of "plunder." Abortion rights were not even on the overwhelming majority of Americans' radar screens in 1973. Many of the proponents had strong financial and personal motivations for supporting abortion rights, and the most influential proponents were all too often not of the groups on whose behalf they claimed to be speaking—the doctors tended to be men, and the women's activists tended to be well off with other means of protecting their interests.[63] The vehicle through which foundational change occurred, the court system, was the branch of government least likely to be driven by consent, and the decision's reasoning did not even clearly arise from the text of the United States Constitution:

> This right of privacy, whether it be founded in the 14th Amendment's concept of personal liberty [as] we feel it is, or, as the District Court determined, in the [Ninth Amendment], is broad enough to encompass a woman's decision whether or not to terminate her pregnancy.[64]

The nature of the *Roe* rights scheme further cut off, legislative refinement of the law and therefore slams the door to opportunities for the sort of political trading through which the Irish now can be said to have consented to a constitutional order. Some, such as the most dogmatic liberal women and a subset of those who had abortions, benefited. For the losers, the loss was total. *Roe* and its progeny tangibly damaged many American citizens—via damage to their principles, lifestyles, and communities—so that other citizens' conception of the good society might exclusively be vindicated, an act that can be described only as the plunder of one group to protect the interests of another.

The Irish abortion regulation experience has numerous lessons for Americans. Individualism and liberalism offer many important building blocks for liberty and fulfillment, but for the many people who find a significant amount of their fulfillment in social interaction and group membership, a wholly individualistic law and culture will be detrimental to them. Some reasonable balancing of liberal democratic and communitarian ideals will best promote individual flourishing, and in the United States, where individualism is so predominant, extra attention to communitarianism may be necessary to maximize the flourishing of all citizens. Decisions about issues such as abortion and divorce, where consensus may be difficult, are issues for polities large enough to constitute a community but small enough to permit consensus and with enough competition from polities of the same size to permit citizens to vote with their feet. True, communities will make different choices about their law, and purists on both sides will be unhappy about that, but to the extent that the abortion debate is about what is good for women, wide-scale rights to abortion are not obviously the answer. For many women, the best opportunities for flourishing, fulfillment, and achievement of aspirations will lie elsewhere, and they should be permitted to say through their law where that might be.

TEN

Conclusion

How do I know what I think until I see what I say?
—Fintan O'Toole[1]

On October 31, 1997, the Irish people elected Belfast-native and long-time legal scholar Mary McAleese to be their next president. If Mary Robinson's election in 1991 can be said to have opened the curtains on a period of social revolution, McAleese's election closed those curtains just a little, signaling that the Irish might not want to turn back the clock, but that the "revolution" had gone just far enough for now, thanks.

Superficially, outsiders might have made the mistake of thinking the Irish had chosen "Mary Robinson II" as their president. Both were distinguished female law professors and law reform activists. Both had been active in the abortion and divorce debates of the 1980s. McAleese bears a strong physical resemblance to Robinson, and they share the same first name. As *The Irish Family* observed during the campaign, "[t]he careers of Mary McAleese and Mary Robinson appear to have shadowed each other so closely over the past decade that it's perhaps not surprising that Mary MacAleese now finds herself in the position of being the favourite to succeed her as President."[2]

But superficialities are where the similarities end. Mary McAleese had never held an important government or legislative office, the traditional background for Irish presidents, including Robinson, all of whom had been distinguished former legislators and loyal party activists. Robinson was a seasoned Labour party politician, while McAleese had been nominated for the presidency by the long-time establishment party of Irish government, Fianna Fáil. McAleese had also served as legal counsel and an advisor to both the prolife and antidivorce campaigns in the 1980s, while Mary Robinson was on the opposite side, representing the Dublin Well Woman Centre before both the Irish Supreme Court and the European Court of Justice. Like President Robinson, President McAleese did not make her views on abortion and divorce a centerpiece of her campaign, but they were known and discussed, even while she dressed herself in more modern philosophical garb, striking a pose as a modern Catholic woman whose religiosity was private and individualistic, with little impact on what her public life as President of Ireland would be.[3] Her alleged connections to Sinn Féin, the political party often linked to the Irish Republic Army, got much more press than her former social activism, and her campaign theme, "Building Bridges," was taken to refer to North-South relations. But not unlike Robinson, McAleese was herself a social bridge as well.

The public conversation in the fall of 1997 as the election heated up indicated some foreboding about what the changing social roles for women had wrought. Betty Friedan had written in 1963 of housewives imprisoned in their homes lacking the fulfillment that careers and public lives—lives in the world of men—might provide. In late September 1997, *Irish Times* columnist Kevin Myers questioned the continued viability of that concern:

> [Friedan's] sentiments ring as true today as they did 34 years ago; but the buried and unspoken problem, that strange sense of stirring, has changed: the problem is no longer women being imprisoned by home, but women being imprisoned from home by the very financial necessity their economic liberalization has brought about.... The price women are paying in Ireland and all over the world is in that part of their personality which feminism declared should be shared equally with males or with the state: the care and duties of child-rearing.[4]

Myers indicted an economic system increasingly fueled by female workers, only the lucky few of whom could now retreat into their "life in the home":

> [F]or many other women, the notion of life as a homemaker, the minder of families, the baker of breads and the creator of the bewitching Sunday kitchen smells of their childhood, is the fantasy which besets them in the bus and traffic-jam, just as once the prospects of freedom from domestic begrudgery tantalised that earlier generation of women for whom the words of Friedan were words of freedom.
>
> It did not work like that. Some of the happiest—and indeed most envied—women I know are those who opted for the once coveted, then reviled, and now coveted again job of home-maker, housekeeper and mother. We leapt from the frying pan into the fire; and some prefer the frying pan but are economically compelled to stay in the flames. Friedan begat freedom begat fiefdom.[5]

Myers's statement was no shot in the dark. A week later, the *Irish Times* published a long feature that was inspired by former American publishing executive Elizabeth Perle McKenna's *When Work Doesn't Work Anymore*, about Irish career women who walked away from lucrative and challenging careers to rear children and live more balanced lives.[6] If *When Work Doesn't Work Anymore* was an exposé of the dissatisfactions of many liberal women with career-as-identity, Anne B. Ryan's 2002 release, *Balancing Your Life: A Practical Guide to Work, Time, Money and Happiness*, was the self-help book, and the annual conferences of the Rural Resource Development and its successor, the Céifin Institute, about the challenges the Celtic Tiger presented to daily life and community, organized and motivated a broader group of activists concerned about the decline of community in Ireland. The "de Valera vision" is hardly back in style, but the gentle breeze of reassessment, or "rebalancing," may be in the wind.

Father Harry Bohan of the Céifin Institute hopes he is a herald of "a new era of 'communitarianism.'"[7] Recalling a question of one attendee at a Céifin conference—"who will raise the next generation?"—Father Bohan remarked that

> When she asked that question, she was pointing out how we have become a very work-friendly society but not family-friendly. But she was also touching into the disconnecting of people generally from institutions of all kinds—family, community, church, state—and how the world of the marketplace, or the world of money, had become central to people's lives.[8]

From the decline in the relevance of the church, cultural sporting groups, and schools, as well as the decline of the extended family of grandparents, aunts, uncles and cousins in raising children and the rise of an economy-oriented culture, Father Bohan sees a fraying of relationships of all kinds in Ireland. "We took the whole world of relationships for granted," he argues,[9] and now there is no time to lose in reinvigorating Ireland's communitarian roots.

The fate of her competitors underscores the symbolic message of Mary McAleese's election at the end of the social revolution which saw both abortion and divorce legalized in certain instances but potentially strong, substantive restrictions imposed on both. The top four presidential candidates were women, but each with very different views. The Labour candidate, antinuclear activist Adi Roche, who had also campaigned against the Eighth Amendment all those years ago, cloaked herself in the liberal agenda and spoke of a "quiet revolution in the kitchens of Ireland."[10] Association with that revolution failed to win her votes, however, as her early lead in the polls collapsed to less than 7 percent during the six-week campaign, amid a public row with former members of her charity. The Fine

Gael candidate, Mary Banotti, symbolized some of the key features of the 1990s' revolution, having divorced her Italian husband abroad at a time when divorce was illegal in Ireland, and she even claimed kinship with Michael Collins, Eamon de Valera's early nemesis. Nevertheless, Banotti, the only elected official in the race, could not crack 30 percent of the first-preference votes on election day, and head to head with transfers reallocated under Ireland's single-transferable vote scheme, McAleese trounced her, 59 percent to 41 percent.

Ironically it was Independent Rosemary Scallon, an inspirational singer known as Dana, who surged on election day, virtually doubling her support to almost 14 percent. Dana's platform was almost purely prolife, and she has the distinction of being the first presidential candidate in history nominated not by a political party, but by local government councils. Dana appealed to those scratching their heads at what was becoming the conventional wisdom of the liberal revolution:

> How can we call ourselves a tolerant and pluralist society if the views of people like me are not represented? We can't claim to be a tolerant country if we are intolerant of people who believe in God and in the family.... A mature confident democracy like Ireland values all its people equally whether they be singers, or sandwich makers or lawyers, whether they be employed or not. It respects the inherent dignity of liberals and conservatives, atheists and believers.[11]

Experts chuckled at her candidacy, but Dana ultimately earned both the grudging respect of many opinion makers and admiration for rising above much of the six-week campaign's pettiness. She has since been elected to the European Parliament on the same platform.

Irish Times columnist Fintan O'Toole wrote at the end of the Robinson presidency that her election had taught the Irish what they thought about the impending social revolution she symbolized. Yet, taken in light of President McAleese's election, Dana's surprising double-digit results, and the enigmatic results of the convoluted 2002 abortion referendum, perhaps the more apt observation is that once the Irish saw what they were saying about social change and what that told them about who they were as a people, they stopped saying it quite so shrilly. President McAleese was open, though not out in front, about her prolife views, but she also told an important Catholic publication that she had advised the Irish bishops in 1992 to support the information amendment to the Irish Constitution.[12] Her campaign slogan, "Building Bridges," was roundly criticized for its vacuity, but perhaps its soothing tones appealed subconsciously to a people seeking hope in community from the philosophical wreckage that their gruelingly serious politics, the meltdown of their church and social upheaval had left in the past six years—a "kinder, gentler" form of social change.

The compromises of the 1990s on abortion and divorce arose from deep roots in Irish cultural soil: the constant tension between the English legacy of liberal democracy and the homegrown Catholic communitarianism. In the 1990s and early years of the new millennium, the Irish reconfirmed a commitment to a substantive notion of the common good respecting the life of both the born and unborn as well as the importance of marriage and familial commitment, while also accepting procedures to avoid tyranny toward dissenting minorities where possible. In other words, the Irish tinkered with the balance between liberalism and Catholic communitarianism during the 1980s and 1990s, but the balance still holds. The compromises made in the process are not wholly satisfactory to prochoice or prolife and those favoring or disapproving of divorce, and they are certainly no one's ideas of philosophical purity. What they may be is a sufficient basis for the Irish people to continue to hazard their fortunes together in a society everyone can live with during tumultuous modern times.

The United States has clearly not done so well. "If you don't like what's on television, just turn it off" and "people who don't believe in abortions shouldn't have one." Americans are used to these rejoinders, the unanswerables of modern radical individualism, that values are purely private and "to each his own." But modern individualism is increasingly about "to each *my* own." In *Apollo 13*, Tom Hanks, as astronaut James Lovell, stares up at the night sky after watching the live broadcast of Neil Armstrong's moon landing and foreshadows its immeasurable effect on American and world culture: "From now on we live in a world where man has walked on the moon," he marvels. Social barriers have also been shattered, with similar effect; Americans now live in a world where abortion is legal, divorce is commonplace, birth control devices are openly available on the shelves of the local Wal-Mart store and fertility drugs are frankly discussed on network television. Only the naive would think we, our neighbors, our communities and our society at large are not indelibly formed and changed by such things. The shared good of a certain kind of community that better facilitates our flourishing and fulfillment and might better facilitate the flourishing and fulfillment of many to come may be gone in many parts of the United States forever. As the example of American women facing the almost fifty-fifty chance of divorce shows, once the individualism train starts to leave the station, the dangers from being left behind are too great not to get on board. And neither is abortion much of a choice where the fact that it is labeled a choice at all simply means that bearing the child has become an optional extra undertaken at a woman's own risk. When modern individualists insist on the recognition of ever more rights without a corresponding recognition of duties, communities and costs, they remake the world in their image and take from those who dissent the building blocks required for their flourishing and happiness. Radical individualists are quick to complain about those who, in an effort to account for duties and communities, "impose their morality on others," but their inability to see the world through anyone else's eyes blinds them to their own sins of this nature.[13] Not surprisingly, *Habits of the Heart* uncovers latent ambivalence about individualism in America.[14] We may be ready for new approaches.

In 1996, the Irish-government-appointed Constitution Review Group issued a report of recommendations for substantive and technical amendments to the Irish Constitution that would remove or sanitize most of its religious and communitarian underpinings, such as the preamble and Article 41 on the family. Gerry Whyte raised a polite hand in mild protest, less at the notion of secularizing change and more from concern that the changes would "threaten the balance" between individualism and a substantive notion of the common good (Catholic communitarianism), which would "reduce[] the potential of the Constitution for promoting the communitarian goal of social inclusion"[15] and eliminate the vehicle for so many Irish citizens' flourishing and community aspirations. The report barely glimpsed the light of day before being quickly consigned to the dark again, but as secularizing constitutional change proceeds less directly through the courts and changes in the mores of the Irish people, Whyte's observations remain urgent. The balance between liberalism and communitarianism holds, but how long will that last? If Catholic communitarianism or communitarianism in any form loses too much of its force in Ireland, are the Irish people prepared for what unbridled individualism will mean? What kind of country would the Irish have as a result? Is it the sort of country they would want? Is it the sort of country they could even live with?

Modern Irish history is the story of strong communal and national voices balanced by individual voices of varying dynamics, with almost constant reevaluation. From this balance, the Irish have nurtured circumstances conducive to human flourishing without tyranny. Their skepticism of abortion and divorce in particular reflects and promotes at a foundational level the vibrancy of the collective and communal voice in Ireland, which in turn respects and promotes the aspirations of many Irish people to flourish and live within the common good. Corresponding compromises protect those who would describe the common good differently from becoming complete outsiders in their own country. The Irish cannot claim an ideal society or even an ideal law of abortion and divorce, but neither have those of societies such as the United States (with a more extensive grounding in and commitment to individualism) been clearly less ideal. In the past two decades, however, the balance between individual and group voices, and by extension, the accepted definition of the common good has come under greater fire than ever before. A temporary and perhaps longer-term calm has been restored, but how the Irish proceed—fine tuning the balance or swerving onto the road of radical individualism—is the key decision for their future. But the Irish really are lucky. Their nation is small enough that mature deliberation may continue to inspire a general consensus to which their history leaves them open. In any event, regardless of the outcome, others can still learn much from their past.

As this book goes to press, the world faces a deadly threat from nations holding weapons of mass destruction. Only a few years ago, our high-tech everyday lifestyles seemed to turn against us when terrorists flew commercial airliners into the World Trade Center. For several days as 2002 turned to 2003, a European cult continued to claim it has cloned human beings, raising ethical imperatives many thought were far in the future. Passion for science fiction in the popular culture has waned; medieval fantasy is now the rage. Though the most advanced weapons may turn out to be our saving grace, it is a time when technology is serving up a generous slice of dismay. Depending on the hands wielding it and the purposes to which it is applied, Eamon de Valera's warning that technology can lead to "sturdiness and vigour and confidence" or alternatively "through demoralisation to decadence and dissolution"[16] has rarely seemed more apt.

Yet we also live in a time when a combination of technology and purpose could render obsolete one of our greatest political and moral problems: abortion. Scientific and technological advances have made both natural and artificial contraception more reliable than ever before. In the twenty years between *Roe* and *Casey*, advances in neonatal care shortened the time to viability by several weeks, and now it is more than another ten years later.[17] Perhaps a time when abortion is wholly unnecessary is within the foreseeable future and when what might in a prior age have been an abortion becomes an effort to save unborn children's lives outside the womb.

The prospect of a postabortion society will cheer most on both sides of the American abortion debate, but that prospect should not serve as a current excuse for the counterproductive state of U.S. law that impedes the liberty it was intended to promote; shows disrespect for the needs of women in crisis; robs citizens of the opportunity to engage their fellow citizens meaningfully in foundational, public decision making; and damages for all members of society key sources of flourishing and fulfillment. Those problems are no less urgent because they are intangible and difficult to measure; that very latency makes them all the more deadly. Why Ireland matters—why this still relatively poor, undeveloped, tiny, homogeneous, and somewhat troubled country is so terribly important to wealthy, powerful American society—is that as individual Americans, we may not be flourishing as well as we should be, and the Irish can show us how we could do better.

This book opens with an Irish exhortation to Ireland, and it ends with a quintessentially American suggestion:

> I'm going out to clean the pasture spring;
> I'll only stop to rake the leaves away
> (And wait to watch the water clear, I may):
> I shan't be gone long.–You come too.
> I'm going out to fetch the little calf
> That's standing by the mother. It's so young
> It totters when she licks it with her tongue.
> I shan't be gone long
> You come too.[18]

Chapter Notes

Chapter One

1. Kevin Myers, *An Irishman's Diary*, March 21, 1997, at 13.
2. J.M. Kelley, *Fundamental Rights in the Irish Law and Constitution* 67 (Dublin: Allen Figgis, 2d ed., 1967).
3. Richard Sinnott, *Irish Voters Decide: Voting Behavior in Elections and Referendums Since 1918*, 278 (1995).
4. Fintan O'Toole, "The State We're In, Fintan O'Toole on the Oddest Political Contest in the History of the State," *Irish Times*, Sept. 23, 1997.
5. See K. Wilson-Davis, "Irish Attitudes to Family Planning," 3 *Social Studies*, 260 (1974).
6. *Irish Constitution* art. 40.3.3.
7. *Attorney General* v. *X* [1992]. 1 I. R. 1, 53 (Ir. S. Ct. 1992) (Finlay, C. J.).
8. Nuala O'Faolain, "Catholicism Needs More Articulate Voices Now," *Irish Times*, June 19, 1995.
9. Myers, supra note 1.
10. Id.
11. Twenty-Fifth Amendment of the Constitution (Protection of Human Life in Pregnancy) Bill, 2001, Key Questions, at §A.4, available at http://www.doh.ie/publications/propkeyq.html.
12. Rory O'Connell, "Natural Law: Alive and Kicking?" 9 *Ratio Juris*, 258, 280 (1996).
13. Garrett Barden, "Discovering a Constitution," in *Ireland's Evolving Constitution, 1937–97: Collected Essays 1*, 9 (Tim Murphy and Patrick Twomey, eds., 1998). See also Donald P. Kommers, "Liberty and Community in Constitutional Law: The Abortion Cases in Comparative Perspective," 1985 *Brigham Young University Law Review*, 371, 175 (1985).
14. Barden, supra note 10, at 9. As Barden points out, this sense of constitutionalism is somewhat different from the more formalized "contractual" view of constitutionalism so characterized by the American founding period. See also Adam Smith, *The Wealth of Nations* (Edwin Cannan, ed., Modern Library, 1937); F. A. Hayek, *The Road to Serfdom* (Fiftieth Anniversary ed., University of Chicago Press, 1994); Frank Easterbrook, "The State of Madison's Vision of the State: A Public Choice Perspective," 107 *Harvard Law Review*, 1328, 1333 (1994).
15. O'Connell, supra note 9, at 279.
16. Gerry Whyte, "Discovering the Philosophical Premises of the Report of the Constitution Review Group: An Analysis of the Recommendations on Fundamental Rights," preliminary draft received from author, at 6.
17. Brian Stiltner, *Religion and the Common Good: Catholic Contributions to Building Community in a Liberal Society*, 7 (1999).
18. Gerry Whyte, "Constitutional Adjudication, Ideology and Access to the Courts," in *Law and Liberty in Ireland*, 149, 162 (Anthony Whelan, ed., 1993).
19. Id. at 163.
20. For a complete development of this point, see Mary Ann Glendon, *Abortion and Divorce in Western Law*, 112–42 (1987) (hereinafter Glendon, *Abortion and Divorce*).
21. *Planned Parenthood* v. *Casey*, 505 U.S. 833, 846 (1992) (plurality opinion written by Justice O'Connor).
22. See, e.g., *Roe* v. *Wade*, 410 U.S. 113, 162 (1973) ("We do not agree that, by adopting

one theory of life, Texas may override the rights of the pregnant woman that are at stake. We repeat, however, that the State does have an important and legitimate interest in preserving and protecting the health of the pregnant woman [and] that it has still *another* important and legitimate interest in protecting the potentiality of human life"); *Casey*, 505 U.S. at 846 (reaffirming "the essential holding of *Roe*," which includes "a recognition of the right of the woman to choose to have an abortion before viability and to obtain it without undue interference from the States"; "a confirmation of the States' power to restrict abortions after fetal viability, if the law contains exceptions for pregnancies which endanger a woman's life or health"; and "the principle that the State has legitimate interests from the outset of the pregnancy in protecting the health of the woman and the life of the fetus that may become a child").

23. See, e.g., Elizabeth K. Spahn, "Waiting for Credentials: Feminist Theories of Enforcement of International Human Rights," 44 *American University Law Review*, 1053 (1995).

24. See, e.g., Mary Boyle, *Re-Thinking Abortion: Psychology, Gender, Power and the Law*, 96–98 (1997). For example, early in a relationship, a woman may shrink from upsetting a man or interfering with his pleasure due to the risk that he will reject her or become angry during intimate and vulnerable moments. Later on in the relationship, giving up condom use can be associated with a trust and commitment threshold the couple has reached.

25. Catharine MacKinnon, "*Roe* v. *Wade*: A Study in Male Ideology," in *Abortion: Moral and Legal Perspectives*, 45, 53 (Jay L. Garfield and Patricia Hennessey, eds., 1984).

26. E.g., *Muller* v. *Oregon*, 208 U.S. 412, 420–23 (1908).

27. E.g., *Mississippi University for Women* v. *Hogan*, 458 U.S. 718, 725 (1982).

28. Glendon, *Abortion and Divorce*, supra note 17, at 10, 13.

29. James M. Buchanan and Gordon Tullock, *The Calculus of Consent*, 89–90 (1962) (explaining that the "rule of unanimity" in constitutional decision making eliminates negative externalities that impose costs on individuals from collective action).

30. William Binchy, "Pluralism, Liberty and the Right to Life," in *Law and Liberty in Ireland*, 132, 145 (Anthony Whelan, ed., 1993).

31. Kenneth L. Grasso, "Beyond Liberalism," in *Catholicism, Liberalism, and Communitarianism*, 29, 54 (Kenneth L. Grasso et al., eds., 1995).

Chapter Two

1. Brian Friel, *Dancing at Lughnasa*, 71 (1990).

2. See Thomas Cahill, *How the Irish Saved Civilization*, 158–96 (1995).

3. Katharine Scherman, *The Flowering of Ireland*, 166 (1981). By comparison, the Roman Church, which had not yet asserted its authority over the unruly Irish, was hierarchical, with high standards of obedience, "materialistic, tightly organized, widely social in intent, intolerantly conformist."

4. Maureen Wall, *The Penal Laws, 1691–1760*, 13 (Irish History Series, No. 1, 1967).

5. Basil Chubb, *The Government and Politics of Ireland*, 4 (1993).

6. Quoted in Gearóid Ó'Tuathaigh, "Ireland's Land Questions: A Historical Perspective," in *Rural Change in Ireland*, 16, 17 (John Davis, ed., 1999).

7. Giovanni Costigan, *A History of Modern Ireland*, 144 (1969).

8. Cormac Ó Gráda, *Ireland: A New Economic History, 1780–1939*, 173 (1994) (calling the famine "the main event in modern Irish history").

9. Leslie Clarkson, "The Modernisation of the Irish Diet, 1740–1920," in *Rural Change in Ireland*, 32, 36–37 (John Davis, ed., 1999). During the late 1700s, other potential foodstuffs, including the grains and meat which had previously figured more prominently in the Irish diet than potatoes, had become so lucrative on the international market that poor Irish could not afford them.

10. F. S. L. Lyons, *Ireland Since the Famine*, 35 (1973).

11. Ó'Gráda, supra note 8, at 214.

12. Cecil Woodham-Smith, *The Great Hunger, Ireland 1845–1849*, 30 (1962) (quoting the Catholic bishop of Raphoe addressing the Irish Poor Enquiry of 1835).

13. Id. at 76.

14. Ó'Gráda, supra note 8, at 192 (quoting *The Economist*).

15. Id. at 192 (quoting Charles Wood).

16. Woodham-Smith, supra note 12, at 122 (quoting *The Times*, Sept. 8, 1847).

17. Id. at 89 (quoting Charles Trevelyan to Sir Randolph Routh, July 17, 1845).

18. Ó'Gráda, supra note 8, at 192 (quoting Charles Trevelyan).

19. Id. at 236.

20. R. F. Foster, *Modern Ireland, 1600–1972*, 340 (1988).

21. Terence Brown, *Ireland: A Social and Cultural History, 1922 to the Present*, 23–24 (1985).

22. Though Liam Kennedy and the researchers working with him question whether the famine caused Irish marriage ages to rise significantly, they do not seriously debate the conclusion that the famine increased the trend toward nonmarriage in Ireland. See Liam Kennedy et al., *Mapping the Great Irish Famine*, 51–59, 209–10 (1999) (hereinafter Kennedy, *Mapping*).

23. See Liam Kennedy, "Farm Succession in Modern Ireland," in *Rural Change in Ireland*, 116, 120–21 (John Davis, ed., 1999).

24. J. J. Lee, *Ireland, 1912–1985*, 522 (1986).

25. I am indebted to Ronan Fanning for helping me understand this point when I met him at University College Dublin in October 1997.

26. See Ó'Gráda, supra note 8, at 218.

27. See Kennedy, *Mapping*, supra note 22, at 50–53.

28. Id. at 54–59; see generally Ó'Gráda, supra note 8, at 214–18.

29. I am again indebted to Ronan Fanning for helping me understand this point.

30. Brown, supra note 21, at 19–20.

31. Tom Garvin, *1922: The Birth of Irish Democracy*, 11 (1996).

32. John A. Murphy, "The 1937 Constitution: Some Historical Reflections," in *Ireland's Evolving Constitution, 1937–97: Collected Essays*, 11, 14 (Tim Murphy and Patrick Twomey, eds., 1998).

33. That the people have "no right to do wrong" is a famous remark of Eamon de Valera's. See Garvin, supra note 31, at 14.

34. Lee, supra note 24, at 67.

35. Garvin, supra note 31, at 18.

36. Brown, supra note 21, at 14–16.

37. Ronan Fanning, "*The Four-Leaved Shamrock*": *Electoral Politics and the National Imagination in Independent Ireland*, Address at University College Dublin, 6 (Feb. 22, 1983).

38. Mary Kenny, *Goodbye to Catholic Ireland*, 11 (1997).

39. Brown, supra note 21, at 34.

40. Brown, supra note 21, at 30.

41. For a concise history of Western philosophy as it relates to abortion and contraception, see John T. Noonan, Jr., "An Almost Absolute Value in History," in *The Morality of Abortion: Legal and Historical Perspectives* (John T. Noonan, Jr., ed., 1970).

42. Pauline Jackson, "Outside the Jurisdiction: Irish Women Seeking Abortion," in *The Abortion Papers Ireland*, 119, 127 (Ailbhe Smyth, ed., 1992).

43. [1939] 1 K.B. 687.

44. Infant Life (Preservation) Act, 1929, 19 and 20 Geo. 5, c. 34 §1.

45. *Bourne* [1939] 1 K.B. at 692 (emphasis added). According to Kingston and Whelan, *English Reports* includes an additional phrase: "Is there a perfectly clear line between danger to life and danger to health? I should have thought not." James Kingston and Anthony Whelan, *Abortion and the Law*, 63, note 48 (1997).

Chapter Three

1. T. Ryle Dwyer, *De Valera: The Man and the Myths*, 94 (1991) (quoting Eamon de Valera) (emphasis added).

2. Raymond James Raymond, "De Valera, Lemass and Irish Economic Development: 1933–1948," in *De Valera and His Times*, 113 (J. P. O'Carroll and John A. Murphy, eds., 2d ed., 1986).

3. This is the apt title of Tim Pat Coogan's sprawling biography of Eamon de Valera.

4. Ronan Fanning, *Independent Ireland* 93 (1983) (hereinafter "Fanning, *Independent Ireland*").

5. R. F. Foster, *Modern England, 1600–1972*, 538 (1988).

6. Eamon de Valera, "The Ireland That We Dreamed of," in *Great Irish Speeches of the Twentieth Century* 206 (Michael McLoughlin, ed., 1996). According to *Irish Times* columnist John Waters, cultural elites in Ireland have been at war with de Valera and the sentiments (such as these)

that he represented since the 1960s, using this speech as primary source material. Waters is certain that while the term "comely maidens" appears in the official text, de Valera actually said "happy maidens" on the air. Because Waters is convinced that the speech became known as the "comely maidens" speech in an effort to ridicule the now embarrassing Taoiseach, I have followed his lead and substituted "happy" in the text. John Waters, *An Intelligent Person's Guide to Modern Ireland*, 41–44 (1997).

7. Quoted in Ronan Fanning, "*Four-Leaved Shamrock*": *Electoral Politics and the National Imagination in Independent Ireland*, Address at University College Dublin, 16 (Feb. 22, 1983).

8. Waters, supra note 6, at 39.

9. J. J. Lee, *Ireland, 1912–1985: Politics and Society*, 540–41 (1989).

10. Gearóid Ó'Crualaoich, "The Primacy of Form: A 'Folk Ideology' in de Valera's Politics," in *De Valera and His Times*, 47, 55 (J. P. O'Carroll and John A. Murphy, eds., 2d ed., 1986).

11. Patrick Kavanagh, "The Great Hunger," in Patrick Kavanagh, *Collected Poems*, 34, 55 (W. W. Norton, 1973).

12. Ronan Fanning, "Mr. de Valera Drafts a Constitution," in *De Valera's Constitution and Ours*, 33, 42–43 (Brian Farrell, ed., Thomas Davis Lecture Series, 1988) (hereinafter "Fanning, 'Mr. de Valera'").

13. John A. Murphy, "The 1937 Constitution, Some Historical Reflections," in *Ireland's Evolving Constitution, 1937–1997: Collected Essays*, 11, 16 (Tim Murphy and Patrick Twomey, eds., Institute of Public Administration, 1998).

14. Tim Pat Coogan, *Eamon de Valera: The Man Who Was Ireland*, 36 (1993).

15. John A. Murphy, "The Achievement of Eamon de Valera," in *De Valera and His Times*, 1, 6–7 (J. P. O'Carroll and John A. Murphy, eds., 2d ed., 1986).

16. John Kelly, TD, "The Constitution: Law and Manifesto," in *The Constitution of Ireland, 1937–1987*, 208, 211 (Frank Litton, ed., Institute of Public Administration, 1988).

17. For a definitive study on the step-by-step drafting and criticism of the constitution, see Dermot Keogh, "The Irish Constitutional Revolution: An Analysis of the Making of the Constitution," in *The Constitution of Ireland, 1937–1987* (Frank Litton, ed., Institute of Public Administration, 1988).

18. Basil Chubb, *The Politics of the Irish Constitution*, 30 (1991) (referring to Loewenstein's colloquial definition of a normative constitution as a "suit that fits and is actually worn").

19. *Irish Constitution* pmbl.

20. Mary Kenny, *Goodbye to Catholic Ireland*, 183 (1997).

21. Brian Walsh, "The Constitution and Constitutional Rights," in *The Constitution of Ireland 1937–1987*, 86, 94 (Frank Litton, ed., Institute of Public Administration, 1988) (emphasis added).

22. Quoted in Fanning, *Independent Ireland*, supra note 4, at 130. This provision was removed from the constitution in 1972.

23. Dermot Keogh, "Church, State and Society," in *De Valera's Constitution and Ours*, 103, 113 (Brian Farrell, ed., Thomas Davis Lecture Series, 1988).

24. F. S. L. Lyons, *Ireland Since the Famine*, 545 (Fontana Press, 1983).

25. Anthony Whelan, "Constitutional Democracy, Community and Corporatism in Ireland," in *Irish Human Rights Yearbook 1995*, 97, 101 (Gerard Quinn, ed., 1995).

26. John Paul II, *Centesimus Annus*, §13 (St. Paul Books and Media 1991) (hereinafter *Centesimus Annus*).

27. Francis Canavan, S. J., "The Image of Man in Catholic Thought," in *Catholicism, Liberalism, and Communitarianism: The Catholic Intellectual Tradition and the Moral Foundations of Democracy*, 15, 18 (Kenneth L. Grasso et al., eds., 1995).

28. *Gaudium et Spes*, §§12, 25, in *Vatican Council II, Volume I: The Conciliar and Post Conciliar Documents* (Austin Flannery, O. P., ed., Costello Printing, 1998) (hereinafter *Gaudium et Spes*); John Paul II, *Familiaris Consortio* §22 (St. Paul editions) (hereinafter *Familiaris Consortio*).

29. Kenneth L. Grasso, "Beyond Liberalism: Human Dignity, the Free Society, and the Second Vatican Council," in *Catholicism, Liberalism, and Communitarianism: The Catholic Intellectual Tradition and the Moral Foundations of Democracy*, 29, 37 (Kenneth L. Grasso et al., eds., 1995).

30. *Gaudium et Spes*, supra note 28, at §25.

31. Canavan, supra note 27, at 22.

32. Id.
33. *Gaudium et Spes*, supra note 28, at §52.
34. *Centesimus Annus* supra note 26, at §13.
35. Canavan, supra note 27, at 25.
36. *Gaudium et Spes*, supra note 28, at §26.
37. E.g., John Finnis, *Natural Law and Natural Rights*, 155 (1980).
38. See, e.g., *Cathechism of the Catholic Church* §§1905–12 (Libraria Editrice Vaticana, Wanderer Press, 1994) (hereinafter *Catechism*).
39. *Gaudium et Spes*, supra note 28, at §30.
40. *Catechism*, supra note 38, at para. 1910.
41. Grasso, supra note 29, at 35.
42. Id. at 43.
43. *Gaudium et Spes*, supra note 28, at §74.
44. Quoted in John Courtney Murray, S. J., *We Hold These Truths: Catholic Reflections on the American Proposition*, 36 (1960).
45. *Catechism*, supra note 38, at para. 1731.
46. Id. at para. 1733.
47. Murray, supra note 44, at 36.
48. Mary Ann Glendon, *Rights Talk: The Impoverishment of Political Discourse*, 9 (1991).
49. Loren P. Beth, *The Development of Judicial Review in Ireland, 1937–1966*, 43–44 (Institute of Public Administration, 1967).
50. David Hollenbach, "A Communitarian Reconstruction of Human Rights: Contributions from Catholic Tradition," in *Catholicism and Liberalism: Contributions to American Public Philosophy*, 127, 141 (R. Bruce Douglas and David Hollenbach, eds., 1994).
51. See Gerry Whyte, "Constitutional Adjudication, Ideology and Access to the Courts," in *Law and Liberty in Ireland*, 149, 161–63 (Anthony Whelan, ed., 1993).
52. See, e.g., T. John O'Dowd, "Dignity and Personhood in Irish Constitutional Law," in *Justice and Legal Theory in Ireland*, 163, 165–67 (Gerard Quinn et al., eds., 1995).
53. See, e.g., Alexis de Toqueville, *Democracy in America I*, 311 (Phillips Bradley, ed., 1945).
54. Id.
55. *Irish Constitution* art 40.1.
56. Id.
57. *Irish Constitution* art. 40.3.1.
58. See W. N. Hohfeld, *Fundamental Legal Conceptions as Applied in Judicial Reasoning*, 35–50 (1923); Mary Redmond, "Towards a Hohfeldian View of the Rights and Freedoms in the Irish Constitution," 1979–1980 *Dublin University Law Review*, 52.
59. *Irish Constitution* art. 40.3.3.
60. *Irish Constitution* art. 40.3.2.
61. *Irish Constitution* art. 40.4.1.
62. *Irish Constitution* art. 40.6.1.
63. See, e.g., *Attorney General* v. *Paperlink Ltd.*, [1984] I. L. R. M. 373, 381 (Ir. H. Ct.) (right to communicate).
64. James Casey, *Constitutional Law in Ireland*, 395 (2000); Gerard Hogan and Gerry Whyte, *J. M. Kelly's The Irish Constitution*, 755–89 (3d ed., 1994).
65. *Const. of Saorstat Eireann*, art. 3.
66. *Proclamation of Poblacht na Eireann, The Provisional Government of the Irish Republic to the People of Ireland*, quoted in its entirety in Lyons, supra note 24, at 369–70.
67. *Familiaris Consortio*, supra note 28, at §42.
68. The article on family, along with that related to education, is "generally thought to have been inspired by papal encyclicals and by Catholic teaching." Hogan and Whyte, supra note 64, at 991.
69. *Irish Constitution* art. 41.1.1.
70. *Irish Constitution* art. 41.1.2.
71. *Gaudium et Spes*, supra note 28, at §52.
72. See Declan Costello, "The Natural Law and the Irish Constitution," 45 *Studies* 403, 410 (1956).
73. *Irish Constitution* art. 41.2.1.
74. *Irish Constitution* art. 41.2.2.
75. While Pope John Paul II has recognized the legitimacy of women's roles in public life as well, his *Familiaris Consortio* specifically insists that women ought not be compelled to work outside the home for financial reasons. *Familiaris Consortio*, supra note 28, at §23.
76. *Irish Constitution* art. 41.3.1.
77. *Irish Constitution* art. 41.3.2. This provision has since been substantially amended.
78. See, e.g., Yvonne Scannell, "The Constitution and the Role of Women," in *De Valera's Constitution and Ours*, 123, 123 (Brian Farrell, ed., 1988); Kenny, supra note 20, at 183. "Until recently there was something approaching a consensus in Irish society regarding the values underlying Article 41." William Binchy, "Marking a Watershed in Irish Family Law," *Irish Times*, Jan. 8, 1996.

79. *Irish Constitution* art. 42.1.
80. *Irish Constitution* art. 44.1.
81. *Irish Constitution* art. 44.2.1.
82. *Irish Constitution* art. 44.2.2.
83. *Irish Constitution* art. 44.2.3.
84. In his dissent in *Lochner v. New York,* 198 U.S. 45, 75 (1905) (Holmes, J., dissenting), Justice Oliver Wendell Holmes railed against the notion that the U.S. Constitution includes an "economic theory."
85. *Irish Constitution* art. 43.1.1.
86. *Irish Constitution* art. 43.1.2.
87. *Irish Constitution* art. 43.2.2.
88. *Irish Constitution* art. 45.2.v.
89. *Irish Constitution* art 45.1.
90. *McGee* v. *Attorney General,* [1974] I. R. 284, 319 (Ir. S. Ct.) 1973 (opinion of Walsh, J.).
91. See *Catechism,* supra note 38, at para. 1826.
92. Id. at para. 1823.
93. Whyte, supra note 51, at 157–64.
94. Mary Ann Glendon, *Abortion and Divorce in Western Law,* 114–19 (1987).
95. Garrett Barden, "Discovering a Constitution," in *Ireland's Evolving Constitution, 1937–1997: Collected Essays,* 1, 9 (Tim Murphy and Patrick Twomey, eds., 1998).
96. See Keogh, supra note 22, at 104–106.
97. Chubb, supra note 18, at 41–42. See also, e.g., *Cook* v. *Carroll,* [1945] I. R. 515, 519 (Ir. S. Ct.); *In re Tilson,* [1951] I. R. 1, 19 (Ir. S. Ct. 1950).
98. As R. F. Foster describes it, the practical effect of the de Valera vision was "to institute a state of 'protectionism', both economic and cultural." Foster, supra note 5, at 536.
99. Gerard W. Hogan, "Law and Religion: Church-State Relations in Ireland from Independence to the Present Day," 35 *America Journal of Comparative Law,* 47, 55 (1987).
100. Enda McDonagh, "Philosophical-Theological Reflections on the Constitution," in *The Constitution of Ireland, 1937–1987,* 192, 198–203 (Frank Litton, ed., Institute of Public Administration, 1987).
101. Id.; S. I. Strong, "Christian Constitutions: Do They Protect Internationally Recognized Human Rights and Minimize the Potential for Violence Within a Society?" 29 *Case Western Reserve Journal of International Law,* 1, 48–58 (1997).
102. McDonagh, supra note 100, at 198.
103. Fanning, *Mr. de Valera,* supra note 12, at 43.
104. Id.

Chapter Four

1. Liam Clancy, quoted in *The Story of the Clancy Brothers and Tommy Makem* (Shanachie Video, 1991).
2. John Waters, *An Intelligent Person's Guide to Modern Ireland,* 39 (1997).
3. *The Story of the Clancy Brothers and Tommy Makem* (Shanachie Video, 1991).
4. Ronan Fanning, *Independent Ireland,* 191 (1983).
5. David B. Rottman and Philip J. O'Connell, "The Changing Social Structure," *in Unequal Achievement: The Irish Experience, 1957–1982,* 63, 65 (Frank Litton, ed., Institute for Public Administration, 1982).
6. Alexis Guilbride, "A Woman's Crime," *Irish Times,* Oct. 30, 1995.
7. Pauline Conroy Jackson, "Outside the Jurisdiction Irish Women Seeking Abortion" in *The Abortion Paper, Ireland,* 119, 128 (Ailbhe Smyth, ed., 1992) (quoting Judge Davitt in *The Irish Times,* 1944).
8. For a discussion of this case, see Peter Charleton, "Judicial Discretion in Abortion: The Irish Perspective," 6 *International Journal of Law and Family,* 349, 350 (1992).
9. Jackson, supra note 7, at 128.
10. *The People (A-G)* v. *Cadden,* [1957] 91 I.L.T.R. 97.
11. Infanticide Act, No. 16, §1(3) (1949) (Ir.).
12. Alexis Guilbride, "Out of Sight, Out of Mind," *Irish Times,* Oct. 31, 1995.
13. Katherine O'Donovan, "The Medicalisation of Infanticide," [1984] *Criminal Law Review,* 259, 263 (citing Criminal Law Revision Committee, Fourteenth Report, Offences Against the Person, Cmnd. 7844 (1980), para. 103). The British Criminal Law Revision Committee addressing the British law in 1980 appeared to adopt the position that the best justification for infanticide laws was a means of excusing certain crimes due to social problems such as poverty, incapacity to cope with the child and failure to bond with the child.
14. Guilbride, supra note 12.
15. O'Donovan, supra note 13, at 263

(quoting A. J. Ashworth, "The Butler Committee and Criminal Responsibility," [1975] *Criminal Law Review*, 687, 694).

16. F. S. L. Lyons, *Ireland Since the Famine*, 357–58 (Fontana Press, 1985) (describing Ireland's neutrality experience as one in which its people were "condemned to live in Plato's cave").

17. Terence Brown, *Ireland: A Social and Cultural History, 1922 to the Present*, 165–66 (1985).

18. Fanning, supra note 4, at 159.

119. Rottman and O'Connell, supra note 5, at 65.

20. Tim Pat Coogan, *Eamon de Valera: The Man Who Was Ireland*, 660 (1993).

21. J. J. Lee, *Ireland, 1912–1985: Politics and Society*, 348–49 (1989).

22. Fanning, supra note 4, at 190–91.

23. Id. at 159 (quoting Dr. Dignan, Bishop of Clonfert).

24. Dermot Keogh, *Twentieth-Century Ireland: Nation and State*, 211 (1995) (quoting correspondence between the secretary to the hierarchy and the government). These were not the hierarchy's only objections, but they were important.

25. Christopher Wolfe, "Subsidiarity: The 'Other' Ground of Limited Government," in *Catholicism, Liberalism, and Communitarianism: The Catholic Intellectual Tradition and the Moral Foundations of Democracy*, 81, 87 (Kenneth L. Grasso et al., eds., 1995).

26. Pius XI, "Quadragesimo Anno," in *Five Great Encyclicals*, 125, 147 (Paulist Press, 1943) (*hereinafter* "Quadragesimo Anno").

27. Wolfe, supra note 25, at 88.

28. J. H. Whyte, *Church and State in Modern Ireland, 1923–1970*, 287 (1971).

29. In *Gaudium et Spes*, for example, the bishops of Vatican II write that political authority "must be exercised within the limits of the moral order and directed toward the common good" and warn that citizens may defend their rights against the abuses and oppression of political authority "which oversteps its competence." *Gaudium et Spes*, §74, in *Vatican Council II, Volume I: The Concilar and Post Concilar Documents* (Austin Flannery, O. P., ed., Costello Printing, 1998) (*hereinafter Gaudium et Spes*).

30. Quoted in Keogh, supra note 24, at 209 (quoting John Costello).

31. See Whyte, supra note 28, at 374–75.

32. Keogh, supra note 24, at 220.

33. See John W. Whitehead, "Accommodation and Equal Treatment of Religion: Federal Funding of Religiously Affiliated Child Care Facilities," 26 *Harvard Journal of Legislation*, 573, 581–84 (1989); Mark Tushnet, "The Constitution of Religion," 18 *Connecticut Law Review* 701, 709–11 (1986); Jennifer E. Spreng, "Failing Honorably: Balancing Tests, Justice O'Connor and the Free Exercise of Religion," 38 *St. Louis University Law Journal* 837, 870–71 (1995).

34. Brown, supra note 17, at 173. Brown symbolizes the tentative change by describing the experiences of the playright Brendan Behan, the novelist Brian O'Nolan, and the poet Patrick Kavanagh, whose modern and personalist works flourished in the 1940s and 1950s despite the obscurity and penury in which they lived.

35. Michael Adams, "Censorship of Publications," in *Morality and the Law*, 71, 72–73 (Desmond M. Clarke, ed., 1983).

36. Id. at 74–75.

37. Id. at 75–76.

38. Brown, supra note 17, at 181.

39. See Adams, supra note 35, at 78; Whyte, supra note 28, at 343–46.

40. Anthony Coughlan, "The Constitution and Social Policy," in *The Constitution of Ireland*, 143, 157 (Frank Litton, ed., Institute of Public Administration, 1988).

41. T. Ryle Dwyer, *De Valera: The Man and the Myths*, 314 (1991) (quoting the inaugural address by Eamon de Valera at the opening of the national television service, Radio Telefís Éireann, on December 31, 1961).

42. Keogh, supra note 24, at 253.

43. Abbreviation for the Irish word for a member of the Dáil, or parliament.

44. John Ardagh, *Ireland and the Irish: Portrait of a Changing Society*, 181 (1994).

45. Mary Kenny, *Goodbye to Catholic Ireland*, 283 (1997).

46. Id. at 267.

47. See Brown, supra note 17, at 226; Nuala O'Faolain, "Catholicism Needs More Articulate Voices Now," *Irish Times*, June 19, 1995.

48. Patrick McCabe, *The Dead School*, 142–43 (Delta Books, 1996).

49. Whyte, supra note 28, at 353 (quoting Cardinal Conway).

50. Basil Chubb, *The Politics of the Irish Constitution*, 50 (1991).

51. Id.

52. Brian Walsh, "The Constitution and Constitutional Rights," in *The Constitution of Ireland, 1937–1987*, 86, 104 (Frank Litton, ed., Institute of Public Administration, 1988).

53. Pope Paul VI, *Humana Vitae* §11 (St. Paul Books and Media, 1968) (*hereinafter Humana Vitae*).

54. Id. at §14. Natural family planning, then limited to rhythm, was a licit means of birth control, according to the encyclical, where there were "serious motives to space out births." Id. at 16.

55. Keogh, supra note 24, at 267.

56. *Humana Vitae,* supra note 53 at §15; cf. Pope Pius XI, *On Christian Marriage*, 32 (St. Paul Books and Media, 1930) (*hereinafter On Christian Marriage*) ("however much we may pity the mother whose health and even life is gravely imperiled in the performance of the duty allotted to her by nature, nevertheless what could ever be a sufficient reason for excusing in any way the *direct* murder of the innocent?" [emphasis added]).

57. That hardening had occurred at the beginning of the century, not in the 1960s, which was the culmination of almost seventy years of consistent pronouncements on the issue. John T. Noonan, Jr., "An Almost Absolute Value in History," in *The Morality of Abortion: Legal and Historical Perspectives*, 40–46 (John T. Noonan, Jr., ed., 1970).

58. *On Christian Marriage,* supra note 56, at 28.

59. Id. at 32.

60. Pope John Paul II, *Evangelium Vitae* ("The Gospel of Life") §62 (Times Books 1995) (emphasis in original) (*hereinafter Gospel of Life*).

61. Bryan M. E. McMahon, "Developments in the Irish Legal System Since 1945," in *Ireland, 1945–1970*, 83, 87 (J. J. Lee, ed., Thomas Davis Lecture Series, 1979).

62. William Binchy, "Marking a Watershed in Irish Family Law," *Irish Times*, Jan. 8, 1996.

63. Loren P. Beth, *The Development of Judicial Review in Ireland, 1937–1966*, 11 (Institute of Public Administration, 1967).

64. *State (Healy)* v. *Donoghue,* [1976] I. R. 344, 347 (Ir. S. Ct.) (O'Higgins, C. J.); *McGee* v. *Ireland,* [1974] I. R. 284, 319 (Ir. S. Ct. 1973); Gerard Hogan and Gerry Whyte, *J. M. Kelly's The Irish Constitution*, cxii–cxiii (3d ed., 1994)

65. See, e.g., Rory O'Connell, "Natural Law: Alive and Kicking?" 9 *Ratio Juris*, 258, 269 (1996) (discussing opinion of the Chief Justice in *Norris* v. *Ireland* and suggesting that his justification for upholding the criminal law against homosexual activity was that the constitution was based on the 1937 community's vision of the good life and that it was improper to deviate too much from that vision in constitutional adjudication).

66. *Tormey* v. *Ireland,* [1985] I. R. 289, 296 (Ir. S. Ct.).

67. Cf. G. W. Hogan, "Unenumerated Personal Rights: *Ryan*'s Case Re-evaluated," 25–27 *Irish Jurisprudence*, 95 (1990–1992) with Richard Humphreys, "Interpreting Natural Rights," 28–30 *Irish Jurisprudence*, 221 (1993–1995).

68. E.g., *People* v. *Shaw,* [1982] I. R. 1, 63 (Ir. S. Ct.) (Kenny, J.).

69. E.g., *Tormey,* [1985] I. R. at 296.

70. E.g., *Shaw,* [1982] I. R. at 53–54 (Ir. S. Ct.) (Griffin, J.).

71. Declan Costello, "The Natural Law and The Irish Constitution," 45 *Studies*, 403, 404–09 (1956).

72. Beth, supra note 63, at 44–45.

73. [1965] I. R. 294 (Ir. S. Ct. 1964).

74. *Ryan* [1965] I. R. at 314.

75. See Paul W. Butler and David L. Gregory, "A Not So Distant Mirror: Federalism and the Role of Natural Law in the United States, The Republic of Ireland, and the European Community," 25 *Vanderbilt Journal of Transnational Law*, 429 (1992).

76. Desmond M. Clarke, "The Role of Natural Law in Irish Constitutional Law," [1982] *Irish Jurisprudence*, 204–13.

77. Examples of Justice Walsh's explicit use of a religious natural law paradigm are *McGee* v. *Attorney General,* [1974] I. R. 284, 305–20 (Ir. S. Ct. 1973) and *G.* v. *An Bord Uchtala,* [1980] I. R. 32, 66–69 (Ir. S. Ct. 1978), as well as his extrajudicial writings, such as Brian Walsh, "The Constitution and

Constitutional Rights," in *The Constitution of Ireland* 86–109 (Frank Litton, ed., Institute of Public Administration, 1988).

78. See Anne M. Hilbert, "The Irish Abortion Debate: Substantive Rights and Affecting Commerce Jurisprudential Models," 26 *Vanderbilt Journal of Transnational Law*, 1117 (1993).

79. T. John O'Dowd, "Dignity and Personhood in Irish Constitutional Law," in *Justice and Legal Theory in Ireland* 163, 163–66 (Gerard Quinn et al., eds., 1995).

80. *Attorney General* v. *Paperlink*, [1984] I. R. 373, 386 (Ir. H. Ct. 1983) (Costello, J.).

81. *State (M)* v. *Attorney General*, [1979] I. R. 73, 80–81 (Ir. H. Ct. 1978).

82. *McGee*, [1974] I. R. at 325 (Henchy, J.).

83. [1974] I. R. 284 (Ir. H. Ct. 1972); [1974] I. R. 284 (Ir. S. Ct. 1973).

84. Criminal Law Amendment Act, No. 6 §17(3) (1935); see also Bryan M. E. McMahon, "The Law Relating to Contraception in Ireland," in *Morality and the Law*, 20, 23 (Desmond M. Clarke, ed., 1982).

85. O'Connell, supra note 65, at 262–64.

86. Justice Walsh states, for example, that "[i]t is a matter exclusively for the husband and wife to decide how many children they wish to have; it would be quite outside the competence of the State to dictate or prescribe the number of children which they might have or should have." *McGee*, [1974] I. R. at 311 (Walsh, J.).

87. Quoted in James O'Reilly, "Marital Privacy and Family Law," 66 *Studies*, 8, 20–21 (1977) (quoting episcopal statement of 1973).

88. *McGee*, [1974] I. R. at 319 (Walsh, J.).

89. Id. at 312.

90. 381 U.S. 479 (1965).

91. 410 U.S. 113 (1973).

92. William Binchy, "Marital Privacy and Family Law: A Reply to Mr. O'Reilly," 66 *Studies* 330, 331 (1977); K. Wilson-Davis, "Irish Attitudes to Family Planning," 3 *Social Studies*, 260 (1974); Michael Fogarty et al., *Irish Values and Attitudes: The Irish Report of the European Value Systems Study*, 13–22 (1984).

93. *McGee*, [1974] I. R. at 335 (Griffin, J.) (the decision did not apply to abortifacients); *McGee*, [1974] I. R. at 312 (Walsh, J.) ("any action ... to limit family sizes by endangering or destroying human life must necessarily not only be an offense against the common good but also against the guaranteed personal rights of the human life in question"); *G.* v. *An Bord Uchtala*, [1980] I. R. 32, 69 (Walsh, J.) (stating in dicta that an unborn child has a right to life); *Norris* v. *State*, [1984] I. R. 36, 103 (Ir. S. Ct.) (McCarthy, J.) (the right to life of the unborn is a "sacred trust to which all organs of government must lend their support).

94. *Norris*, [1984] I. R. at 103 (McCarthy, J.).

95. See, e.g., *SPUC* v. *Coogan*, [1989] I. R. 735, 747 (Ir. S. Ct.) (Walsh, J. discussing the Civil Liability Act, 1961, and the Succession Act, 1965).

96. Ann Sherlock, "The Right to Life of the Unborn and the Irish Constitution," 24 *Irish Jurisprudence*, 13, 16–20 (1989).

97. See Charleton, supra note 8, at 350.

98. *Irish Family Planning* v. *Ryan*, [1979] I. R. 295 (Ir. S. Ct. 1978).

Chapter Five

1. Indignant statement of 19-year-old protagonist Sharon Curley while informing her parents of her unwed pregnancy during the film of the Roddy Doyle novel "The Snapper." *The Snapper* (BBC Films).

2. 67 *Studies*, 1, et seq. (1979).

3. Michael Fogarty et al., *Irish Values and Attitudes: The Irish Report of the European Value Systems Study*, 13–22 (1984).

4. 381 U.S. 479 (1965).

5. 410 U.S. 113 (1973).

6. See *Norris* v. *Attorney General*, [1984] I. R. 36, 103 (Ir. S. Ct.) (McCarthy, J., dissenting); *G.* v. *An Bord Uchtala*, [1980] I. R. 32, 69 (Ir. S. Ct.) (Walsh, J., concurring); *McGee* v. *Attorney General*, [1974] I. R. 284, 312 (Ir. S. Ct.) (Walsh, J., concurring).

7. Paraphrasing Chief Justice Taney in *Dred Scott* v. *Sandford*, 19 How. 393, 407 (1857).

8. *Roe* v. *Wade*, 410 U.S. at 153.

9. Id. at 162.

10. Id. at 163.

11. Id. at 163.

12. Id. at 163–64.

13. Id. at 164–65.

14. See, e.g., John T. Noonan, Jr., "An Almost Absolute Value in History," in *The Morality of Abortion: Legal and Historical*

Perspectives, 1, 1–59 (John T. Noonan, Jr., ed., 1970).

15. William Binchy, "The American Revolution in Family Law," 27 *Northern Ireland Law Quarterly*, 371, 398 and notes 56, 58 (1976) (quoting Byrn, Wade and Bolton, "Fundamental Legal Errors and Dangerous Implications, 19 *Cath. Lawyer*, 243, 245 [1973] and Dittfurth, "Judicial Reasoning and Social Change," 50 *Indiana Law Journal*, 258, 273 [1975]).

16. See James O'Reilly, "Marital Privacy and Family Law," 66 *Studies*, 8, 15–19 (1977).

17. William Binchy, "Marital Privacy and Family Law: A Reply to Mr. O'Reilly," 66 *Studies*, 330, 332–33 (1977).

18. Abortion Act, §1(a) (1967) (U.K.).

19. Nicolas P. Terry, "England," in *Abortion and Protection of the Human Fetus*, 75, 82–83 (Stanislaw Frankowski and George F. Cole, eds., 1987).

20. Cornelius O'Leary and Tom Hesketh, "The Irish Abortion and Divorce Referendum Campaigns," 3 *Irish Political Studies*, 43, 44 (1988) (quoting Mary Robinson).

21. William Binchy, "Pluralism, Liberty and the Right to Life," in *Law and Liberty in Ireland*, 132, 145 (Anthony Whelan, ed., 1993).

22. The notion of the substantive content of the rise of "rights talk" in the United States and, to a lesser extent, elsewhere has primarily been developed by Harvard law professor Mary Ann Glendon. See, e.g., Mary Ann Glendon, *Abortion and Divorce in Western Law*, 112–42 (1987); Mary Ann Glendon, *Rights Talk: The Impoverishment of Political Discourse* (1991).

23. Mary Kenny, *Goodbye to Catholic Ireland*, 342 (1997). *Humana Vitae* does not speak of the right-to-life imperative, but the new catechism addresses openly the right to life of all persons, which implies a duty to defend the embryo from the moment of conception. *Catechism of the Catholic Church*, at paras. 2273–75 (Libreria Editrice Vaticana, 1994).

24. Dermot Keogh, *Twentieth-Century Ireland: Nation and State*, 371 (1995) (quoting the coalition amendment wording proposal).

25. Raymond Byrne and William Binchy, *Annual Review of Irish Law 1992*, 166 (1994).

26. Dolores Dooley-Clarke, "Abortion and the Law," in *Morality and the Law*, 31, 44 (Desmond Clarke, ed., 1982).

27. See, e.g., "Archdiocese of Dublin: Ethical Code for Hospitals," §C.5 (Dec. 11, 1978) and "Ethical Principles of the Coombe Lying-In Hospital, Dublin," §7, both reprinted in *Ethical Issues in Reproductive Medicine*, 156–60, 162–64 (Maurice Reidy, ed., 1982).

28. Teresa Iglesias, "The *X* Case: A Lego-Moral Consideration," 18 *Dublin University Law Review*, 187, 191–92 (1996).

29. John Cooney, *The Crozier and The Dail, Church and State 1922–1986*, 68–69 (1986) (quoting statement from the episcopal conference, Aug. 22, 1983).

30. See Brian Girvin, "Social Change and Moral Politics: The Irish Constitutional Referendum 1983," 34 *Political Studies*, 61, 75–76 (1986).

31. *Planned Parenthood of Missouri* v. *Danforth*, 428 U.S. 52 (1976).

32. *Bellotti* v. *Baird*, 443 U.S. 622 (1979).

33. *Akron* v. *Akron Center for Reproductive Health*, 462 U.S. 416 (1983).

34. *Roe*, 410 U.S. at 162.

35. Peter Mair, "The Party System and Party Competition," in *Politics in the Republic of Ireland*, 86, 88 (John Coakley and Michael Gallagher, eds., 1996).

36. Brian Girvin, "The Divorce Referendum in the Republic: June 1986," 2 *Irish Political Studies*, 93 93–94 (1987) (quoting the proposed amended divorce article).

37. William Binchy, *Is Divorce the Answer?* (1984).

38. Michelle Dillon, *Debating Divorce: Moral Conflict in Ireland*, 41–43 (1993).

39. Id. at 37.

40. Kenny, supra note 23, at 222.

41. Nick Lowry, "Garret's Loaves and Fishes: The Defeat of the Divorce Amendment," in William Binchy et al., *Fusion or Fission: Ireland's Option for the Family*, 48 (1988).

42. William Binchy, "No-Fault Divorce," in *Morality and the Law*, 47, 52 (Desmond M. Clarke, ed., 1982).

43. *Kenny*, supra note 23, at 360.

44. Comment, Anna Margaret McDonough, "When Irish Eyes Aren't Smiling — Legalizing Divorce in Ireland," 14 *Dickinson Journal of International Law*, 647, 651–52 (1996).

45. Dillon, supra note 31, at 103–04.
46. Kenny, supra note 23, at 365.
47. Brian Girvin, "The Divorce Referendum in the Republic: June 1986," 2 *Irish Political Studies*, 93, 97 (1987).
48. *Catechism of the Catholic Church*, paras. 2384–86 (Libraria Editrice Vaticana, Wanderer Press, 1994).
49. John Coakley, "Moral Consensus in a Secularizing Society: The Irish Divorce Referendum of 1986," 10 *Western European Politics*, 291, 293–94; O'Leary and Hesketh, supra note 20, at 57–58.
50. Maeve Binchy, *A Circle of Friends* (1991).
51. *Attorney General (S.P.U.C.)* v. *Open Door Counselling*, [1988] I. R. 593, 598 (Ir. H. Ct. 1986).
52. *Attorney General (S.P.U.C.)* v. *Open Door Counselling*, [1988] I. R. 593, 623 (Ir. S. Ct.).
53. *Attorney General (S.P.U.C.)* v. *Open Door Counselling*, [1987] I.L.R.M. 477, 502 (Ir. H. Ct.).
54. *Open Door*, [1988] I. R. at 599 (Ir. H. Ct.) (quoting in part *Norris* v. *Attorney General*, [1984] I. R. 36,103 (Ir. S. Ct.), a homosexual rights case).
55. Id. at 617.
56. Paul Ward, "Ireland: Abortion: $X + Y = ?!$" 33 *University of Louisville Journal of Family Law*, 385, 393–94 (1995).
57. *Open Door*, [1988] I. R. at 627 (Ir. S. Ct.).
58. Id. at 620.
59. E.g., James Friedman, "On the Dangers of Moral Certainty and Sacred Trusts: The Judgments in the *SPUC* Case and the Issue of Free Speech," 10 *Dublin University of Law Journal*, 71, 83–89 (1988); Ann Sherlock, "The Right to Life of the Unborn and the Irish Constitution," 24 *Irish Jurisprudence*, 13, 31–43 (1989).
60. Friedman, supra note 59, at 84.
61. Michael Adams, "Censorship of Publications," in *Morality and the Law*, 71, 71–72 (Desmond M. Clarke, ed., 1983).
62. *NEA* v. *Finley*, 100 F.3d 671 (1997) (Kleinfeld, J., dissenting), approved in 524 U.S. 569, 585–88 (1998).
63. See John Ardagh, *Ireland and the Irish*, 190 (1994). Dennis Murphy, executive director of the prolife campaign in Dublin told me that despite having the benefits of top legal minds in his organization, the group would not dream of orchestrating "test cases," as occurs in the United States, because any such effort would provoke backlash. The students in *Grogan* may have learned this the hard way when a high court judge recommended that the director of public prosecutions consider their case for a criminal contempt suit. *SPUC* v. *Grogan*, [1994] 1 I. R. 46, 58 (Ir. H. Ct. 1992).
64. *SPUC* v. *Coogan*, [1989] I. R. 734, 742 (Ir. S. Ct.) (Finlay, C. J.) (quoting *Open Door*, [1988] I. R. at 623).
65. *Coogan*, [1989] I. R. at 743 (Ir. S. Ct.) (Walsh, J.).
66. Sherlock, supra note 59, at 29; Ward, supra note 56, at 392.
67. See Ward, supra note 56, at 392.
68. *Coogan*, [1989] I. R. at 743 (Ir. S. Ct.) (Walsh, J. concurring) (emphasis added).
69. Id. at 751 (McCarthy, J., dissenting).
70. *SPUC* v. *Grogan*, [1989] I. R. 753, 758 (Ir. H. Ct.) (*hereinafter Grogan I*).
71. *SPUC* v. *Grogan*, [1992] I. L. R. M. 461, 464 (E.C.J. 1991) (*hereinafter Grogan III*).
72. *SPUC* v. *Grogan*, [1989] I. R. 753, 763 (Ir. S. Ct.) (Finlay, C.J.) (*hereinafter Grogan II*).
73. Id. at 768.
74. *Grogan II*, [1989] I. R. at 771 (Ir. S. Ct.) (McCarthy, J.).
75. Id. at 767 (Walsh, J.).
76. A person in a situation identical to the latter case was found guilty of a felony under Kentucky law and served a prison sentence after the burglary of the house of some former clients of mine.
77. See generally M. J. Findlay, "Criminal Liability for Complicity in Abortions Committed Outside Ireland," 25 *Irish Jurisprudence*, 88 (1980).
78. *Grogan II*, [1989] I. R. at 767 (Ir. S. Ct.) (Walsh, J.) ("When a woman becomes pregnant she acquires rights which cannot be taken from her, namely the right to protect the life of her unborn child and the right to protect her own bodily integrity against any effort to compel her by law or by persuasion to submit herself to an abortion. Such rights also carry obligations the foremost of which is not to endanger or to submit to or bring about the destruction of that unborn life").
79. Byrne and Binchy, supra note 25, at 194.
80. Diarmuid Rossa Phelan, "Right to Life of the Unborn v. Promotion of Trade in

Services: The European Court of Justice and the Normative Shaping of European Union," 55 *Modern Law Review*, 670, 688 (1992).

81. Id. at 684.

82. *Open Door Counselling* v. *Ireland*, 14 Eur. H. R. Rep. 131, 136 (Eur. Comm'n H. R. 1991).

83. Id. at 137.

84. Christopher Wolfe, "The 'Other' Ground of Limited Government," in *Catholicism, Liberalism and Communitarianism: The Catholic Intellectual Tradition and the Moral Foundations of Democracy*, 81, 87 (Kenneth Grasso et al., eds., 1995).

85. 13 Eur. H. R. Rep. 212 (Eur. Ct. H. R. 1991).

86. *Open Door*, 14 Eur. H. R. Rep. at 149 (opinion of E. Busuttil).

87. Id. at 149–50 (dissenting opinion of F. Machinez); see also id. at 152 (dissenting opinion of L. Loucaides).

88. See Angela Thompson, "International Protection of Women's Rights: An Analysis of *Open Door Counselling, Ltd., and Dublin Well Woman Centre* v. *Ireland*," 12 *Boston University International Law Journal*, 371, 379 (1994).

89. Glendon, *Abortion and Divorce*, supra note 22, at 14.

90. *Martin* v. *Hunter's Lessee*, 1 Wheat (14 U.S.) 304 (1816).

91. *Cooper* v. *Aaron*, 358 U.S. 1 (1958).

92. See *United States* v. *Carolene Products Co.*, 304 U.S. 144, at note 4 (1938).

Chapter Six

1. Traditional as adapted by Sarah Makem, "The Butcher Boy," in *The Irish Songbook*, 120, 121 (Joy Graeme, ed., 1979).

2. See generally *Attorney General* v. *X*, [1992] 1 I. R. 1 (Ir. H. Ct.).

3. Id. at 12 (emphasis added).

4. Id.

5. Id.

6. Id. at 12–13.

7. *Attorney General* v. *X*, [1992] 1 I. R. 1, 53 (Ir. S. Ct.) (Finlay, C. J.).

8. Id. at 55.

9. Id. at 76 (Hederman, J., dissenting).

10. Justice Hederman is referring to Article 40.3.2 [the abortion amendment is Article 40.3.3], which states: "The State shall, in particular, by its laws protect as best it may from unjust attack and, in the case of injustice done, vindicate the life, person, good name, and property rights of every citizen."

11. *X*, [1992] 1 I. R. at 76.

12. See Kay Redfield Jamison, *Night Falls Fast: Understanding Suicide*, 114–15 (1999); Patricia Ainsworth, M. D., *Understanding Depression*, 12–13 (2000).

13. Id. at 13; Aaron T. Beck, M. D., "Suicide Intent Scale," reprinted in Kay Redfield Jamison, *Night Falls Fast: Understanding Suicide*, 41 (1999) (thinking about or making some arrangements for a suicide is deemed an indicator of suicidal intent, while making definite plans or completing arrangements is indicative of a severe suicide intent).

14. *X*, [1992] 1 I. R. at 8 (Ir. H. Ct.).

15. Id. at 66 (Ir. S. Ct.) (Hederman, J., dissenting).

16. Id. at 66.

17. Id. at 54 (Finlay, J.).

18. Id. at 54.

19. The failure to describe definite plans or make preparations for a suicide attempt suggests that X was at less risk of committing suicide than those in the severe risk category. Beck, supra note 13.

20. *X*, [1992] 1 I. R. at 67 (Hederman, J., dissenting).

21. Id. at 70.

22. Gerard Hogan, "Law, Liberty and the Abortion Controversy," in *Law and Liberty in Ireland*, 113, 116–17 (Anthony Whelan, ed., 1993).

23. James Kingston and Anthony Whelan, *Abortion and the Law*, 9 (1997).

24. Raymond Byrne and William Binchy, *Annual Review of Irish Law 1992*, 176–78 (1994).

25. Peter McKenna, "Abortion Proposals Are in the Right Direction," *Irish Times*, Oct. 6, 2001.

26. Ivana C. Bacik, "Hypocrisy, Fear in Debate on Abortion," *Irish Times*, Dec. 24, 2001.

27. Medb Ruane, "Ignoring Women's Opinions," *Irish Times*, Oct. 5, 2001.

28. See Teresa Iglesias, "The *X* Case: A Lego-Moral Consideration," 18 *Dublin University Law Review*, 187, 195–96 (1996).

29. *X*, [1992] 1 I. R. at 11 (Costello, J.).

30. Iglesias, supra note 28, at 194.
31. Gerard Hogan and Gerry Whyte, *J. M. Kelly's The Irish Constitution*, 803 (3d ed., 1994). Byrne and Binchy cite competing evidence in their treatise. Byrne and Binchy, supra note 24, at 177.
32. Kingston and Whelan, *supra* note 23, at 16.
33. Byrne and Binchy, supra note 24, at 168 (quoting the attorney general).
34. Id. (quoting the attorney general).
35. See id. at 168–69.
36. *X*, [1992] 1 I. R. at 53 (Finlay, C. J.) (emphasis added).
37. *X*, [1992] 1 I. R. at 79 (McCarthy, J., concurring).
38. The relevant portion of Article 41 states: "The State, therefore, guarantees to protect the Family in its constitution and authority, as the necessary basis of social order and as indispensable to the welfare of the Nation and the State." *Irish Constitution* art. 41.1.2.
39. The relevant portion of Article 42 states: "The State acknowledges that the primary and natural educator of the child is the Family and guarantees to respect the inalienable right and duty of parents to provide, according to their means, for the religious and moral, intellectual, physical and social education of their children." *Irish Constitution* art. 42.1.
40. *X*, [1992] 1 I. R. at 88 (O'Flaherty, J., concurring).
41. *X*, [1992] 1 I. R. at 80 (McCarthy, J.).
42. See R. Randall Rainey, S. J. et al., "Introduction," in *Abortion and Public Policy: An Interdisciplinary Investigation within the Catholic Tradition*, 1, 7 (R. Randall Rainey and Gerard Magill, eds., 1996).
43. Byrne and Binchy, supra note 24, at 185.
44. *Irish Constitution* art. 41.2.1.
45. *X*, [1992] 1 I. R. at 72 (Hederman, J., dissenting).
46. See Patrick Riordan, S. J., "Abortion: The Aftermath of the Supreme Court's Decision," 81 *Studies*, 293, 300–01 (1992).
47. William Binchy, "Pluralism, Liberty and the Right to Life," in *Law and Liberty in Ireland*, 132, 138–39 (Anthony Whelan, ed., 1993).
48. *X*, [1992] 1 I. R. at 87 (O'Flaherty, J., concurring).
49. *Irish Constitution* art. 40.3.2.
50. See Ruth Fletcher, "'Pro-Life' Absolutes, Feminist Challenges: The Fundamentalist Narrative of Irish Abortion Law 1986–1992," 2 *Osgoode Hall Law Journal*, 1, 61 (1998).
51. Attracta Ingram, "Home and Away: The Unequal Vista for Irish Women," in *The Abortion Papers Ireland* 149, 154 (Ailbhe Smyth, ed., 1992).
52. Breda O'Brien, "Time to Tackle Reasons for Choosing Abortion," *Irish Times*, July 21, 2001.
53. See Tom Garvin, *1922: The Birth of Irish Democracy*, 18 (1996).
54. *X* [1992] 1 I. R. at 52.
55. See Peter Charleton, "Judicial Discretion in Abortion: The Irish Perspective," 6, *International Journal of Law and Family*, 363 (1992) (citing poll results immediately after the high court issued its opinion in *X*), but compare Byrne and Binchy, supra note 24, at 170 ("the political voices in favour of legalised abortion within the State were, if anything, even fainter in 1992 than in 1983").
56. *McGee*, [1974] I. R. at 319 (Walsh, J.).
57. Byrne and Binchy, supra note 24, at 170.
58. *Open Door Counselling and Dublin Well Woman Centre* v. *Ireland*, 15 Eur. H. R. Rep. 244 (Eur. Ct. H. R. 1992).
59. Kingston and Whelan, supra note 23, at 163–64.
60. Gerard Hogan, "Protocol 17," in *Maastricht and Ireland: What the Treaty Means*, 109 (Patrick Keatinge, ed. 1992) (quoting Protocol 17).
61. Id. at 118 (quoting Solemn Declaration).
62. Kingston and Whelan, supra note 23, at 19 (quoting proposed Twelfth Amendment referendum).
63. Paul Ward, "Ireland: Abortion: X + Y = ?!" 33 *University of Louisville Journal of Family Law*, 385, 406 (1995).
64. *Open Door Counselling and Dublin Well Woman Centre* v. *Ireland*, 15 Eur. H. R. Rep 244 (Eur. Ct. H. R. 1992).
65. Binchy and Byrne, supra note 24, at 190.
66. *Open Door*, 15 Eur. H. R. Rep. at 266 (quoting *The Observer and the Guardian* v. *United Kingdom*, 14 Eur. H. R. Rep. 153 at para. 59 [1991]).

67. Id. at 267

68. Id. at 277 (Pettiti, Russo, Lopes Rossa and Bigi, J.J., dissenting) (emphasis in original).

69. Id. at 274 (Matscher, J., dissenting).

70. Byrne and Binchy, supra note 24, at 194.

71. *Society for the Protection of Unborn Children* v. *Grogan,* [1994] I. R. 46 (Ir. H. Ct. 1992).

72. Id. at 56.

73. Ward, supra note 63, at 406.

74. See Brendan Kennelly and Eilis Ward, "The Abortion Referendums," in *How Ireland Voted 1992,* 128–31 (Michael Gallagher and Michael Laver, eds., 1993); Richard Sinnott, *Irish Voters Decide: Voting Behavior in Election and Referendums Since 1918,* 230–31 (1995). There may have been some who voted "yes" inexplicably when their true position was closer to that of the supreme court.

Chapter Seven

1. See Mary Ann Glendon, *Rights Talk: The Impoverishment of Political Discourse,* 47–75 (1991).

2. Boris Johnson, "For Richer, for Poorer, but Maybe No Longer for Ever," *Daily Telegraph,* Oct. 16, 1995, at 22.

3. Glendon, supra note 1, at 47–75.

4. *Roe* v. *Wade,* 410 U.S. 133, 159 (1973).

5. *In re Article 26 and the Regulation of Information (Services Outside the State for Termination of Pregnancies) Bill, 1995,* [1995] 1 I. R. 1, 35 (Ir. S. Ct.) (*hereinafter Information Bill*).

6. Id. at 43.

7. See James Kingston and Anthony Whelan, *Abortion and the Law,* 209 (1997); Gerry Whyte, "Natural Law and the Constitution," 47; *Doctrine and Life,* 481, 487–88 (1997).

8. *Information Bill,* [1995] 1 I. R. at 45.

9. Id. at 50.

10. *In re A Ward of Court,* [1996] 2 I. R. 79 (Ir. S. Ct. 1995).

11. Id. at 85.

12. See G. F. Whyte, "The Right to Die and the Irish Constitution," 3 *European Public Law,* 235, 259–60 (1997) (*hereinafter* Whyte, "Right to Die").

13. *Ward of Court,* [1996] 2 I. R. at 119.

14. See id. at 122–28; Whyte, "Right to Die," supra note 12, at 259.

15. [1965] I. R. 294 (Ir. S. Ct. 1964).

16. Noreen O'Carroll, "The Right to Die: A Critique of the Supreme Court Judgment in 'The Ward' Case," 84 *Studies,* 375, 378 (1995).

17. Whyte, "Right to Die," supra note 12, at 245.

18. *Ward of Court* [1996] 2 I. R. at 127.

19. Id. at 128.

20. *Ward of Court* [1996] 2 I. R. at 130 (O'Flaherty, J., concurring).

21. Whyte, "Right to Die," supra note 12, at 252.

22. Id.

23. Dermot Feenan, "Death, Dying and the Law," *Irish Law Times,* April 1996, at 93.

24. See Patrick Hanafin, *Last Rights: Death, Dying and the Law in Ireland,* 40 (1997) (quoting the Irish Medical Council, "Statement of the Council After Their Statutory Meeting on 4th August, 1995" [Dublin, The Medical Council, 1995]).

25. John Paul II, *The Gospel of Life* (*Evangelium Vitae*) §65 (Times Books 1995) (*hereinafter Gospel of Life*); Richard S. Myers, "An Analysis of the Constitutionality of Laws Banning Assisted Suicide from the Perspective of Catholic Moral Teaching," 72 *University of Detroit Mercy Law Review,* 771, 782–83 (1995).

26. *Gospel of Life,* supra note 25, at §65.

27. For a discussion of the "slippery slope" problem in the assisted suicide context, see Yale Kamisar, "Against Assisted Suicide — Even a Very Limited Form," 72 *University of Detroit Mercy Law Review,* 736 (1995).

28. *Ward of Court,* [1996] 2 I. R. at 151 (Denham, J.).

29. Feenan, supra note 23, at 92.

30. Id. at 93.

31. *Ward of Court,* [1996] 2 I. R. at 142 (Blayney, J.) (emphasis added).

32. Id. at 130, 134 (O'Flaherty, J.).

33. O'Carroll, supra note 16, at 379.

34. John T. Noonan, Jr., *A Private Choice: Abortion in America in the Seventies,* 67 (1979) (paraphrasing Jérome Lejeune, who discovered the genetic basis for Down's Syndrome).

35. O'Carroll, supra note 16, at 379.

36. See Hanafin, supra note 24, at 36–37; Feenan, supra note 23, at 90.

37. Liam Hamilton, "Matters of Life and Death," 65 *Fordham Law Review*, 543, 558 (1996).
38. *Roe*, 410 U.S. at 153.
39. *Attorney General* v. *X*, [1992] 1 I. R. 1, 53 (Ir. S. Ct.) (Finlay, C. J.).
40. *Ward of Court*, [1996] 2 I. R. at 136 (Egan, J., dissenting).
41. Id.
42. Id.
43. Id. at 130–37.
44. Hanafin, supra note 24, at 40; John A. Harrington, Note, "Constitutional Law—Withdrawal of Treatment from an Incompetent Patient," 17 *Dublin University Law Review*, 120, 133 (1995); Feenan, supra note 23, at 92.
45. O'Carroll, supra note 16, at 376 (quoting Dr. James Clinch in *The Irish Times*, Aug. 5, 1995).
46. Harrington, supra note 44, at 133.
47. Domicile and Recognition of Foreign Divorces Act, No. 24 (1986) (Ir.).
48. *Judicial Separation and Family Law Reform Act*, No. 6 (1989) (Ir.).
49. *In the Matter of Article 26 of the Constitution and in the Matter of the Matrimonial Home Bill 1993*, [1994] 1 I.L.R.M. 241 (Ir.).
50. Anna Margaret McDonagh, Note, "When Irish Eyes Aren't Smiling—Legalizing Divorce in Ireland," 14 *Dickinson Journal of International Law*, 647, 654–55 (1996).
51. See *The Right to Remarry: A Government Information Paper on the Divorce Referendum* (1995).
52. *McKenna* v. *An Taoiseach*, [1995] 2 I. R. 10 (Ir. S. Ct.). Based on this holding, which was made right before the referendum was scheduled to occur, the courts agreed to hear a challenge to the result of the referendum. Despite the illegal expenditure, the Irish Supreme Court essentially considered the outcome of the referendum to be a nonjusticiable, political question and allowed the result to stand. *Hanafin* v. *Minister for the Environment* [1996] 2 I.L.R.M. 161 (Ir. S. Ct.).
53. Fifteenth Amendment of the Constitution Act, 1995 (Ir.).
54. Draft Family Law (Divorce) Bill, in *The Right to Remarry: A Government Information Paper on the Divorce Referendum*, 31 (1995); see generally Jennifer Carter, Note, "Breaking the Bonds and Splitting the Assets: Women and Divorce in Ireland," 15 *Boston University International Law Journal*, 511, 519–20 (1997).
55. McDonough, supra note 50, at 655 (describing unpublished *VS* v. *RS*).
56. Andy Pollak, "Key Tactician Behind Anti Divorce Campaign," *Irish Times*, Nov. 25, 1995.
57. *Gaudium et Spes*, in *Vatican Council II, the Conciliar and Post Conciliar Documents* §48 (Austin Flannery, O. P., Costello Publishing 1998) (*hereinafter Gaudium et Spes*).
58. *Murray* v. *Ireland*, [1985] I. R. 532, 535–37 (Ir. H. Ct.) (Costello, J.), affirmed [1991] I.L.R.M. 465 (Ir. S. Ct.).
59. Gerard Clarke, "Law and Morals: Which Law? Whose Morals?" 83 *Studies* 64, 68 (1994).
60. Seamus Murphy, "Against Divorce," 84 *Studies* 7, 12 (1995) (*hereinafter* Murphy, "Against Divorce").
61. William Binchy, "Referendum Will Decide Shape of Society for Generations," *Irish Times*, Nov. 23, 1995.
62. McDonough, supra note 50, at 662.
63. Michele Dillon, *Debating Divorce: Moral Conflict in Ireland*, 15 (1993).
64. Murphy, "Against Divorce," supra note 60, at 12–13.
65. William Binchy, "Pluralism, Religious Freedom, and Marriage Law," 45 *Doctrine and Life*, 71, 72 (1995). ("The retention of freedom as to future options does not necessarily make a person a better, or even a freer, human being. Commitment is integral to true human freedom.")
66. Id.
67. *Catechism of the Catholic Church* paras. 1638–40 (Libraria Editrice Vaticana, The Wanderer Press, 1994).
68. *Gaudium et Spes*, supra note 57, at §48.
69. "Defying Church, Ireland Votes to Legalize Divorce; Margin is Slimmest in Country's History," *Associated Press*, Nov. 26, 1995.
70. [1998] 1 I.L.R.M. 460 (Ir. H. C.) (*hereinafter C*).
71. *C*, [1998] 1 I.L.R.M. at 469.
72. Id.
73. Raymond Byrne and William Binchy,

Annual Review of Irish Law 1992, 177–78 (1994).

74. *C*, [1998] 1 I.L.R.M. at 473.

75. *C*, [1998] 1 I.L.R.M. at 478.

76. Amy M. Buckley, Note, "The Primacy of Democracy over Natural Law in Irish Abortion Law: An Examination of the C Case," 9 *The Duke Journal of Comparative and International Law*, 275, 305 (1998).

77. Id. at 307–08.

Chapter Eight

1. Maeve Binchy, *Tara Road* (1999).

2. Tommy Sands, "The Age of Uncertainty," in Sean Keane, *Turn a Phrase* (Sound recording, Kells Music).

3. Iseult Honohan, "The Common Good and the Politics of Community," in *Questioning Ireland: Debates in Political Philosophy and Public Policy*, 73, 79–80 (Joseph Dunne et al., eds., 2000).

4. Id. at 81.

5. Kevin J. Worthen, "The Role of Local Governments in Striking the Proper Balance Between Individualism and Communitarianism," 1993 *Brigham Young University Law Review*, 475, 479.

6. Mary Ann Glendon, *Abortion and Divorce in Western Law* 112 (1987) (*hereinafter* Glendon, *Abortion and Divorce*).

7. Id. at 112–19.

8. Alexis de Toqueville, *Democracy in America*, vol. 1, 66–71 (Phillips Bradley, ed., 1945).

9. Edmund Burke, *Reflections on the Revolution in France*, 59 (Doubleday Anchor, 1973).

10. See Alexis de Toqueville, *Democracy in America*, vol. 2, 109–118 (Phillips Bradley, ed., 1945).

11. See Alexander Hamilton et al., *The Federalist Papers*, no. X, at 77–84 (Clinton Rossiter, ed., 1961).

12. Glendon, *Abortion and Divorce*, supra note 6, at 114–19.

13. See, e.g., Burke, supra note 9; Herbert J. Storing, *What the Anti-Federalists Were For*, 72–73 (1981); Mary Ann Glendon, *The Transformation of Family Law: State, Law, and Family in the United States and Western Europe*, 298–304 (1996).

14. Robert Bellah et al., *Habits of the Heart* (1996).

15. *Meyer* v. *Nebraska*, 262 U.S. 390 (1923).

16. Donald P. Kommers, "Liberty and Community in Constitutional Law: The Abortion Cases in Comparative Perspective," 1985 *Brigham Young University Law Review*, 371, 374–75.

17. Id., at 375–76 (quoting *Meyer* v. *Nebraska*, 262 U.S. at 399).

18. Kenneth L. Grasso, "Introduction: Catholic Social Thought and the Quest for an American Public Philosophy," in *Catholicism, Liberalism, and Communitarianism: The Catholic Intellectual Tradition and the Moral Foundations of Democracy*, 1, 11 (Kenneth L. Grasso et al., eds., 1995).

19. John Courtney Murray, S. J., *We Hold These Truths: Catholic Reflections on the American Proposition*, 91 (1960).

20. 381 U.S. 479 (1965).

21. Kommers, supra note 16, at 376.

22. 405 U.S. 438 (1972).

23. Id. at 453 (emphasis in original).

24. *Roe*, 410 U.S. at 163.

25. Id. at 137.

26. *Roe*, 410 U.S. at 164.

27. Cf., id. at 159.

28. Kommers, *supra* note 16, at 376–77.

29. Id. at 386–88 (citing *Bellotti* v. *Baird*, 443 U.S. 622, 637–39 [1979]).

30. Id. at 391.

31. *Casey*, 505 U.S. at 877.

32. Id.

33. Id. at 885.

34. The court also held a parental consent provision with a judicial bypass procedure to be valid, but the law was long established on this subject.

35. *Casey*, 505 U.S. at 898 (emphasis added). O'Connor appears to have been particularly worried about the possibility of violence toward women who notify their spouses about their decision to abort but gives little weight in balancing this serious concern to the also serious relationship and interest of a father in the life of his child, stating simply that a man has a "deep and proper concern and interest" in his unborn child as well as a "cognizable and substantial interest in" his born children's custody. Id. at 895.

36. Glendon, *Abortion and Divorce*, supra note 11, at 17.

37. *Casey*, 505 U.S. at 933 (Blackmun, J., dissenting).

38. Id. at 914–15.

39. Bellah, supra note 14, at 153 (A community of memory is "one that does not forget its past. In order not to forget that past, a community is involved in retelling its story, its constitutive narrative, and in so doing, it offers examples of the men and women who have embodied and exemplified the meaning of the community.")

40. Michele Dillon, *Debating Divorce: Moral Conflict in Ireland*, 15 (1993).

41. Kristin Luker, *Abortion and the Politics of Motherhood*, 6 (1984).

42. Id. at 7.

43. William Binchy, "The Right to Life Touches on Wider Issues," *Irish Times*, Jan. 31, 1997.

44. Frederica Mathewes-Green, "Finding Common Ground in the Abortion Debate," at 52, 53 in *The Ethics of Abortion* (Jennifer A. Hurley, ed., An Opposing Viewpoints Series, 2001).

45. Catharine MacKinnon, *Feminism Unmodified: Discourses on Life and Law*, 101–02 (1987).

46. Mary Ann Glendon, *Rights Talk: The Impoverishment of Political Discourse*, 101–02 (1991).

47. See, e.g., Ruth Colker, "Feminism, Theology, and Abortion: Toward Love, Compassion, and Wisdom," 77 *California Law Review*, 1011, 1043–44 (1989).

48. Justice Blackmun, author of *Roe*, has since argued that the right also arises from the guarantee of equal protection of the laws. See *Casey*, 510 U.S. at 928–29.

49. Catharine A. MacKinnon, *Toward a Feminist Theory of the State*, 128 (1989).

50. Kathy Rudy, *Beyond Pro-Life and Pro-Choice: Moral Diversity in the Abortion Debate*, 70 (1996) (emphasis in original).

51. Ruth Colker, *Abortion and Dialogue: Pro-Choice, Pro-Life, and American Law*, 33–34 (1992) (*hereinafter Abortion and Dialogue*).

52. Id.

53. Susan Estrich, *Sex and Power*, 204 (2000).

54. Rudy, supra note 50, at 98.

55. Germaine Greer, *The Whole Woman*, 329 (1999).

56. Marshall McLuhan, *Understanding Media: The Extensions of Man*, 23–35 (1964).

57. *Family Support Act*, P.L. 100–485, compiled as 5 U.S.C. §5315; 26 U.S.C. §§21nt, 6109; 30 U.S.C. §§1229, 1230; 42 U.S.C. §§602 et seq., 1301, 1308, 1315, 1318, 1320, 1395 et seq., 1396.

58. 11 U.S.C. §523(a)(5).

59. See, e.g., Elijah Anderson, *Code of the Street: Decency, Violence, and the Moral Life of the Inner City*, 158, 171–72 (1999). Noting that since Temporary Assistance to Needy Families (TANF) has replaced the old entitlement welfare system, not only do poor and inner-city teens have new incentives to avoid pregnancy, but the incentive has increased for them to identify the fathers of their children so that the government now or they later (when their TANF eligibility ends) can bleed what support they can out of the fathers through wage garnishments.

60. Cf. Natalie Klashtorny, "Ireland's Abortion Law: An Abuse of International Law," 10 *Temple International and Comparative Law Journal*, 419, 432 (1996) (citing Berta E. Hernandez, "To Bear or Not to Bear: Reproductive Freedom as an International Human Right," 17 *Brooklyn Journal of International Law*, 309, 320 [1991]).

61. See, e.g., Mary Boyle, *Re-Thinking Abortion: Psychology, Gender, Power and the Law*, 96–99 (1997) (describing what are profoundly complex, interpersonal problems with women demanding that men use contraceptives, including "the extent to which women may have to step outside their culturally prescribed, feminine role and become dominant in sexual encounters in order to protect themselves from pregnancy").

62. Colker, *Abortion and Divorce*, supra note 51, at 43–46.

63. Boyle, supra note 61, at 96–98.

64. Colker, *Abortion and Divorce*, supra note 51, at 48 (quoting Carol Levine and Nancy Neveloff Dubler, "Uncertain Risks and Bitter Realities: The Reproductive Choices of HIV-Infected Women," 68, *The Millbank Quarterly*, 321, 330–31 [1990]).

65. E.g., Dianne Jntl Forte and Karen Judd, "The South Within the North: Reproductive Choice in Three U.S. Communities," in *Negotiating Reproductive Rights: Women's Perspectives Across Countries and Cultures*, 279 (Rosalind P. Petchesky and Karen Judd, eds., 1998) (noting

that poor women in several communities described even unwed motherhood as a way to improve economically, a source of pride and self-respect, empowering, and self-fulfilling); Colker, *Abortion and Divorce*, supra note 51, at 49.

66. See Linda Hogan, "Procreative Choice: A Feminist Theological Comment," in *The Abortion Papers Ireland*, 181–82 (Ailbhe Smyth, ed., 1992) (*hereinafter* Hogan, "Procreative Choice").

67. John Hart Ely, "The Wages of Crying Wolf: A Comment on *Roe* v. *Wade*," 82 *Yale Law Journal*, 920, 933 (1973).

68. Christopher Jencks, "Is the American Underclass Growing?" in *The Urban Underclass*, 28, 91 (Christopher Jencks and Paul E. Peterson, eds., 1991).

69. See, e.g., Hogan, "Procreative Choice," supra note 66, at 175, 182; Glendon, *Abortion and Divorce*, supra note 11, at 23, 27, 52–57.

70. See KRS 403.044.

71. See KRS 403.170.

72. Id.

73. KRS 403.200.

74. See David Hollenbach, "A Communitarian Reconstruction of Human Rights," in *Catholicism and Liberalism: Contributions to American Public Philosophy*, 127, 139, 146–47 (R. Bruce Douglass and David Hollenbach, eds., 1994).

75. See *Loving* v. *Virginia*, 388 U.S. 1 (1967).

76. See *Pierce* v. *Society of Sisters*, 268 U.S. 510 (1925).

77. *Meyer* v. *Nebraska*, 262 U.S. 390 (1923).

78. See *Zablocki* v. *Redhail*, 434 U.S. 374 (1978) (referring to the "right to procreate" of *Griswold* as undergirding the fundamental right to marry).

79. See *Griswold* v. *Connecticut*, 381 U.S. 479 (1965).

80. See *Roe* v. *Wade*, 410 U.S. 133 (1973).

81. I do not argue that the United States recognizes no rights related to sociality — the First Amendment to the U.S. Constitution would belie that notion — only that the emphasis and character are different.

82. Andy Pollak, "Key Tactician Behind Anti Divorce Campaign," *Irish Times*, Nov. 25, 1995. Binchy explains elsewhere that the 1995 divorce amendment is actually "the introduction of an entitlement to seek social legitimacy for abandoning one's spouse." William Binchy, "Referendum Will Decide Shape of Society for Generations," *Irish Times*, Nov. 23, 1995.

83. E.g., William Binchy, "Pluralism, Religious Freedom, and Marriage Law," 45 *Doctrine and Life* 72 (Bernard Treacy and Gerry Whyte, eds., 1995) ("The retention of freedom as to future options does not necessarily make a person a better, or even a freer, human being. Commitment is integral to true human freedom.")

84. The text of this paragraph is taken from my regular newspaper column. Jennifer E. Spreng, "Are We Really Ready to Live in a Community with a Casino?" *Messenger-Inquirer* (Owensboro, Ky), Aug. 21, 2001, at 6A.

Chapter Nine

1. Neil Hannon (lead singer, Divine Comedy), in *From a Whisper to a Scream — The Living History of Irish Rock* (video recording, 1999).

2. See *The All-Party Oireachtas Committee on the Constitution, Fifth Progress Report: Abortion* (2000).

3. *Green Paper on Abortion*, reprinted in *Irish Times*, Sept. 10, 1999.

4. 410 U.S. 113 (1973).

5. James A. Gardner, "The Ambiguity of Legal Dreams: A Communitarian Defense of Judicial Restraint," 71 *North Carolina Law Review*, 805, 842 (1993).

6. I am indebted to William Binchy for discussing this point with me during an interview with him in Dublin during October 1997.

7. Donald P. Kommers, "Liberty and Community in Constitutional Law: The Abortion Cases in Comparative Perspective," 1985 *Brigham Young University Law Review*, 371, 407.

8. Frank Bryan and John McClaughry, *The Vermont Papers: Recreating Democracy on a Human Scale*, 3 (1989) (emphasis in original).

9. Mary Ann Glendon, "Irish Family Law in Comparative Perspective: Can There Be Comparative Family Law?" 23 *Irish Jurisprudence*, 1 (1988).

10. See David Hollenbach, "A Communitarian Reconstruction of Human Rights: Contributions from the Catholic Tradi-

tion," in *Catholicism and Liberalism: Contributions to American Public Philosophy*, 117, 141 (R. Bruce Douglass and David Hollenbach, eds., 1994).

11. William Binchy, "Pluralism, Liberty and the Right to Life," in *Law and Liberty in Ireland*, 132, 143 (1993).

12. Breda O'Brien, "No Simple Answers to Complex Abortion Issue," *Irish Times*, Nov. 3, 2001.

13. Mary Ann Glendon, *Abortion and Divorce in Western Law*, 16–19 (1987) (*hereinafter* Glendon, *Abortion and Divorce*).

14. Ruth Colker, "Feminism, Theology, and Abortion: Toward Love, Compassion, and Wisdom," 77 *California Law Review*, 1011, 1066–69 (1989).

15. *Roe*, 410 U.S. at 159.

16. Peter McKenna, "Abortion Proposals Are in the Right Direction," *Irish Times*, Oct. 6, 2001.

17. Glendon, *Abortion and Divorce*, supra note 13, at 23.

18. Roddy Doyle, *The Snapper*, 6 (Penguin Books, 1992).

19. Id.

20. Id.

21. Id. at 65.

22. Id.

23. Id. at 160.

24. Id. at 162.

25. "Moving Ahead: Initiatives for Expanding Opportunity in America" 19–24 (House Wednesday Group white paper, 1991).

26. "New Directions: Welfare Reform in Twelve States" 1 (House Wednesday Group white paper, 1992).

27. Lawrence Mead, *Beyond Entitlement: The Social Obligations of Citizenship*, 218, 240 (1986).

28. "Moving Ahead," supra note 25, at 31.

29. "New Directions," supra note 26, at 1.

30. Isabel Sawhill and Ron Haskins, "Welfare Reform and the Work Support System," in *Welfare Reform and Beyond* 107, 109–15 (Isabel Sawhill et al, eds., 2002).

31. See generally Ron Haskins, "The Effects of Welfare Reform on Family Income and Poverty," in *The New World of Welfare*, 103 (Rebecca Blank and Ron Haskins, eds., 2001).

32. *Irish Constitution* art. 41.3.1.

33. Rosemary Horgan, "Divorce—The Irish Experience," in *The Divorce Act in Practice*, 1, 9–10 (Geoffrey Shannon, ed., 1999). The Judicial Separation Act requires separation of households for a separation on that basis, but a separation may also be granted on the grounds that a normal marital relationship has not existed for a year, which could involve the partners living in the same residence.

34. See, e.g., *R.C.* v. *C.C.*, [1997] 1 I.L.R.M. 401 (Ir. H. Ct.) (noting concern over possible collusion where a wife who did not want a divorce did not oppose the divorce proceedings but still granting decree).

35. See Judicial Separation and Family Law Reform Act, No. 6, §2(1) (1989) (Ir.).

36. See Horgan, supra note 33, at 11–12.

37. See discussion in Jennifer A. Carter, Note, "Breaking the Bonds and Splitting the Assets: Women and Divorce in Ireland," 15 *Boston University International Law Journal*, 511, 526–27 (1997).

38. Sinead Conneely, "*The Family Law (Divorce) Act 1996*: Some Observations," *Irish Law Times*, Apr. 1997, at 78.

39. See Seamus Murphy, "Marriage and Divorce: In Support of Marriage," 84 *Studies*, 239, 240 (1995).

40. Id. at 280–81.

41. *The Right to Remarry: A Government Information Paper on the Divorce Referendum*, 9 (1995).

42. William Binchy, "Pluralism, Religious Freedom, and Marriage Law," in *Religion, Morality and Public Policy*, 71, 72 (*Doctrine and Life* special, 1995).

43. Id. (emphasis in original). I struggle, as I always do, with Binchy's insistence on categorizing the interests he champions as "rights," but his meaning is clear.

44. Iseult Honohan, "The Common Good and the Politics of Community," in *Questioning Ireland: Debates in Political Philosophy and Public Policy*, 73, 81 (Joseph Dunne et al., eds., 2000).

45. See William Binchy, "Pluralism in Ireland: A Comment," 68 *Studies*, 7, 9–10 (1979).

46. James M. Buchanan and Gordon Tullock, *The Calculus of Consent: Logical Foundations of Constitutional Democracy*, 72 (1965). A unanimity rule may impose such excessively high decision-making costs on some individuals that they may agree to a

less-than-unanimous decision rule in their own interests. This situation does not result in tyranny.

47. Richard E. Wagner and James D. Gwartney, "Public Choice and Constitutional Order," in *Public Choice and Constitutional Economics*, 29, 30 (James D. Gwartney and Richard E. Wagner, eds., 1988) (emphasis in original).

48. Id.

49. Id. at 31.

50. Barbara Sinclair, "Leadership Strategies in the Modern Congress," in *Congressional Politics*, 135, 149–52 (Christopher Deering, ed., 1989)

51. Buchanan and Tullock, supra note 46, at 252 (emphasis added).

52. Id. at 72, 115.

53. Richard Sinnott, *Irish Voters Decide: Voting Behaviour in Elections and Referendums Since 1918*, 227 (1995).

54. Buchanan and Tullock, supra note 46, at 115–16.

55. Id. at 114–15.

56. Frank H. Easterbrook, "The State of Madison's Vision of the State: A Public Choice Perspective," 107 *Harvard Law Journal*, 1328, 1344 (1994).

57. Thomas S. Ulen, "Economic and Public-Choice Forces in Federalism," 6 *George Mason Law Review*, 921, 933 (1998); Jeffrey Rosen, "Class Legislation, Public Choice, and the Structural Constitution," 21 *Harvard Journal of Law and Public Policy*, 181, 203 (1997).

58. See Ulen, supra note 57, at 940.

59. Wagner and Gwartney, supra note 47, at 31.

60. See Buchanan and Tullock, supra note 46, at 88–91.

61. See William H. Riker and Barry R. Weingast, "Constitutional Regulation of Legislative Choice: The Political Consequences of Judicial Deference to Legislatures," 74 *Virginia Law Review*, 373 (1988).

62. Wagner and Gwartney, supra note 47, at 31–33.

63. See John T. Noonan, Jr., *A Private Choice: Abortion in America in the Seventies*, 33–46 (1979).

64. *Roe*, 410 U.S. at 53.

Chapter Ten

1. Fintan O'Toole, "The State We're In, Fintan O'Toole on the Oddest Political Contest in the History of the State," *Irish Times*, Sept. 23, 1997.

2. Simon Rowe, "The Race for the Park ... Where Do They Stand?" *Irish Family*, Oct. 17, 1997, at 6.

3. See, e.g., David Quinn, "McAleese Right on Fertility," *Irish Times*, Oct. 5, 1997, at 21.

4. Kevin Myers, "An Irishman's Diary," *Irish Times*, Sept. 30, 1997, at 13.

5. Id.

6. Karen Holmquist, "When Work Stops Working," *Irish Times*, Oct. 6, 1997, at 6.

7. Fr. Harry Bohan, with Frank Shouldice, *Community and the Soul of Ireland: The Need for Values-Based Change*, 19 (2002).

8. Id. at 2.

9. Id. at 26.

10. Alison O'Connor, "Roche Tells Voters of Fears for the Liberal Agenda," *Irish Times*, Oct. 20, 1997.

11. Rowe, supra note 2, at 6.

12. Id.

13. The material in this paragraph is based significantly on my newspaper column, *Are We Really Ready to Live in a Community with a Casino?* published in the *Owensboro Messenger-Inquirer* on August 21, 2001.

14. Robert N. Bellah et al., *Habits of the Heart*, 144 (1996).

15. Gerry Whyte, "Discerning the Philosophic Premises of the Report of the Constitution Review Group: An Analysis of the Recommendations on Fundamental Rights," draft received from author.

16. T. Ryle Dwyer, *De Valera: The Man and the Myths*, 314 (1991) (quoting Eamon de Valera).

17. *Planned Parenthood* v. *Casey*, 505 U.S. 833, 860 (1992).

18. Robert Frost, "The Pasture," in *The Poetry of Robert Frost: The Collected Poems, Complete and Unabridged*, 1 (Edward Connery Lathem, ed., First Owl Book Edition, 1979).

Bibliography

Books

Abortion in Northern Ireland: the Report of an International Tribunal. Belfast: The Northern Ireland Abortion Law Reform Association and Beyond the Pale Publications, 1989.

Abortion Now. Dublin: Life Education and Research Network, 1983.

Ackerman, Bruce. *We the People: Foundations*. Cambridge, MA: Belknap Press, 1991.

Ainsworth, Patricia, M.D. *Understanding Depression*. Jackson: University Press of Mississippi, 2000.

Anderson, Elijah. New York & London: W. W. Norton & Co., *Code of the Street: Decency, Violence, and the Moral Life of the Inner City*, 1999.

Ardagh, John. *Ireland and the Irish: Portrait of a Changing Society*. London: Hamish Hamilton, 1994.

Arnold, Bruce. *What Kind of Country?: Modern Irish Politics, 1968–1983*. London: Jonathan Cape, Ltd., 1984.

Arnold, Mavis, and Peadar Kirby, eds. *The Abortion Referendum: The Case Against*. Dublin: Anti-Referendum Campaign, 1982.

Baumgardner, Jennifer, and Amy Richards. *Manifest A*. New York: Farrar, Strauss & Giroux, 2000.

Bellah, Robert, et al. *Habits of the Heart*. Berkeley: University of California Press, 1996.

Berman, Harold J. *Faith and Order: The Reconciliation of Law and Religion*. Atlanta: Scholar's Press and Emory University Studies in Law and Religion, 1993.

Beth, Loren P. *The Development of Judicial Review in Ireland, 1937–1966*. Dublin: Institute of Public Administration, 1967.

Binchy, Maeve. *Tara Road*. New York: Dell, 2000.

Binchy, William. *Is Divorce the Answer?* Dublin: Irish Academic Press, 1984.

_____, ed. *Fusion or Fission: Ireland's Option for the Family*. Dublin: Life Education and Research Network, 1988.

Blank, Rebecca, and Ron Haskins, eds. *The New World of Welfare*. Washington, D.C., Brookings Institution Press, 2001.

Bohan, Harry, with Frank Shouldice. *Community and the Soul of Ireland: The Need for Values-Based Change*. Dublin: The Liffey Press, 2002.

Boyle, Mary. *Re-Thinking Abortion: Psychology, Gender, Power and the Law*. London and New York: Routledge, 1997.

Brown, Terence. *Ireland: A Social and Cultural History, 1922 to the Present.* Ithaca and London: Cornell University Press, 1985.

Bryan, Frank, and John McClaughry. *The Vermont Papers: Recreating Democracy on a Human Scale.* Post Mills, Vermont: Chelsea Green Publishing Company, 1989.

Buchanan, James M. *The Limits of Liberty: Between Anarchy and Leviathan.* Chicago and London: University of Chicago Press, 1975.

_____, and Gordon Tullock, *The Calculus of Consent: Logical Foundations of Constitutional Democracy.* Ann Arbor: University of Michigan Press, 1965.

Byrne, Raymond, and William Binchy. *Annual Review of Irish Law 1987.* Dublin: Round Hall Press, 1988.

_____, and _____. *Annual Review of Irish Law 1988.* Dublin: Round Hall Press, 1989.

_____, and _____. *Annual Review of Irish Law 1989.* Dublin: Round Hall Press, 1990.

_____, and _____. *Annual Review of Irish Law 1992.* Dublin: Round Hall Press, 1994.

_____, and _____. *Annual Review of Irish Law 1993.* Dublin: Round Hall Press, 1996.

_____, and _____. *Annual Review of Irish Law 1995.* Dublin: Round Hall Press, 1997.

Cahill, Thomas. *How the Irish Saved Civilization: The Untold Story of Ireland's Heroic Role from the Fall of Rome to the Rise of Medieval Europe.* New York: Nan A. Talese, 1995.

Casey, James. *Constitutional Law in Ireland.* London: Sweet & Maxwell, 2000.

Chubb, Basil. *The Government and Politics of Ireland.* Dublin: Institute of Public Administration, 3d ed., 1993.

_____. *The Politics of the Irish Constitution.* Dublin: Institute of Public Administration, 1991.

Clarke, Desmond M., ed. *Morality and the Law.* Thomas Davis Lecture Series. Cork: Mercier Press, 1982.

Coakley, John, and Michael Gallagher, eds. *Politics in the Republic of Ireland.* 2d ed. Limerick: PSAI Press, 1996.

Colker, Ruth. *Abortion and Dialogue: Pro-Choice, Pro-Life, and American Law.* Bloomington: Indiana University Press, 1992.

Connelly, Alpha, ed. *Gender and the Law in Ireland.* Dublin: Oak Tree Press, 1993.

Coogan, Tim Pat. *Eamon De Valera: The Man Who Was Ireland.* New York: Harper Collins, 1993.

Cooney, John. *The Crozier & the Dáil: Church & State 1922–1986.* Cork: Mercier Press, Ltd., 1986

Costigan, Giovanni. *A History of Modern Ireland.* New York: Pegasus, 1969.

Davis, John, ed. *Rural Change in Ireland.* Belfast: Institute of Irish Studies, 1999.

de Toqueville, Alexis. *Democracy in America.* Phillips Bradley, ed. The Henry Reeve Text, New York: Vintage Books, 1945.

Devlin, Judith, and Ronan Fanning, eds. *Religion and Rebellion.* Historical Studies XX. Dublin: Irish Committee of Historical Sciences, 1997.

Dillon, Michele. *Debating Divorce: Moral Conflict in Ireland.* Lexington: University Press of Kentucky, 1993.

Donnelly, James S., Jr. *The Great Irish Potato Famine.* Phoenix Mill: Sutton Publishing, 2001.

Douglass, R. Bruce, and David Hollenbach, eds. *Catholicism and Liberalism: Contributions to American Public Philosophy.* Cambridge Studies in Religion and American Public Life. Cambridge: Cambridge University Press, 1994.

Duncan, William, ed. *Law and Social Policy, Some Current Problems in Irish Law.* Dublin: Dublin University Law Journal, 1987.

Dunne, Joseph, et al., eds. *Questioning Ireland: Debates in Political Philosophy and Public Policy.* Dublin: Institute of Public Administration, 2000.
Dwyer, T. Ryle. *Big Fellow, Long Fellow: A Joint Biography of Collins and de Valera.* New York: St. Martin's Press, 1998.
_____. *De Valera: The Man and the Myths.* Dublin: Poolbeg Press, 1991.
Edwards, R. Dudley. *A New History of Ireland.* Toronto and Buffalo: University of Toronto Press, 1972.
Estrich, Susan. *Sex and Power.* New York: Riverhead Books, 2000.
Fanning, Ronan. *Independent Ireland.* Dublin: Helicon, 1983.
Farrell, Brian. *De Valera's Constitution and Ours.* Thomas Davis Lecture Series. Dublin: Gill & Macmillian, 1987.
Fineman, Martha Albertson, and Isabel Karpin. *Mothers in Law: Feminist Theory and the Legal Regulation of Motherhood.* New York: Columbia University Press, 1995.
Finnis, John. *Natural Law and Natural Rights.* Clarendon Law Series. Oxford: Clarendon Press, 1999.
Fogarty, Michael, et al. *Irish Values and Attitudes: The Irish Report of the European Value Systems Study.* Dublin: Dominican Publications, 1984.
Foster, R. F. *Modern Ireland 1600–1972.* London: Penguin Press, 1988.
Frankowski, Stanislaw J., and George F. Cole, eds. *Abortion and Protection of the Human Fetus: Legal Problems in a Cross-Cultural Perspective.* Boston: M. Nijhoff, 1987.
Friel, Brian, *Dancing at Lughnasa.* London and Boston: Faber & Faber Ltd., 1990.
Gallagher, Michael, and Michael Laver, eds. *How Ireland Voted, 1992.* Dublin: Folens, 1993.
Garfield, Jay L., and Patricia Hennessey, eds. *Abortion: Moral and Legal Perspectives.* Amherst: University of Massachusetts Press, 1984.
Garvin, Tom. *1922: The Birth of Irish Democracy.* New York: St. Martin's Press, 1996.
Ginnell, Laurence. *The Brehon Laws: A Legal Handbook.* 1993.
Girvin, Brian, and Roland Sturm, eds. *Politics and Society in Contemporary Ireland.* Gower: Aldershot, 1996.
Glendon, Mary Ann. *Abortion and Divorce in Western Law.* Cambridge, MA: Harvard University Press, 1987.
_____. *Rights Talk.* New York: Free Press, 1991.
_____. *The Transformation of Family Law: State Law and the Family in the United States and Western Europe.* Chicago: University of Chicago Press, 1996.
Grasso, Kenneth L., et al., eds. *Catholicism, Liberalism and Communitarianism: The Catholic Intellectual Tradition and the Moral Foundations of Democracy.* London: Rowman & Littlefield, 1995.
Greer, Germaine. *The Whole Woman.* New York: A. A. Knopf, 1999.
Gwartney, James D., and Richard E. Wagner, eds. *Public Choice and Constitutional Economics.* Greenwich, CT: JAI Press, Inc., 1988.
Hanafin, Patrick. *Last Rights: Death, Dying and the Law in Ireland.* Cork: Cork University Press, 1997.
Harris, D. J., M. O'Boyle, C. Warbrick. *Law of the European Convention on Human Rights.* London: Butterworths, 1995.
Hayek, F. A. The Road to Serfdom Fiftieth Anniversary ed. Chicago: University of Chicago Press, 1994.

Hogan, Gerard, and Gerry Whyte. *J. M. Kelly's The Irish Constitution.* Dublin: Butterworths, 1994.

Hohfield, W. N. *Fundamental Legal Conceptions as Applied in Judicial Reasoning.* New Haven: Yale University Press, 1923.

Heffernan, Liz, ed. *Human Rights: A European Perspective.* Dublin: Blackrock Co. and Portland, OR: Round Hall Press in association with Irish Centre for European Law, Dublin, 1994.

Hurley, Jennifer A., ed. *The Ethics of Abortion.* An Opposing Viewpoints Series Book. San Diego: Greenhaven Books, 2001.

Jamison, Kay Redfield. *Night Falls Fast: Understanding Suicide.* New York: Knopf, 1999.

Keatinge, Patrick, ed. *Maastricht and Ireland.* Dublin: Institute of European Affairs, 1992.

Kelly, Fergus. *A Guide to Early Irish Law.* Dublin: Dublin Institute for Advanced Studies, 1995.

Kennedy, Liam, et al. *Mapping the Great Irish Famine.* Dublin: Dublin Institute for Advanced Studies, 1999.

Kenny, Mary. *Goodbye to Catholic Ireland.* London: Sinclair-Stevenson, 1997.

Keogh, Dermot. *Twentieth-Century Ireland: Nation and State.* New York: St. Martin's Press, 1995.

_____. *The Vatican, The Bishops and Irish Politics, 1919–1939.* Cambridge: Cambridge University Press, 1986.

Kingston, James, and Anthony Whelan. *Abortion and the Law.* Dublin: Round Hall Sweet & Maxwell, 1997.

Landes, Joan B., ed. *Feminism, the Public and the Private.* Oxford and New York: Oxford University Press, 1998.

Lasch, Christoper. *Women and the Common Life: Love, Marriage and Feminism.* Elisabeth Lasch-Quinn, ed. New York: W. W. Norton, 1997.

Lee, J. J., ed. *Ireland: 1945–1970.* New York: Harper & Row, 1979.

_____. *Ireland, 1912–1985: Politics and Society.* Cambridge, Cambridge University Press, 1989.

Litton, Frank, ed. *The Constitution of Ireland.* Dublin: Institute of Public Administration, 1987.

_____, ed. *Unequal Achievement: the Irish Experience, 1957–1982.* Dublin: Institute of Public Administration, 1982.

Luker, Kristen. *Abortion and the Politics of Motherhood.* Berkeley: University of California Press, 1984.

Lyons, F.S.L. *Ireland Since the Famine.* London: Fontana Press, 1973.

MacKinnon, Catharine A. *Feminism Unmodified: Discourses on Life and Law.* Cambridge, MA: Harvard University Press, 1987.

_____. *Toward a Feminist Theory of the State.* Cambridge, MA: Harvard University Press, 1989.

McBrien, Richard P. *Catholicism.* Study edition. San Francisco: HarperSan Francisco, 1980.

McCabe, Patrick. *The Dead School.* New York: Delta Books, 1996.

McKenna, Elizabeth Perle. *When Work Doesn't Work Anymore: Women, Work and Identity.* New York: Delacorte Press, 1997.

McLoughlin, Michael, ed. *Great Irish Speeches of the Twentieth Century.* Dublin: Poolbeg Press, 1996.

Mead, Lawrence. *Beyond Entitlement: The Social Obligations of Citizenship*. New York: Free Press, 1986.
Morgan, Lynn M., and Meredith W. Michaels, eds. *Fetal Subjects, Feminist Positions*. Philadelphia: University of Pennsylvania Press, 1999.
Murphy, Tim, and Patrick Twomey, eds. *Ireland's Evolving Constitution, 1937–1997: Collected Essays*. Oxford: Hart Publishing, 1998.
Murray, John Courtney, S. J., *We Hold These Truths: Catholic Reflections on the American Proposition*. Kansas City: Sheed and Ward, 1960.
Nelson, Hilde Lindemann, ed. *Feminism and Families*. New York: Routledge, 1997.
Noonan, John T., Jr., ed. *The Morality of Abortion: Legal and Historical Perspectives*. Cambridge, MA: Harvard University Press, 1970.
_____. *A Private Choice: Abortion in American in the Seventies*. New York: The Free Press, 1979.
Novak, Michael. *Free Persons and the Common Good*. Lanham, MD: Madison Books, 1989.
O'Brien, Conor Cruise. *Ancestral Voices: Religion and Nationalism in Ireland*. Dublin: Poolbeg Press, 1994.
O'Carroll, J. P., and John A. Murphy, eds. *De Valera and His Times*. 2d ed. Cork: Cork University Press, 1986.
Ó Gráda, Cormac. *Ireland: A New Economic History 1789–1939*. Oxford and New York: Oxford University Press, 1994.
O'Halloran, Kerry. *Family Law in Northern Ireland*. Dublin: Gill & Macmillan (1997).
O'Leary, Cornelius. *Irish Elections, 1918–1977: Parties, Voters and Proportional Representation*. New York: St. Martin's Press, 1979.
Petchesky, Rosalind P., and Karen Judd, eds. *Negotiating Reproductive Rights: Women's Perspectives Across Countries and Cultures*. London and New York: Zed Brooks, 1998.
Quinn, Gerard, ed. *Irish Human Rights Yearbook*. Dublin: Round Hall Sweet & Maxwell, 1995.
_____. *Justice and Legal Theory in Ireland*. Oak Tree Press, 1995.
Rainey, Randall, S. J., and Gerard Magill, eds. *Abortion and Public Policy: An Interdisciplinary Investigation within the Catholic Tradition*. Omaha, NE: Creighton University Press, 1996.
Reid, Madeleine. *The Impact of Community Law on the Irish Constitution*. Dublin: Irish Centre for European Law, 1990.
Reidy, Maurice, ed. *Ethical Issues in Reproductive Medicine*. Dublin: Gill and Macmillan, 1983.
Rossiter, Clinton, ed. *The Federalist Papers*. New York: New American Library, 1961.
Rudy, Kathy. *Beyond Pro-Life and Pro-Choice: Moral Diversity in the Abortion Debate*. Boston: Beacon Press, 1996.
Ryan, Anne B. *Balancing Your Life: A Practical Guide to Work, Time, Money and Happiness*. Dublin: The Liffey Press, 2002.
Rynne, Andrew. *Abortion: The Irish Question*. Dublin: Ward River Press, Swords Co., 1982.
Sawhill, Isabel, et al., eds. *Welfare Reform and Beyond*. Washington: Brookings Institute Press, 2002.
Scherman, Katharine. *The Flowering of Ireland: Saints, Scholars and Kings*. Boston: Little, Brown, 1981.

Shannon, Geoffrey, ed. *The Divorce Act in Practice.* Dublin: Round Hall, 1999.
Shrage, Laurie. *Moral Dilemmas of Feminism: Prostitution, Adultery, and Abortion.* New York: Routledge, 1994.
Sinnott, Richard. *Irish Voters Decide: Voting Behaviour in Elections and Referendums Since 1918.* Manchester: Manchester University Press, 1995.
Smith, Adam. *The Wealth of Nations.* Edwin Cannan, ed. New York: Modern Library, 1937.
Smith, Herbert F., S. J. *Natural Family Planning: Why It Succeeds.* Boston: Daughters of St. Paul, 1987.
Smyth, Ailbhe, ed. *The Abortion Papers Ireland.* Dublin: Attic Press, 1992.
Sorenson, Leonard R. *Madison on the "General Welfare" of America: His Consistent Constitutional Vision.* Lanham, MA: Rowman & Littlefield Publishers, Inc., 1995.
Stetson, Dorothy McBride, ed. *Abortion Politics, Women's Movements, and the Democratic State: A Comparative Study of State Feminism.* Oxford & New York: Oxford University Press, 2001.
Stiltner, Brian. *Religion and the Common Good: Catholic Contributions to Building Community in a Liberal Society.* Lanham: Rowman & Littlefield Publishers, Inc., 1999.
Storing, Herbert J. *What the Anti-Federalists Were For: The Political Thought of the Opponents of the Constitution.* Chicago and London: University of Chicago Press, 1981.
The Tain. Thomas Kinsella, trans. New York & London: Oxford University Press, 1970.
Treacy, Bernard, and Gerry Whyte, eds., *Religion, Morality and Public Policy.* A *Doctrine & Life* Special. Dublin: Dominican Publication, 1995.
Walker, Samuel. *The Rights Revolution: Rights and Community in Modern America.* New York: Oxford University Press, 1988.
Wall, Maureen. *The Penal Laws, 1691–1760.* Irish History Series, No. 1. Dundalk: Dundalgan Press, 1967.
Ward, Alan J. *The Irish Constitutional Tradition: Responsible Government and Modern Ireland, 1782–1992.* Washington, D.C.: Catholic University of America Press, 1994.
Waters, John. *Every Day Like Sunday?* Dublin: Poolbeg Press, 1995.
_____. *Intelligent Person's Guide to Modern Ireland, An.* London: Gerald Duckworth & Co., 1997.
Weschler, Toni. *Taking Charge of Your Fertility: The Definitive Guide to Natural Birth Control and Pregnancy Achievement.* New York: Harper Perennial, 1995.
Whelan, Anthony, ed. *Law and Liberty in Ireland.* Dublin: Oak Tree Press, 1993.
Whyte, J. H. *Church and State in Modern Ireland, 1923–1970.* New York: Barnes & Noble Publishers, 1971.
Wood, Kieron, and Paul O'Shea. *Divorce in Ireland: The Options, The Issues, The Law.* Dublin: O'Brien Press, 1997.
Woodham-Smith, Cecil. *The Great Hunger: Ireland, 1845–1849.* New York and Evanston: Harper & Row, 1962.

Articles

Andrews, J. A. "The European Jurisprudence of Human Rights," 43 *Maryland Law Review* 463 (1984).

Barnes, Anthony Tyler. Note, "Ireland's Divorce Bill: Traditional Irish and International Norms of Equality and Bodily Integrity at Issue in a Domestic Abuse Context," 31 *Vanderbilt Journal of Transnational Law* 643 (1998).

Barrett, Richard. "Church and State in Light of the Report of the Irish Constitution Review Group," 20 *Dublin University Law Journal* 51 (1998).

Binchy, William. "The American Revolution in Family Law," 27 *Northern Ireland Law Quarterly* 371 (1976).

_____. "Marital Privacy and Family Law: A Reply to Mr. O'Reilly," 66 *Studies* 330 (1977).

Buckley, Amy. Note, "The Primacy of Democracy Over Natural Law in Irish Abortion Law: An Examination of the *C* Case," *The Duke Journal of Comparative and International Law* 275 (1998).

Butler, Andrew, and Rory O'Connell. "A Critical Analysis of Ireland's Constitutional Review Group Report," 33 *Irish Jurisprudence* 237 (1998).

Butler, Paul, and David Gregory. "A Not So Distant Mirror: Federalism and the Role of Natural Law in the United States: The Republic of Ireland and the European Community," 25 *Vanderbilt Journal of Transnational Law* 429 (1992).

Cannon, Ruth. "Matters of Irish Constitutional Debate: Originalism, Democracy and Natural Law," 5 *Irish Student Law Review* 22 (1995).

Carder, Kristen. Note, "Liberalizing Abortion in Ireland: *In re Article 26* and the Passage of the Regulation of Information (Services Outside the State for the Termination of Pregnancies) Bill, 3 *Tulsa Journal of Comparative and International Law.* (1996).

Carter, Jennifer. Note, "Breaking the Bonds and Splitting the Assets: Women and Divorce in Ireland," 15 *Boston University International Law Journal* 511 (1997).

Charleton, Peter. "Judicial Discretion in Abortion: The Irish Perspective," 6 *International Journal of Law and Family* 349 (1992).

Clarke, Desmond M. "The Constitution and Natural Law: A Reply to Mr. Justice O'Hanlon," *Irish Law Times*, at 177 (Aug. 1993).

_____. "The Role of Natural Law in Irish Constitutional Law," *Irish Jurisprudence* 187 (1982).

Coakley, John. "Moral Consensus in a Secularizing Society: The Irish Divorce Referendum of 1986," 10 *Western European Politics* 291 (1987).

Cole, David. "Going to England: Irish Abortion Law and the European Community," *Hastings International and Comparative Law Review* (1993).

Colker, Ruth. "Feminism, Theology, and Abortion: Toward Love, Compassion, and Wisdom," 77 *California Law Review* 1011 (1989).

Conneely, Sinead. "The Family Law (Divorce) Act 1996: Some Observations," *Irish Law Times* 79 (Apr. 1997).

Costello, Declan. "The Terminally Ill: The Law's Concerns," 21 *Irish Jurisprudence* 35 (1986).

Cross, Frank B. "The Judiciary and Public Choice," 50 *Hastings Law Journal* 355 (1999).

Curtin, Deirdre. "Case C-159/90, *The Society for the Protection of Unborn Children* v. *Grogan*," 29 *Common Market Law Review* 585 (1992).

Dallen, Russell M., Jr., "An Overview of European Community Protection of Human Rights, With Some Special References to the U.K.," 27 *Common Market Law Review* 761 (1990).

Davies, Michael. Note, "Selective Non-Treatment of the Newborn: In Whose Best Interests? In Whose Judgment?" 49 *Northern Ireland Law Quarterly* 82 (1998).

Duncan, William R. Note, "Family Law: The Financial and Property Provisions of the Judicial Separation and Family Law Reform Act of 1989," 13 *Dublin University Law Journal* 143 (1991).

Easterbrook, Frank A. "The State of Madison's Vision of the State: A Public Choice Perspective," 107 *Harvard Law Review* 1328 (1994).

Ely, John Hart. "The Wages of Crying Wolf: A Comment on *Roe* v. *Wade*," 82 *Yale Law Journal* 920 (1973).

Engle, Karen. "International Human Rights and Feminism: When Discourses Meet," 13 *Michigan Journal of International Law* 517 (1992).

Epstein, Richard A. "Substantive Due Process by Any Other Name: The Abortion Cases," *Supreme Court Review* 159 (1973).

Ewing, K. D., and C. A. Gearty. "Terminating Abortion Rights?" *New Law Journal* 1696 (Dec. 4, 1992).

Farley, Ryan P. Note, "Ireland and Divorce: Is a Little Rebellion Now and Then a Good Thing?" 11 *Emory Law Review* 515 (1997).

Feenan, Dermot. "Death, Dying and the Law," *Irish Law Times*, at 90 (April 1996).

Fette, Sarah E. Comment, "Learning from Our Mistakes: The Aftermath of the American Divorce Revolution as a Lesson in Law to the Republic of Ireland," 7 *Indiana International and Comparative Law Review* 391 (1997).

Findlay, M. J. "Criminal Liability for Complicity in Abortions Committed Outside Ireland," *Irish Jurisprudence* 88 (1980).

Fletcher, Ruth. "Post Colonial Fragments: Representations of Abortion in Irish Law and Politics," 28 *Journal of Law and Society* 568 (2001).

_____. "Pro-Life' Absolutes, Feminist Challenges: The Fundamentalist Narrative of Irish Abortion Law 1986–1992," 36 *Osgoode Hall Law Journal* 1 (1998).

Freeman, Katherine. "The Unborn Child and the European Convention on Human Rights: To Whom Does 'Everyone's Right to Life' Belong?" 8 *Emory International Law Review* 615 (1994).

Friedman, James. "On the Dangers of Moral Certainty and Sacred Trusts: The Judgments in the *SPUC* Case and the Issue of Free Speech," 10 *Dublin University Law Review* 71 (1988).

Gardner, James A. "The Ambiguity of Legal Dreams: A Communitarian Defense of Judicial Restraint," 71 *North Carolina Law Review* 805 (1993).

Garet, Ronald R. "Communality and Existence: The Rights of Groups," 56 *Southern California Law Review* 1001 (1983).

Garvin, Tom. "The Politics of Denial and of Cultural Defence: The Referenda of 1983 and 1986 in Context," 3 *Irish Review* 1 (1988).

Girvin, Brian. "The Divorce Referendum in the Republic: June 1986," 2 *Irish Political Studies* 93 (1987).

_____. "Social Change and Moral Politics: The Irish Constitutional Referendum 1983," 34 *Political Studies* 61 (1986).

Glendon, Mary Ann. "A Beau Mentir Qui Vient de Loin: The 1988 Canadian Abortion Decision in Comparative Perspective," 83 *Northwestern University Law Review* 569 (1989).

_____. "Irish Family Law in Comparative Perspective: Can There Be Comparative Family Law?" 23 *Irish Jurisprudence* 1 (1988).
Grey, Thomas C. "Do We Have an Unwritten Constitution?" 27 *Stanford Law Review* 703 (1975).
Hamilton, Liam. "Matters of Life and Death," 65 *Fordham Law Review* 543 (1996).
Harrington, John A. Note, "Constitutional Law: Withdrawal of Treatment from an Incompetent Patient," 17 *Dublin University Law Journal* 120 (1995).
Harris, Ian. "Professor Dworkin, The American Constitution and a Third Way," 57(2) *Cambridge Law Review* 284 (1998).
Highet, Keith. "Freedom to Provide Services: Prohibition of Dissemination of Information About Hospitals in Other Member States That Perform Abortion," 86 *American Journal of International Law* 367 (1992).
Hilbert, Anne M. Note, "The Irish Abortion Debate: Substantive Rights and Affecting Commerce Jurisprudential Models," 26 *Vanderbilt Journal of Transnational Law* 1117 (1994).
Hogan, G. W. Note, "Constitutional Law: The Matrimonial Homes Bill Reference," 16 *Dublin University Law Journal* 175 (1994).
_____. "Irish Nationalism as a Legal Ideology," 75 *Studies* 528 (1986).
_____. "Law and Religion: Church and State Relations in Ireland from Independence to the Present Day," 35 *American Journal of Comparative Law* 47 (1987).
_____. "The Supreme Court and the Single European Act," 22 *Irish Jurisprudence* 55 (1987).
_____. "Unenumerated Personal Rights: *Ryan*'s Case Re-Evaluated," 25–27 *Irish Jurisprudence* 95 (1990–1992).
Humphreys, Richard. "Interpreting Natural Rights," 28–30 *Irish Jurisprudence* 221 (1993–1995).
Iglesias, Teresa. "The *X* Case: A Lego-Moral Consideration," 18 *Dublin University Law Journal* 187 (1996).
Inglis, Tom. "Sacred and Secular in Catholic Ireland," 74 *Studies* 38 (1985).
Jackson, Nuala E. Note, "Family Law: The Constitution and Beneficial Ownership of the Family Home," *Dublin University Law Journal* 153 (1992).
Kamisar, Yale. "Against Assisted Suicide: Even a Very Limited Form," 72 *University of Detroit Mercy Law Review* 735 (1995).
Kavanagh, Aileen. "The Quest for Legitimacy in Constitutional Interpretation," 33 *Irish Jurisprudence* 195 (1998).
Keown, I. J. "Miscarriage: A Medico-Legal Analysis," *Criminal Law Review* 604 (1984).
Kirby, Peadar. "The Death of Innocence: Whither Now? Trauma in Church and State," 54 *Studies* 257 (1995).
Klashtorny, Natalie. Comment, "Ireland's Abortion Law: An Abuse of International Law," 10 *Temple International and Comparative Law Journal* 419 (1996).
Koegler, Keith. "Ireland's Abortion Information Act of 1995," 29 *Vanderbilt Journal of Transnational Law* 1117 (1996).
Kommers, Donald P. "Liberty and Community in Constitutional Law: The Abortion Cases in Comparative Perspective," *Brigham Young University Law Review* 371 (1985).
Lang, John Temple. "The Development of European Community Constitutional Law," 25 *International Lawyer* 455 (1991).
Maclean, Donald A. Note, "Can the EC Kill the Irish Unborn?: An Investigation

of the European Community's Ability to Impinge on the Moral Sovereignty of Member States," 28 *Hofstra Law Review* 527 (1999).

Maclean, Mavis. "Child Support in the U.K.: Making the Move from Court to Agency," 31 *Houston Law Review* 515 (1994).

Marshall, Laura A. "What God Has United Man Will Now Divide: Divorce Referendum Changes Law of 60 Years," 26 *Georgia Journal of International and Comparative Law* 505 (1997).

Martin, Frank. "Judicial Discretion in Family Law," *Irish Law Times* 226 (Dec. 1997).

McAuley, Barry. "Abortion and the Law," *Irish Law Times* 8 (May 1983).

McDonough, Anna Margaret. "When Irish Eyes Aren't Smiling: Legalizing Divorce in Ireland," 14 *Dickinson Journal of International Law* 647 (1996).

McGinnis, John O. "The Original Constitution and Its Decline: A Public Choice Perspective," 21 *Harvard Journal of Law and Public Policy* 195 (1997).

McGleenan, Tony. Note, "*Bourne*" Again? Abortion Law in Northern Ireland After *Re K* and *Re A*," 45 *Northern Ireland Law Quarterly* 389 (1994).

Merrill, Thomas W. "Does Public Choice Theory Justify Judicial Activism After All?" 21 *Harvard Journal of Law and Public Policy* 219 (1997).

Morison, John. "A Disposition to Preserve and an Ability to Improve: The Report of the Constitution Review Group in the Republic of Ireland," *Public Law* 55 (1997).

Murphy, Séamus, S. J. "Against Divorce," 84 *Studies* 333 (1995).

_____. Marriage and Divorce: In Support of Marriage," 84 *Studies* 239 (1995).

Murphy, Tim. "Democracy, Natural Law and the Irish Constitution," *Irish Law Times* at 81 (Apr. 1993).

Myers, Richard S. "An Analysis of the Constitutionality of Laws Banning Assisted Suicide from the Perspective of Catholic Moral Teaching," 72 *University of Detroit Mercy Law Review* 771 (1995).

O'Carroll, J. P. "Bishops, Knights— and Pawns? Traditional Thought and the Irish Abortion Referedum Debate of 1983," 6 *Irish Political Studies* 53 (1991).

O'Carroll, Noreen. "The Right to Die," 84 *Studies* 375 (1995).

O'Connell, Rory. "Natural Law: Alive and Kicking? A Look at the Constitutional Morality of Sexual Privacy in Ireland," 9(3) *Ratio Juris* 258 (1996).

O'Connor, David. Note, "Limiting 'Public Morality' Exceptions to Free Movement in Europe: Ireland's Role in a Changing European Union," 22 *Brooklyn Journal of International Law* 695 (1997).

O'Donnell, Rory, and Teresa Brannick. "The Influence of Turnout on the Results of the Referendum to Amend the Constitution to Include a Clause on the 'Rights of the Unborn': A Review of Walsh's Findings," 16 *Economic and Social Review* 59 (1984).

O'Donovan, Katherine. "The Medicalisation of Infanticide," *Criminal Law Review* 259 (1984).

O'Hanlon, Roderick. "Natural Rights and the Irish Constitution," *Irish Law Times*, at 8 (Jan. 1993).

O'Leary, Cornelius, and Tom Hesketh. "The Irish Abortion and Divorce Referendum Campaigns," 3 *Irish Political Studies* 43 (1988).

O'Reilly, James. "Marital Privacy and Family Law," 66 *Studies* 8 (1977).

Perry, Michael J. "Abortion, The Public Morals, and the Police Power: The Ethical Function of Substantive Due Process," 23 *U.C.L.A. Law Review* 689 (1976).

Phelan, Diarmuid Rossa. "Right to Life of the Unborn v. Promotion of Trade in

Services: The European Court of Justice and the Normative Shaping of the European Union," 55 *Modern Law Review* 670 (1992).

Price, Christopher. Comment, "Finding Fault with Irish Divorce Law," *Loyola of Los Angeles International and Comparative Law Journal* 669 (1997).

Quinlan, John A. "The Right to Life of the Unborn: An Assessment of the Eighth Amendment to the Irish Constitution," *Brigham Young University Law Review* 371 (1984).

Redmond, Mary. "Towards an Hohfeldian View of the Rights and Freedoms in the Irish Constitution," *Dublin University Law Journal* 53 (1979–1980).

Riker, William H., and Barry R. Weingast. "Constitutional Regulation of Legislative Choice: The Political Consequences of Judicial Deference to Legislatures," 74 *Virginia Law Review* 373 (1988).

Riordan, Patrick, S. J. "Abortion: The Aftermath of the Supreme Court's Decision," 81 *Studies* 293 (1992).

_____. "The Church and Culture," 83 *Studies* 331 (1994).

Rosen, Jeffrey. "Class Legislation, Public Choice, and the Structural Constitution," 21 *Harvard Journal of Law and Public Policy* 181 (1997).

Sacco, Deno, and Alexia Brown. "Regulation of Abortion in the European Community: *Society for the Protection of Unborn Children of Ireland Ltd.* v. *Grogan*, Judgment of the Court of Justice of 4 October 1991 in Case C-159/90 (1991)," 33 *Harvard International Law Journal* 291 (1992).

Sherlock, Ann. "Constitutional Change, Referenda and the Courts in Ireland," *Public Law* 125 (1997).

_____. "The Right to Life of the Unborn and the Irish Constitution," *Irish Jurisprudence* 13 (1989).

Spahn, Elizabeth. "Waiting for Credentials: Feminist Theories of Enforcement of International Human Rights," 44 *American University Law Review* 1053 (1995).

Spreng, Jennifer E. Comment, "Failing Honorably: Balancing Tests, Justice O'Connor and the Free Exercise of Religion," 38 *St. Louis University Law Journal* 837 (1995).

Sterling, Abigail-Mary E. W. Note, "The European Union and Abortion Tourism: Liberalizing Ireland's Abortion Law," 20 *Boston College International and Comparative Law Review* 385 (1997).

Stoffregen, Seth. Comment, "Abortion and the Freedom to Travel in the European Economic Community: A Perspective on *Attorney General* v. *X*," 28 *New England Law Review* 543 (1993).

Strong, S. I. "Christian Constitutions: Do They Protect Internationally Recognized Human Rights and Minimize the Potential for Violence Within a Society?" 29 *Case Western Reserve Journal of International Law* 1 (1997).

Studies 67 (1) (1978) (entire issue devoted to pluralism in Ireland).

Thompson, Angela. "International Protection of Women's Rights: An Analysis of *Open Door Counselling, Ltd. and Dublin Well Woman Centre* v. *Ireland*," 12 *Boston University International Law Journal* 371 (1994).

Tiedemann, Scott. Comment, "The Abortion Controversy in the Republic of Ireland and Northern Ireland and Its Potential Effect on Unification," 17 *Loyola of Los Angeles International and Comparative Law Journal* 737 (1995).

Tribe, Laurence H. "Childhood, Suspect Classifications, and Conclusive Presumptions: Three Linked Riddles," 39(3) *Journal of Law and Contemporary Problems* 8 (Summer 1975).

_____. "Structural Due Process," 10 *Harvard Civil Rights— Civil Liberties Law Review* 269 (1975).

Tushnet, Mark. "The Constitution of Religion," 18 *Connecticut Law Review* 701 (1986).

Ulen, Thomas S. "Economic and Public-Choice Forces in Federalism," 6 *George Mason Law Review* 921 (1998).

Viteritti, Joseph P., and Gerald J. Russello. "Community and American Federalism: Images Romantic and Real," 4 *Virginia Journal of Social Policy and Law* 683 (1997).

Walsh, Brendan M. "The Influence of Turnout on the Results of the Referendum to Amend the Constitution to Include a Clause on the Rights of the Unborn," 15 *Economic and Social Review* 227 (1984).

_____. "The Influence of Turnout on the Results of the Referendum to Amend the Constitution to Include a Clause on the Rights of the Unborn," 16 *Economic and Social Review* 71 (1984).

Ward, Paul. "Ireland: Abortion: 'X' + 'Y' = ?!" 33 *University of Louisville Journal of Family Law* 385 (1995).

Weiler, Joseph H. H. "Eurocracy and Distrust: Some Questions Concerning the Role of the European Court of Justice in the Protection of Fundamental Human Rights," 61 *Washington Law Review* 1103 (1986).

Weinstein, Jeffrey. Comment, "An Irish Solution to an Irish Problem: Ireland's Struggle with Abortion Law," 10 *Arizona Journal of International and Comparative Law* 165 (1993).

Whitehead, John W. "Accommodation and Equal Treatment of Religion: Federal Funding of Religiously Affiliated Child Care Facilities," 26 *Harvard Journal of Legislation* 573 (1989).

Whyte, Gerry. "The Application of the European Convention on Human Rights Before the Irish Courts," 31 *International and Comparative Law Quarterly* 856 (1982).

_____. "Discerning the Philosophical Premises of the Report of the Constitution Review Group: An Analysis of the Recommendations on Fundamental Rights," copy from author.

_____. "Natural Law and the Constitution," 47 *Doctrine and Life* 481 (1997).

_____. "Religion and the Irish Constitution," 30 *John Marshall Law Review* 725 (1997).

_____. "The Right to Die and the Irish Constitution," 3 *European Public Law* 235 (1997).

Wilkinson, Brian. Note, "Moving Towards Equality: Homosexual Law Reform in Ireland," 45 *Northern Ireland Law Quarterly* 252 (1994).

Wilson, William. "Is Life Sacred?" 17(2) *Journal of Social Welfare and Family Law* 131 (1995).

Wilson-Davis, K. "Irish Attitudes to Family Planning," 3 *Social Studies* 260 (1974).

Worthen, Kevin J. "The Role of Local Governments in Striking the Proper Balance Between Individualism and Communitarianism: Lessons for and from Americans," *Brigham Young University Law Review* 475 (1993).

Zenkich, Sabina. Note, "X Marks the Spot While *Casey* Strikes Out: Two Controversial Abortion Decisions," 23 *Golden Gate Law Review* 1001 (1993).

Constitutions and Treaties

Bunreacht na hÉireann

Constitution of the Irish Free State

European Convention on Human Rights
European Economic Community Treaty
United States Constitution

Cases

A and B v. *Eastern Health Board,* [1998] I.L.R.M. 460 (Ir. H. Ct. 1997).
Akron v. *Akron Center for Reproductive Health,* 462 U.S. 416 (1983).
Article 26 and the Regulation of Information (Services Outside the State for Termination of Pregnancies) Bill, In re, [1995] 1 I.R. 1(Ir. Sup. Ct. 1995).
Article 26 and the Matrimonial Home Bill, In re, [1993] 1 I.L.R.M. 241 (Ir. S. Ct.).
Article 26 in the Matter of the Criminal Law (Jurisdiction) Bill, In re, [1977] I.R. 129 (Ir. S. Ct. 1976).
Attorney General and Minister for Posts and Telegraphs v. *Paperlink,* [1984] I.L.R.M. 373 (Ir. H. Ct. 1983).
Attorney General ex rel. Society for the Protection of Unborn Children, [1988] I.R. 593 (Ir. H. Ct. 1986).
Attorney General ex rel. Society for the Protection of Unborn Children, [1988] I.R. 593 (Ir. S. Ct.).
Attorney General ex rel. Society for the Protection of Unborn Children, [1994] I.L.R.M. 256 (Ir. S. Ct. 1992)
Attorney General v. *Cadden,* 91 I.L.T.R. 97 (1957).
Attorney General v. *Paperlink,* [1984] I.L.R.M. 373, 381 (Ir. H. Ct.).
Attorney General v. *X,* [1992] 1 I.R. 1 (Ir. H. Ct.).
Attorney General v. *X,* [1992] 1 I.R. 1 (Ir. S. Ct.).
Bank of Ireland v. *Caffin,* [1971] I.R. 123 (Ir. S. Ct.).
Bellotti v. *Baird,* 443 U.S. 622 (1979).
Cook v. *Carroll,* [1945] I.R. 515 (Ir. S. Ct.).
Cooper v. *Aaron,* 358 U.S. 1 (1958).
Dred Scott v. *Sandford,* 19 How. (60 U.S.) 393 (1857)
Eisenstat v. *Baird,* 405 U.S. 438 (1972).
Ennis v. *Butterly,* [1997] 1 I.L.R.M. 28 (Ir. H. Ct. 1996).
G. v. *An Bord Uchtála,* [1980] I.R. 32 (Ir. S. Ct.).
Gaffney v. *Gaffney,* [1975] I.R. 133 (Ir. H. Ct. 1973).
Gaffney v. *Gaffney,* [1975] I.R. 133 (Ir. S. Ct.).
Griswold v. *Connecticut,* 381 U.S. 479 (1965).
Irish Family Planning v. *Ryan,* [1979] I.R. 295 (Ir. H. Ct. 1977).
Irish Family Planning v. *Ryan,* [1979] I.R. 295 (Ir. S. Ct. 1978).
K v. *K,* [1986] I.L.R.M. 75 (Ir. H. Ct. 1984).
K v. *K,* [1986] I.L.R.M. 75 (Ir. S. Ct. 1985).
Kerry Co-Operative Creamery v. *An Bord Bainne,* [1991] I.L.R.M. 851 (Ir. S. Ct.).
Lochner v. *New York,* 198 U.S. 45 (1905).
Loving v. *Virginia,* 388 U.S. 1 (1967).
M and M v. *An Bord Uchtála,* [1975] I.R. 81 (Ir. H. Ct. 1974).
M v. *Attorney General,* [1979] I.R. 73 (Ir. S. Ct.).
Martin v. *Hunter's Lessee,* 1 Wheat (14 U.S.) 304 (1816).
McGee v. *Attorney General,* [1974] I.R. 284 (Ir. H. Ct. 1972).
McGee v. *Attorney General,* [1974] I.R. 284 (Ir. S. Ct. 1972).
McKenna v. *An Taoiseach,* [1996] I.L.R.M. 81 (Ir. S. Ct. 1995).

Meyer v. *Nebraska*, 262 U.S. 390 (1923).
Mississippi University for Women v. *Hogan*, 458 U.S. 718 (1982).
Mueller v. *Switzerland*, 13 Eur. H.R. Rep. 212 (Eur. Ct. H.R. 1991).
Muller v. *Oregon*, 208 U.S. 412 (1908).
Murray v. *Ireland*, [1985] I.R. 532 (Ir. H. Ct.).
Murray v. *Ireland*, [1991] I.L.R.M. 465 (Ir. S. Ct.).
NEA v. *Finley*, 100 F.3d 671 (1997).
NEA v. *Finley*, 524 U.S. 569, 585 (1998).
Norris v. *Attorney General* [1984] I.R. 103 (Ir. S. Ct.).
O'Bryan v. *Keogh*, [1972] I.R. 144 (Ir. H. Ct. 1970).
O'Bryan v. *Keogh*, [1972] I.R. 144 (Ir. S. Ct.).
Open Door Counselling v. *Ireland*, 14 Eur. H.R. Rep. 131 (Eur. Comm'n H.R. 1991).
Open Door Counselling v. *Ireland*, 15 Eur. H.R. Rep. 244 (Eur. Ct. H.R. 1992).
People v. *Shaw*, [1982] I.R. 1 (Ir. S. Ct.).
Pierce v. *Society of Sisters*, 268 U.S. 510 (1925).
Planned Parenthood v. *Casey*, 505 U.S. 833 (1992).
Planned Parenthood v. *Danforth*, 428 U.S. 52 (1976).
R.C. v. *C.C.*, [1997] I.L.R.M. 401 (Ir. H. Ct.).
Rex v. *Bourne*, 1 K.B. 687 (Eng. C.C.C. 1938).
Roe v. *Wade*, 410 U.S. 113 (1973).
Ryan v. *Attorney General*, [1965] I.R. 294 (Ir. S. Ct. 1964).
Society for the Protection of Unborn Children v. *Coogan*, [1989] I.R. 734 (Ir. H. Ct.).
Society for the Protection of Unborn Children v. *Coogan*, [1989] I.R. 734 (Ir. S. Ct.).
Society for the Protection of Unborn Children v. *Grogan*, [1989] I.R. 753 (Ir. H. Ct. & Ir. S. Ct.).
Society for the Protection of Unborn Children v. *Grogan*, [1992] I.L.R.M. 461 (Eur. Ct. J.).
Society for the Protection of Unborn Children v. *Grogan*, [1992] 2 I.R. 471 (Ir. H. Ct.).
Society for the Protection of Unborn Children v. *Grogan*, [1992] 1 I.R. 46 (Ir. H. Ct.).
State (Healy) v. *Donoghue*, [1976] I.R. 344 (Ir. S. Ct.).
Tilson, In re, [1951] I.R. 1 (Ir. H. Ct. 1950).
Tilson, In re, [1951] I.R. 1 (Ir. S. Ct. 1950).
Tormey v. *Ireland*, [1983] I.R. 289 (Ir. S. Ct.).
United States v. *Carolene Products*, 304 U.S. 114 (1938).
Ward of Court, In re A, [1996] 2 I.R. 79 (Ir. S. Ct. 1995).
Zablocki v. *Redhail*, 434 U.S. 374 (1978).

Legislative Materials

Abortion Act, 1967, ch. 87 (U.K.).
Act to prevent the destroying and murthering of bastard children, An, 43 Geo. III, c. 58 (1803).
Adoption Act, No. 2 (1964) (Ir.).
Adoption Act, No. 24 (1974) (Ir.).
Adoption Act, No. 30 (1988) (Ir.).
The All-Party Oireachtas Committee on the Constitution, *Fifth Progress Report: Abortion* (2000).
Censorship of Publications Act, No. 21 (1929) (Ir.).
Censorship of Publications Act, No. 1 (1946) (Ir.).

Censorship of Publications Act, No. 15 (1967) (Ir.).
Constitution Review Group, *Report of the Constitution Review Group* (1996).
Criminal Law Amendment Act, No. 6 (1935) (Ir.).
Domicile and Recognition of Foreign Divorces Act, No. 24 (1986) (Ir.).
Family Home Protection Act, No. 27 (1976) (Ir.).
Family Law Act, No. 26 (1995) (Ir.).
Family Law (Divorce) Act (1996) (Ir.).
Family Law (Maintenance of Spouses and Children) Act, No. 11 (1976) (Ir.).
Fifteenth Amendment of the Constitution Act (1995) (Ir.).
Green Paper on Abortion, reprinted in *Irish Times*, Sept. 10, 1999.
Health (Family Planning) Act, No. 20 (1979) (Ir.).
Human Fertilisation and Embryology Act, 1990, ch. 37 (U.K.).
Infant Life (Preservation) Act, 19 & 20 Geo. 5, ch. 34 (1929) (U.K.).
Infanticide Act, No. 16 (1949) (Ir.).
Judicial Separation and Family Law Reform Act, No. 6 (1989) (Ir.).
K.R.S. ch. 403, et seq. (Ky.).
Married Women's Status Act, No. 5 (1957) (Ir.).
Matrimonial Causes and Marriage Law (Ireland) Amendment Act, 33 & 34 Vict., c. 110 (1870).
Moving Ahead: Initiatives for Expanding Opportunity in America (House Wednesday Group white paper, 1991).
New Directions: Welfare Reform in Twelve States (House Wednesday Group white paper, 1992).
Offences Against the Person Act, 24 & 25 Vict., c. 100 (1861) (U.K.).
Regulation of Information (Services Outside the State for Termination of Pregnancies) Act, No. 5 (1995) (Ir.).
The Right to Remarry: A Government Information Paper on the Divorce Referendum (1995).
Twenty-fifth Amendment of the Constitution (Protection of Human Life in Pregnancy) Bill, 2001 (Ir.).

ENCYCLICALS AND CHURCH DOCUMENTS

Catechism of the Catholic Church. Libreria Editrice Vaticana. The Wanderer Press, 1994.
Five Great Encyclicals. The Paulist Press, 1943.
John Paul, II. *Crossing the Threshold of Hope*. 1994.
John Paul, II. *Evangelium Vitae* [The Gospel of Life] §62. Times Books, 1995.
John Paul, II. *Familiaris Consortio* [The Role of the Christian Family in the Modern World]. St. Paul Editions.
John Paul, II. *Laborem Exercens* [On Human Work]. St. Paul Editions.
John Paul, II. *Muieris Dignitatem* [On the Dignity & Vocation of Women]. St. Paul Books & Media, 1996.
John Paul, II. *Veritatis Splendor* [The Splendor of Truth]. Pauline Books & Media, 1999.
Paul VI. *Humana Vitae* [Of Human Life]. St. Paul Books & Media, July 25, 1968.
Pius XI, *On Christian Marriage* [Official Vatican Text]. St. Paul Books & Media.
Vatican Council II, *The Conciliar and Post Conciliar Documents, Volume 1*. Austin Flannery, O. P., 1998.

NEWSPAPERS

Bacik, Ivana. "Hypocrisy, Fear in Debate on Abortion," *Irish Times*, Dec. 24, 2001.

Binchy, William. "Marking a Watershed in Irish Family Law," *Irish Times*, Jan. 8, 1996.

_____. "Referendum Will Decide Shape of Society for Generations: Divorce Redefines Marriage as a Temporary Arrangement and That Has Far Reaching Consequences," *Irish Times*, Nov. 23, 1995.

_____. "Right to Life Touches on Wider Issues," *Irish Times*, Jan. 31, 1997.

"Defying Church, Ireland Votes to Legalize Divorce; Margin is Slimmest in Country's History," *Assoc. Press*, Nov. 26, 1995.

Fitzgerald, Garret. "Time to Exorcise the Ghosts of the Past British Concerns," *Irish Times*, July 1996.

Giorello, Sibella C. "A Child with Three First Names That Was Proof Enough That Her Irish Mother Must Have Wanted Her," *Rich. Times-Disp.*, July 7, 1996.

Guilbride, Alexis. "Out of Sight Out of Mind," *Irish Times*, Oct. 31, 1995.

_____. "A Woman's Crime," *Irish Times*, Oct. 30, 1995.

Holmquist, Karen. "When Work Stops Working," *Irish Times*, Oct. 6, 1997, at 6.

McKenna, Peter. "Abortion Proposals are in the Right Direction," *Irish Times*, Oct. 6, 2001.

Myers, Kevin. "An Irishman's Diary," *Irish Times*, Jan. 11, 1996.

_____. "An Irishman's Diary," *Irish Times*, Jan. 16, 1996.

_____. "An Irishman's Diary," *Irish Times*, Apr. 19, 1996.

_____. "An Irishman's Diary," *Irish Times*, Sept. 30, 1997, at 13.

_____. "What Price a Down's Child?" *Sun. Telegraph*, May 4, 1997.

O'Brien, Breda. "Time to Tackle Reasons for Choosing Abortion," *Irish Times*, July 21, 2001.

O'Connor, Alison. "Roche Tells Voters of Fears for the Liberal Agenda," *Irish Times*, Oct. 20, 1997.

O'Faolain, Nuala. "Catholicism Needs More Articulate Voices Now," *Irish Times*, June 19, 1995.

O'Toole, Fintan. "The State We're In," *Irish Times*, Sept. 23, 1997.

Pollak, Andy. "Key Tactician Behind Anti Divorce Campaign," *Irish Times*, Nov. 25, 1995.

Quinn, David. "McAleese Right on Fertility," *Irish Times*, Oct. 5, 1997, at 21.

Rowe, Simon. "The Race for the Park.... Where Do They Stand?" *Irish Family*, Oct. 17, 1997, at 6.

Vrazo, Fawn. "Irish Tore Babies from Unwed Moms," *North New Jersey Record*, July 21, 1996.

Whyte, Gerry. "Archbishop's Criticism of Constitution Group May Be Opening Shot," *Irish Times*, Sept. 5, 1996.

Index

www.ingramcontent.com/pod-product-compliance
Ingram Content Group UK Ltd.
Pitfield, Milton Keynes, MK11 3LW, UK
UKHW041835100926
8556IPUK00018B/979

9 780786 416752